Policy, Practice, and Politics
in
Teacher Education

Policy, Practice, and Politics

in

Teacher Education

**Editorials From
the *Journal of
Teacher Education***

Marilyn Cochran-Smith

Foreword by John I. Goodlad

A Joint Publication

CORWIN PRESS
A SAGE Publications Company
Thousand Oaks, California

Serving Learners

For information:

Corwin Press
A Sage Publications Company
2455 Teller Road
Thousand Oaks, California 91320
www.corwinpress.com

Sage Publications Ltd.
1 Oliver's Yard
55 City Road
London EC1Y 1SP
United Kingdom

Sage Publications India Pvt. Ltd.
B-42, Panchsheel Enclave
Post Box 4109
New Delhi 110 017 India

Printed in the United States of America

Library of Congress Cataloging-in-Publication Data

Cochran-Smith, Marilyn, 1951-
Policy, practice, and politics in teacher education:
editorials from the Journal of Teacher Education / Marilyn Cochran-Smith.
    p. cm.
"A Joint Publication of The American Association of Colleges for Teacher Education"—T.p.
Includes bibliographical references and index.
ISBN 1-4129-2811-7 (cloth) — ISBN 1-4129-2812-5 (pbk.)
    1. Teachers—Training of—United States. 2. Education—Research—United States. I. Journal of teacher education. II. Title.
LB1715.C5893 2006
370.71′1—dc22

                                        2005025357

Acquisitions Editor:	Faye Zucker
Editorial Assistant:	Gem Rabanera
Typesetter:	C&M Digitals (P) Ltd.
Cover Designer:	Rose Storey

Contents

**CORWIN
PRESS**

The Corwin Press logo—a raven striding across an open book—represents the union of courage and learning. Corwin Press is committed to improving education for all learners by publishing books and other professional development resources for those serving the field of PreK–12 education. By providing practical, hands-on materials, Corwin Press continues to carry out the promise of its motto: **"Helping Educators Do Their Work Better."**

The American Association of Colleges for Teacher Education (AACTE) ensures the learning of all P-12 students through evidence-based preparation of high-quality school personnel. AACTE provides leadership for the continuing transformation of professional preparation programs to ensure competent and caring educators for all America's children and youth. A national voluntary organization, AACTE is the principal professional association for college and university leaders with responsibility for educator preparation and for all providers of education preparation services who share our commitment to professional standards, leadership, and ethical service to all learners.

This book is dedicated to Larry Ludlow, fellow Lynch School of Education Professor and my husband. He read and critiqued every one of the chapters and editorials in this book. His critique, which was sometimes hard to hear and sometimes at cross purposes to my own, was invaluable. His willingness to consider seriously every draft, even when at the early stages of gestation, was a gift.

—MCS

Foreword

John I. Goodlad

Two rounds of editing educational journals, each for a year, precipitated a lifelong decision: never more! Those of you with similar experiences will know the reason: It is demanding, underappreciated work and involves a never-ending stream of articles to read, tough decisions to make, friends who do not write well to disappoint, deadlines to meet, and more. Rewards notwithstanding, one gives up a great deal. Responsibility increases when the publication is backed by a large professional organization. Such is the case with the *Journal of Teacher Education (JTE)*.

Marilyn Cochran-Smith did not need the brownie points on her academic record that come with the work. She was already a full professor, internationally known for her research and writing, especially in the field of teacher education. She was well aware of the downside in taking on the editing role, warts and all. Unlike my shortsightedness, however, she looked beyond to the opportunity it offered. With years of thought-filled experience behind her, she now possessed a rich ecology of educational belief. Why not test and refine it even more in the challenging tasks of shaping her learnings for a wide and often critical audience? Isn't learning from experience what life is all about?

Even though in my brief editorial experience, I walked the halls where John Dewey walked decades before me, I failed to see the learning opportunities beyond the routines that confronted me. My only excuse is that it was early in my academic career, and the buzzing in my mind had not yet begun to settle down into patterns that would shape and reshape later on. What bully pulpits those two journals of the University of Chicago had offered me!

I thought my main writing task of the editorial responsibility was to briefly introduce the articles to follow in the issue. But why provide an abstract with, perhaps, a fifty-fifty chance of turning the potential reader off or on? When Katrina vanden Heuvel, editor of *The Nation,* writes a piece, it almost invariably provides a larger context that may or may not refer to a specific article. One soon gets to know what the magazine stands for and increasingly is able to judge how well its contents serve its mission.

And so it is with all good editors. And so it is with Cochran-Smith in her editorial service to the *Journal of Teacher Education.* She almost invariably provides a context, historical or contemporary or both, for the themes of each issue, sometimes referring to specific articles, sometimes not. What she does so artfully is introduce the reader to her own perspective on the larger context she sees to be relevant to the current issue of the journal.

At times, in editing, the larger context overrides attention to articles in the magazine, as it should. Katrina vanden Heuvel did not hesitate in the September 19, 2005, issue of *The Nation* to express her disgust over a prominent pundit's repeated reference to one of our nation's worst natural disasters as the work of Hurricane Katrina vanden Heuvel.

The invitation to write a foreword to a book composed of editorials of the *JTE* written by Cochran-Smith from May/June 2000 to January/February 2006 came to me when I was primarily involved each day in climbing out of a life-threatening illness. I did not need a writing responsibility, particularly one that necessitated an early deadline. However, I had read about half of Cochran-Smith's editorials over these years and had been very impressed. Each of the pieces I had read had implications for a much larger educational domain and audience than teacher education and teacher educators. Her writings were just as relevant to teachers, policymakers, school board members, and anyone who cares about our schools and their public purpose. Putting them into a book for wider circulation than characterizes a specialized professional journal simply made sense. I was pleased to have the opportunity to contribute to it.

In my own research and experience, I have become acutely aware of the general absence of well-chosen books on educational matters in the libraries of both secondary and elementary schools. Dialogue, enriched by reading, about highly relevant educational problems and issues is a rare phenomenon. I concluded my reveries about these circumstances with the conclusion that a book of Cochran-Smith's thoughtful editorials deserves attention both within and beyond the professional teacher education community.

I do not know what percentage of readers skip the editorials in the journals and magazines they read. My record is mixed. When I am purposeless, seated, and alone, I reach for something relatively short to read and often settle on a piece because of its title or because the name of the author is familiar to me and I enjoy his or her stuff. Cochran-Smith must be aware that many of us have such habits and probably never get back to anything in a magazine or journal other than what catches our attention during those brief respites.

She gave each of her editorials a title. Try these on for their magnetism: "The Questions That Drive Reform"; "Desperately Seeking Solutions"; "Teacher Education, Ideology, and Napoleon"; "The Unforgiving Complexity of Teaching"; "Sometimes It's *Not* About the Money: Teaching and Heart"; "Stayers, Leavers, Lovers, and Dreamers: Insights About Teacher Retention"; "No Child Left Behind: 3 Years and Counting"; "Teacher Education and the Outcomes Trap." Further, she gets into her topic quickly. Consider these opening sentences: "Teacher education is under attack"; "For a number of years, some of us involved in teacher education have been writing about the importance of learning to teach for social justice, social change, and social responsibility"; "Some policy and political analysts assume that ambiguity, conflict, and competing goals are inherent in human societies"; "In an essay on medical practice, Vivian Wang (2000) questioned what she called the 'fallacy of neutral universalism";' "Three years ago, President Bush signed the No Child Left Behind Act (NCLB) into law."

After pulling us into the narrative, she follows with a few paragraphs that provide a context for what follows. And then she never allows herself to deviate from the central theme of the editorial, employing throughout straightforward, nonacademic language. In my reading, including writing of my own once in print, I encounter sentences I would like to rewrite for greater clarity. I moved along quickly with Cochran-Smith's without encountering any such temptation. There will be readers who will disagree from time to time with Cochran-Smith's take on some issues, but surely they will have admiration for the work of a professional at the top of her form.

Cochran-Smith refers several times to her quarter-century of inquiry into the teacher education enterprise and lessons learned from it. Reading her editorials sequentially revealed to me a strengthening in the major themes of her ecology of educational belief even over the short span of a half dozen years. I have selected four that resonated significantly with me. I chose these because they run through the editorials as organizing threads or elements that hold them together. As a result, this book is not just a collection of miscellaneous articles. The themes I have chosen provide the cohesion a book requires. The careful reader might well draw out a different list. I make no effort to prioritize mine because each is significant for anyone who cares deeply about the role of education and schooling in our social and political democracy.

THE IDEOLOGY TRAP

Among the annoyances that probably bump around in Cochran-Smith's mental space, I suspect that one heading her list might well be called "the ideology trap." She does not attempt to disguise her dislike of advocates of a given persuasion criticizing the persuasion of another individual or group as ideological and lacking evidence. She strongly points out that each of us has at any given time a repertoire of beliefs, some well-supported by evidence and some not. Pushed into argument, we cite such evidence as we can muster. Each of us is entitled to our opinions, but entitlement is not validity. What she insists on—and this perspective emerges frequently—is that both the arguments put forward and the decisions ultimately taken be backed by solid inquiry. One might well wish that this were more often the case.

I have heard it said that Cochran-Smith uses the bully pulpit of editor to advance her own ideology. Of course. What should we expect? A bland citing of the research, pro or con, regarding each issue addressed, leaving it to the reader to choose? No thanks. She has beliefs developed over years of experience, study, and disciplined inquiry that lend authenticity to the positions she takes. I do not expect her to recite a step-by-step litany of how she came to believe what she believes.

The field of education is not characterized by public acknowledgment of credentials such as specialized preparation, certification, and experience. The public is not well versed in educational matters, in spite of its interest and of nearly everyone having attended school for several years. Rarely do general education programs in colleges offer courses on the nation's educational system and the ubiquitous educating that surrounds us night and day. It is little wonder that Cochran-Smith chides educators for their limited engagement in determining the mission and conduct of this system. And it is shocking that, in recent years, those educators most respected by their colleagues for their inquiry and ideas have rarely been invited to the nation's educational summits. Perhaps a change in the word—from ideology to "ideaology"—would both necessitate bringing expertise to the table and substantially improve the quality of outcomes from these periodic rituals.

THE PUBLIC PURPOSE OF SCHOOLING

Early on, Cochran-Smith stays close to the issues of teacher education carried from the 20th century to the 21st: an enterprise under sharp attack, implications of the increasing privatization of education, the standards movement in schooling now moving to include teacher education, the "evidence" question pertaining to the impact of teachers' preparation on students' learning, alternative routes to teaching, politically motivated solutions to complex educational problems, and more. In her first piece, she chides educators for not doing more to "shape the debate and chart the course of policy in teacher education"—a theme that reoccurs.

Initially, her growing concern for the role of schooling and teacher education in sustaining the American democracy merely sneaks into the narrative from time to time. But references to the public purpose of schooling and the increasing dominance of private purpose appear more frequently and more passionately over time. In a concluding editorial, she charges the teacher education community "to help change the terms of the debate about the purpose of schooling (and teacher education) in society. Surely the major purpose is not to produce pupils who can pass tests. . . . The purpose of education needs to be understood as preparing students to engage in satisfying work, function as lifelong learners who can cope with the challenges of a rapidly changing global society, recognize inequities in their everyday contexts, and join with others to challenge them." This is, of course, a moral purpose.

WHAT TEACHERS NEED
TO KNOW AND BE ABLE TO DO

What increasingly becomes clear as one reads the editorials is that what Cochran-Smith perceives to be the purpose of schooling in a democratic society shapes her views on virtually every aspect, every debate, every issue of the teacher education enterprise. It particularly shapes her views of the human beings to whom education of the young in schools is to be entrusted. She addresses this theme obliquely in several editorials but comes firmly to grips with it in "Studying Teacher Education: What We Know and Need to Know."

The articles and books I find to be most satisfying, whether fiction or nonfiction, are those that send me outside the pages, to that ecology of belief I have referred to several times in the preceding pages. How does what is written merge into this ecosystem or does it? What resonated strongly with me in the last editorial is the way in which the perceived purposes of schooling define the work, character, and education required of the teacher.

Earlier on in this foreword to what follows in her book, I wrote that Cochran-Smith's conception of the role of schooling and teacher education in our democratic society "sneaks into the narrative from time to time" as she proceeds through the years of her editorial responsibilities. But in the last two editorials, the pieces fell clearly and firmly into place for me.

For as long as I can remember, I have been well aware that teachers should be prepared, at a minimum, for delivering what we expect our schools to do. But when there is very little discourse about what our schools are for, the domain of possibilities widens, inviting an array of answers to the question of what teachers should know and be able to do. There follow from these answers alternative routes of teacher preparation. Then, should the question of school purpose be raised, the answers frequently are derived from prescribed means instead of the ends. Today, when the purpose mandated for schools is high pupil performance on tests, what teacher education programs must do is prepare future teachers to teach their students to do well on tests.

The common search for scientific evidence in support of good teacher education programs is to find out first what educational experiences contributed to students' high test scores and, of course, what educational experiences provided in teacher preparation programs contributed to the success of the teachers. The work of gaining the sought-for scientific evidence gets a little complicated, doesn't it? But I have not closed the circle yet. There remains the question of what educational experiences contributed to the success of the teacher educators who prepared the teachers whose students did well on tests.

As Cochran-Smith points out, the absence of scientific evidence from educational research to verify effective teacher education programs "seems to suggest that as a profession, teacher education is in sorry shape. . . . But closer analysis reveals that compared with the preparation of professionals in other fields, teacher preparation may actually be at the forefront." Nonetheless, this lack of "scientific" evidence fuels the drive of critics who would abolish schools of education and, indeed, the so-called professional route that, for decades, has been the major path to teaching in the nation's schools. I urge the reader to read very carefully Cochran-Smith's final editorials where she makes very clear why she sees "the outcomes question" as a trap for both teachers and teacher educators, placing on them and them alone accountability in the drive for high test scores.

EDUCATORS AND THE PUBLIC

Implicit in Cochran-Smith's writing is a belief that is, for her, a basic assumption about teachers and teacher educators that flows directly from her beliefs about the public democratic purposes of schooling: Educators must be among our best-educated citizens. It is my agreement with these beliefs and this opportunity to advance them that significantly influenced my decision to write this foreword to a book that should be widely read.

I am in complete agreement also with her advocacy of educators taking a much more active role in what has been described as the struggle for the soul of the American public school. Some are so reluctant to take a public stand on the fundamental issues of educational policy and practice that they nullify their rights under the First Amendment. The public discourse about education and schooling is diminished when well-educated citizens choose not to be involved. When educators are mute, experience and knowledge relevant to the conversation is missing.

Earlier, I stated that public discourse about education and schooling is not well informed. It is highly disturbing to read that 50 % or fewer of those polled know little or nothing about the No Child Left Behind Act, even though it was passed into law in 2001 and directly affects the substance and conduct of children's schooling. Even many much-schooled parents are unaware that satisfactory performance of their children on standardized tests has little to do with becoming well educated. The correlation between test performance and the use of principles and concepts presumably learned in the classroom and their transfer to situations outside of school for which these presumed learnings are relevant is very low. And there is virtually no correlation between test scores and attributes such as honesty, dependability, courage, compassion, respect for others, and other human traits we value.

Polls and studies conducted over the past couple of decades reveal a very broad set of public expectations for schooling. The late Ernest Boyer in his inquiry into secondary schools and that of colleagues and me into both elementary and secondary schools concluded that most people "want it all" from our schools: personal, social, vocational, and academic development. Why is it, then, that the general public is not outraged by a federal mandate that has resulted in a narrowing to just a few subjects what is important in the curriculum? If the test scores do not predict the use out of school of what is judged to be learned in these subjects in school, what predictions might we make about their learnings in the other domains of public expectations?

If high academic achievement in a few subjects considered basic is to be the purpose of schooling, we do not need the apparatus for its conduct we now have: buildings, buses, administrators, teachers, support staff, school boards, and all the rest. Let the economic purpose take over, as it largely has now. The manufacturers of computers and the necessary software will put all of our children and youth on the Internet, day or night or both. The god of economic utility smiles.

This is not to say that we, the people, would be relieved of the taxes we now pay for the schooling of the young. Day care is not the purpose of schooling, but it certainly is a major function—perhaps THE major function. If the home is to be the classroom, the implications for parents in the workplace are enormous. If students are also to attend places of tutoring outside of homes, there arises a need for dependable transportation and a large security force to ensure children's safety. And who is to attend to the physical and artistic needs and interests of the young? How will the ability to get along with others, to function productively in teams, and to develop respect for people of different colors, faiths, and beliefs be fostered? Indeed, what provisions are we to make for inducting our young people into the work in progress we call democracy?

By George, it appears that we need schools. Just this little, rather simplistic analysis causes one to think that universal public schooling is probably the best invention ever tried. The trouble is that we seem to have forgotten what our schools were initially created for and how these expectations expanded as more and more diverse groups of people strained the principle, *e pluribus unum*. The caring for and renewing of our democracy is a delicate, demanding undertaking. No other institution embraces the young as our schools do. No other institution has the ability or holds the promise of educating the young to make the most of themselves, earn a good living, and be responsible citizens. Clearly, we presently are heading down paths that, if followed for much longer, will cripple our schools in the functions we should expect them to perform and endanger the well-being of our democracy.

The late educational historian Lawrence Cremin asked himself the question of what we should do when confronted with problems for which there appear to be no clear answers. He wrote: We talk. Of late, we have not talked much about the directions of our schools and democracy. Just a few decades ago, there were coffee klatches, book clubs, issue-oriented town hall and school board meetings nationwide in which books such as *Why Johnny Can't Read* were intensely discussed. Some exist today, but they are scattered thinly across the country. The educational debate has largely left local communities and, such as it is, gone to state capitals and Washington, D.C. It must be brought back. Perhaps participation in the educational conversation is what Cochran-Smith had in mind for teacher educators—and, I trust, for teachers, principals, and superintendents—when she urged them to get involved. If this is what some are reluctant to do in their roles as educators, I remind them again of their rights and responsibilities as citizens.

There are those who will disagree with me strongly regarding my position on the comprehensive role I perceive for schools. "Put the kids on the Internet. We don't need schools," they will say. My position will be rejected as ideological, and so it is if this is just another word for belief. My critics will endeavor to provide hard evidence for their position, which is, of course, ideological. To repeat, I prefer to add an "a" before the first "o" in that word. My position grows out of beliefs currently embedded in my ecology of mind. My evidence would be regarded by critics as soft. It is historical and philosophical and has to do with what it means to be human and part of the fabric that holds us together in a democratic society. I have stated my position comprehensively elsewhere. If I were asked to provide an abstract of at least the part that refers to democracy, I would borrow the following from my longtime friend and colleague, the late Kenneth Sirotnik:

> America is a collection of multiple communities defined by different interests, races, ethnicities, regions, economic stratifications, religions, and so forth. Celebrating these differences is part of what makes this nation great. But there is a community— a moral community—that transcends the special interests of individuals, families, groups, that stands for what this nation is all about: liberty *and justice* for all. . . . It is a "moral ecology" held together by a political democracy and the fundamental values embedded in the system. . . . What could be more central to education generally and public schooling particularly than moral commitments to inquiry, knowledge, competence, caring, and social justice? (*The Moral Dimensions of Teaching,* edited by John I. Goodlad, Roger Soder, and Kenneth A. Sirotnik, 1990, pp. 307–308)

The public conversation about teacher educators and the teachers they help prepare goes beyond the subject matter and pedagogy of the prescribed academic curriculum. It must also be about the larger context in which we live. The metaphor coming to mind is that of introducing the young to the human conversation, especially the attributes we all must possess if democracy is to be more than an abstraction. Our schools must be places of equity, justice, and respect for one another. For this goal to be attained, the conduct of teacher education must be characterized by equity, justice, and respect for one another. These high expectations will be met only if we are able to agree as a nation on the democratic public purpose of our schools. May the conversation ensue and thrive in all of our communities.

Preface and Acknowledgments

As I began work on my 30th editorial for the *Journal of Teacher Education* (*JTE*)—the very last in the series I wrote over a six-year period—I came across a Web site called "how to write an editorial." This Web site was designed for middle and high school students working on their school newspapers with particular attention to writing editorials about the environment.[1] Explaining that an editorial offers an opinion on current events or issues, the Web site advised writers to develop five-paragraph essays and offered a rhyming set of steps—selecting, collecting, connecting, correcting—to walk would-be editorialists through the writing process. The Web site also explained that editorials have four purposes—informing readers about complex issues, promoting a "worthy activity" to get the reader involved, praising a person or event, and entertaining readers.

Perhaps if I had found this Web site earlier, I would have been more entertaining in my editorials over the last six years or spent precious editorial space praising the many people who do the hard work of teacher education. Perhaps I would have learned how to get complex things said in five paragraphs. And perhaps the whole enterprise would have been for me a simpler, step-by-step process. But none of those things happened. Instead, if I can judge by what regular readers of *JTE* have told me, my editorials were usually helpful, occasionally inspiring, and sometimes downright troubling, but rarely entertaining. And not once was any editorial of mine—or anything else I have written about teacher education—anywhere near as short as five paragraphs.

This is the case, I believe, because over the last six years there has been precious little related to teacher education that was entertaining or humorous and almost nothing that was simple or straightforward. Instead, during the period from 1999, when I wrote the first editorial, to 2006, when I put the last one to bed, teacher education has been a profession under heavy pressure to reform and has been embroiled in multiple highly contentious debates about the research base related to teacher preparation, definitions of teacher quality and effectiveness, the impact on achievement of various pathways into teaching, and the wisdom of policies related to regulation and accountability. Of course, criticism and debate are not new to teacher education. Due to the fact that teaching is a very public profession (and due also in part to multiple other factors such as the feminization of teaching, the low status of its clients, and the marginalization of education as a field of study in the university hierarchy), teacher education has been sharply critiqued for as long as it has existed. Questions about who should teach, what teachers should know, and who should decide are issues that have already endured for a century and will no doubt continue to be debated since it seems safe to assume that we will always face the challenge of how to ensure a cadre of well-prepared teachers for the nation's children.

Despite the very real way that teacher education's current state of affairs is "déjà vu all over again," it is also the case that teacher education has recently taken some new directions and faced challenges that are almost without precedent—defining the role of teacher education in the face of federally mandated annual school accountability measures, the phenomenal growth of alternate pathways into teaching (including for-profit providers and programmed courses of study), the near universal implementation of high-stakes pupil and teacher testing, the shift from input to outcome accountability systems focused on pupils' achievement, and the construction of teacher education as a policy issue judged on the basis of cost-benefit and other econometric analyses. The editorials collected in this book address these and other issues, attempting to explain, analyze, compare, critique, question, and sometimes challenge emerging and prevailing views. In doing so, the book identifies major issues in the field and points to both promising and dangerous directions.

In addition to my *JTE* editorials, this book includes two new pieces—a Prologue and an Epilogue. The Prologue provides one bookend to the editorials by discussing the relationships of policy, practice, and politics, arguing that these are inextricably tied and need to be understood as such. To do this, the Prologue offers two related conceptual frameworks, one for understanding the politics of policy in teacher education and one for understanding the politics of practice. The editorials themselves make connections across various policy, project, and program developments and also raise questions about the directions the field seemed to be going—or, at times, the directions in which the field was being pushed to go by external and internal critics of teacher education or by policymakers. In some cases, such as in the editorial titled, "Teacher Education in Dangerous Times," my purpose was to sound an alarm and urge my colleagues to take a position against emerging policies that, in my view, promoted a far too technical view of teaching and a retrograde training model of teacher education. In others, such as "The Unforgiving Complexity of Teaching" and "What a Difference a Definition Makes," I hoped to point to what I saw as the exceedingly narrow understandings of teaching and learning and of educational research that were either implicit or explicit in recent educational policies. And in others, such as "Sometimes It's *Not* About the Money," my editorial was intended to respond explicitly to what I viewed as the wrong-headedness of an exclusively market-driven approach to reforming teacher education.

In all of the editorials, my intent was to be both opinionated and scholarly, a duality that some might find inappropriate and others might deem contradictory. This is open to debate, of course, with the proof in the eyes and mind of the reader. Nonetheless, since it was my hope to be both erudite and timely, I took pains to document the editorials carefully and often used as texts hot-off-the-press reports, empirical studies, and research syntheses. I also drew on a wide array of my own and others' scholarship—both conceptual and empirical research—related or relevant to the broad topic of teacher education. Taken individually, each editorial offers a "read" of current events and issues in teacher education policy and practice. In this way, each editorial represents a particular moment in time and my professional reactions to and analyses of that moment. The book has carefully retained the "in-the-moment" nature of the editorials, arranging them chronologically and identifying each editorial by volume year and issue number, with minimal editing only in order to update references and bibliographic material.

Despite the careful retention of the in-the-moment nature of the individual editorials, the collection of editorials over a six-year period—and this book as a whole—transcend particular moments.

Taken together as a group, the editorials and the new pieces identify major issues, weave connections across time and space, and link the contemporary to the perennial. As a group, the editorials make the case that in order to understand current issues and events in teacher education, it is necessary to unpack and try to untangle the political purposes and agendas to which policy and practice are attached. In this sense the book provides a compass for "reading" the issues, events, and topics of the present and the future of teacher education, suggesting that it will always be necessary to identify underlying politics and larger agendas in order to make sense of contemporary and future debates.

The Epilogue bookends the editorials on the other end by linking them to the future of teacher education and identifying promising directions as well as pointing out pitfalls. The Epilogue suggests that there is plenty to be worried about regarding the future of teacher education, but also that there are a number of promising practices that have the potential to transform the field. The audience for this book is the broader teacher education community, primarily those working as teacher education practitioners, administrators, researchers, and policymakers at colleges and universities, in the major professional organizations related to the field, and in the think tanks and foundations that include teacher education in their scope of commentary and analysis.

The editorial group at Boston College took on the editorship of the *Journal of Teacher Education* as a professional project related especially to the work of the faculty in teacher education. Our intention was to try to contribute nationally by bringing more inter-disciplinary educational perspectives to bear on the major issues of the field and to use the journal to examine more of the controversial and contested aspects of teacher education policy and practice. Our hope was to contribute locally by using the work of producing the journal as an occasion for faculty development and collaboration. I had the distinct privilege of serving as editor of the journal in collaboration with associate editor David Scanlon, whose common sense, scholarship, and sense of humor were always right on target. We worked with special assistance from associate editor Curt Dudley-Marling, who played a key role in editorial decisions and reviewed most of the editorials in this book, and Jerry Pine, who served as book review editor. We also worked in collaboration with associate editors Audrey Friedman, Andy

Hargreaves, Janice Jackson, Larry Ludlow, Pat McQuillan, and Dennis Shirley, who reviewed many many manuscripts and also served as stewards for the general direction of the journal and its selection of themes.

For nearly its whole tenure at Boston College, the journal relied heavily on the support of managing editor Kevin Koziol, a doctoral student in curriculum and instruction who was remarkably adept at connecting the daily work of the journal with larger intellectual issues in education and a whole range of related areas, and of journal administrator Moira Raftery, a paragon of administrative efficiency, careful attention to detail, and thoughtful colleagueship (and to whom many of us fondly refer as "the mother of the journal"). For four years, we also had the ever-cheerful and efficient help of our journal assistant Marc Banks, an undergraduate and then master's student in teacher education. Along the way, the vast majority of faculty members at the Lynch School of Education, some administrators, and many doctoral students were enlisted as manuscript reviewers. We could never have produced the journal without them or without the support and resources of the Lynch School of Education and Boston College. But more important, the spirit of collaborative work with Lynch School and arts and sciences colleagues at Boston College and with Boston Public School teachers and administrators around the larger enterprise of teacher education was the intellectual context in which these editorials were created. Although I take full responsibility for the ideas and views expressed in my editorials, it was in part the many conversations with colleagues that created a healthy spirit of debate and intellectual engagement and served as grist and sometimes sounding board for the editorials that are collected here.

My colleagues who served on the AACTE Publications Committee, which oversees the organization's publications program and the *Journal of Teacher Education,* were enormous supporters and contributors to the work of *JTE,* especially Donna Wiseman, who served two terms as chair of the Publications Committee and was a staunch supporter of the journal and a loyal reviewer, and who became a good friend. Later, Lin Goodwin and then Richard Ruiz skillfully chaired the Publications Committee. Their contributions and those of the Publications Committee members—Tom Bellamy, Christine Bennett, Renee Clift, Cynthia Dillard, Constance Ellison, Carl Grant, JoAnn Haysbert, Rick Hovda, Bob McNergney, and

Michael Miller—added to the quality and depth of thinking about various *JTE* themes and other issues. AACTE staff members Kristin McCabe and Carol Hamilton were also very supportive and professional. I am especially grateful for the insights, advocacy, and unfailing professionalism—not to mention the friendship—of Judy Beck, vice president of AACTE for professional development and overseer of the Publications Committee. In addition, Corwin/Sage professionals Catherine Rossbach, Douglas Rife, Faye Zucker, Astrid Virding, Jacquelyn Rawson, Jason Dean, and Paul Reis were extremely helpful and supportive of the development of both *JTE* and this book. Finally I want to thank *JTE*'s entire Board of Reviewers—225 strong—whose members reviewed the enormous number of manuscripts we received over the years. I am especially grateful to those who reviewed multiple manuscripts every year, unfailingly offering thoughtful and constructively critical commentary to the authors of journal submissions. I learned a great deal about current thinking and practice in our field by reading the reviews, and I am grateful to every one of these colleagues.

—*Marilyn Cochran-Smith*

NOTE

1. The Web site address is http://projects.edtech.sandi.net/montgomery/sandiegowatershed/how_to_write_an_editorial.htm.

Prologue

Policy, Practice, and Politics:
Taking Stock of the Field

This is a book about policy, practice, and politics in teacher education. Its content is a collection of editorials, which were written five times a year over the six years that I served as editor of the *Journal of Teacher Education,* 2000–2006. As the alliteration of the title suggests, these editorials individually and collectively make the case that the strands of teacher education policy, practice, and politics are indelibly interrelated and braided together. The editorials reveal that practice sometimes complies with policy (or is coerced by policy to reform) and sometimes resists or co-opts policy. The editorials also reveal that policy is sometimes shaped by emerging practice, but also, and probably more often, policy trumps practice, ignoring its realities, creating contradictions, or forgetting its history. Most important, this book suggests that politics hovers over all of this, winding its way around, under, and through practice and policy—sometimes creating snarls that are nearly impossible to untangle, sometimes weaving extensions into existing discussions, and sometimes concentrating on the beads and baubles of policy debates rather than the thicker strands of substance. Although the entanglement of teacher education policy and practice with politics is inevitable—and at times blatantly obvious—it is all too seldom made explicit and visible in the discourse of the field. The impact of politics is often subtle—disguised as "just good policy," masquerading as "what the research shows," or stitched so seamlessly into the logic of the discourse about practice that it is nearly imperceptible. Often, given the amnesia of our field, the much longer political history that is the context for new developments in teacher education policy and practice is either forgotten or ignored. Just as often, given the myopia of our field, the much broader political agendas that are the context for new developments are purported simply to be "common sense."

That teacher education policy and practice are completely intertwined with politics is neither surprising nor revelatory. Teaching is, after all, a public profession with which nearly everybody has extensive experience and about which many people have strong opinions. If teaching—as part of the larger educational system that sponsors it—is understood to be the major shared activity through which our society socializes and inculcates its children, then it stands to reason that it is a high-stakes enterprise. What is taught, how it is taught, who teaches it, who assesses it, how it is paid for, and who decides all of these things are contested areas, reflecting the inevitable disagreements about values, ideals, and purposes that are inherent in all social institutions. In this sense, politics is an inherent and valuable part of human societies and the social institutions they construct. Far from being simply what partisan policymakers engage in, politics represents the tensions and disagreements that inevitably arise when human beings live together and when they create social institutions to organize their lives.

Teaching is not only a high-stakes profession; it is also a huge profession. As sociologist Richard Ingersoll (2004) points out, teachers comprise 4% of the entire civilian workforce, with two times as many teachers as nurses, and five times as many teachers as either lawyers or professors. In addition, teachers' salaries make up the biggest chunk of the overall cost of education (Rice, 2003), and everybody these days seems to agree that providing "well-qualified teachers" (which, although its importance seems unanimous, means a number of quite different things to different individuals and groups) for the nation's children should be a priority. In light of all this, it may well be that the only remarkable thing is that teacher education practice and policy are not debated and critiqued by politicians, policymakers, and the public even more often and more heatedly than they already are.

This prologue has three purposes. First, it provides the background for the editorials included in this book by describing the larger historical, social, and political contexts within which they were written. Along these lines, I suggest that during this period a "new teacher education" was emerging, which, although it had deeper roots, represented a significant departure from the past. In this section, I also discuss the role of editorials as written discourse that "takes stock" of events and issues at particular moments in time, attempting to connect these events to others as well as to the larger issues and perennial questions that define a field. In this sense the prologue is intended to help readers understand the larger contemporary context within which each editorial represents a moment in time. Second, this prologue shows how the editorials transcend particular moments in time by making an argument about the role of politics in policy and practice in a more general sense. The argument here is that in a certain way, policy *is* politics, and that, given the increasingly politicized society in which we live, there is very little policy, and perhaps to a lesser extent but still the case, there is very little practice that is *not* shaped by larger political issues related to ideas, values, morals, and priorities as well as power, influence, and alliances. Finally, the prologue discusses the major recurring themes in the politics of teacher education practice and policy over the last six years: the role of research and science in improving teacher preparation, competing agendas for reform, the impact of the accountability and testing movements on teacher education, defining teacher quality and its connections to desired outcomes, and teacher education for social justice and equity.

TAKING STOCK OF TEACHER EDUCATION

As noted, all of the editorials in this book were written between 1999 and 2006. During this time, as I have argued in detail elsewhere (Cochran-Smith, 2005), a "new teacher education" has emerged out of a convergence of social, economic, professional, and political trends. These were influenced by the changing notions of accountability that emerged in the mid 1960s and, more specifically, the educational reform movements that began in the 1980s. In addition, the new teacher education is influenced by the continuing educational achievement gap, the enlarged role of the federal government in education, the elevation of the science of education, the embrace of a market approach to education policy, and the history and status of the teaching profession and the teacher education field.

The New Teacher Education

Despite the fact that calls for something new and improved are the rule rather than the exception in teacher education, it is clear that what has been called for recently (and what actually appears to have emerged) is qualitatively different from what was demanded in previous cycles of reform and critique. In the 1950s and 1960s, for example, teacher education was urged to reform by addressing its perceived imbalance between liberal arts and humanities, on one hand, and pedagogy and methods, on the other. In the 1970s, teacher education was caught up in the competency movement, pressed to improve by assessing the progress of teacher candidates as they were trained to display explicit teaching behaviors in classrooms. During the 1980s, teacher education was pushed to be more coherent and internally cohesive by focusing on the emerging knowledge base, especially with regard to knowledge about the marriage of content and pedagogy, and the conceptual frameworks that steered the curriculum. In the 1990s, teacher education was propelled by the professionalization agenda, urged to reform itself as a standards-based profession, consistent across accreditation, certification, and licensure and in keeping with professional consensus. Although reminiscent of the 1970s in some ways, the emerging new teacher education of the 2000s is more evidence- and outcomes-oriented than previously. More important, the new teacher education is increasingly driven by a market approach to reform where educational improvement is assessed in terms of cost-benefit analyses and where there is enormous faith in the power of competition and the invisible hand of the market to regulate the economy and our social institutions. These shifts in the practice and policy of the new teacher education are reflected in the many reform documents, position papers, research syntheses, and calls for action that were widely disseminated during the period from just before and after the reauthorization of the Higher Education Act (HEA) in 1998 and continuing until the present.

Of course, teacher education is neither monolithic nor unitary, and there are many variations among programs, pathways, and related projects. When I speak of a new teacher education, then, I am referring to emerging trends, patterns, and directions in the field rather than particular programs or routes. And, of course, it is important to note that the emergence of this new teacher education has been gradual rather than abrupt and that some of the seeds of change have deep historical and epistemological roots. However, the HEA reauthorization in 1998 with its Title II provisions stipulating numerous mandatory reporting and accountability requirements for teacher education, linking state grants to the revision of certification, and providing funding for alternate routes (Earley, 2004), works well as a rough marker for "the new teacher education." As Penelope Earley (2000) pointed out shortly after its reauthorization, the HEA debates, which had accountability as their mantra, "fingered teacher education as the culprit" (p. 37) in the perceived failure of the schools and the impending teacher shortage and thus charted the course for tighter regulation and other interventions. This does not mean, however, that the 1998 HEA requirements brought about the new teacher education. They did not. Rather "the new teacher education" was influenced by the same social forces that influenced HEA. It is also important to note that the new teacher education was not something "done to" the profession by outside forces. Rather, those involved in the profession of teacher education at universities, professional organizations, foundations, and think tanks were shaped by but also helped to shape the directions of the field.

The new teacher education, which is the context for the editorials collected in this book, has three closely coupled pieces: it is constructed as a public policy problem, based on research and evidence, and driven by outcomes. These pieces of the new teacher education are elaborated in many of the editorials collected in this book. As these pieces are put together in the context of additional— sometimes conflicting—regulations and in light of the commitments that have historically animated teacher education, a number of tensions have surfaced: the trade-off between selectivity and diversification, the balance between subject matter and pedagogy, the competition between university and multiple other locations as the site for teacher preparation, and the contradictions of tightly regulated deregulation. Each of these issues is also considered in the editorials that follow.

Editorializing the Field

If it is true that teacher education, like all social institutions, is always in part an ideological practice, then it also true that the time period during which the editorials in this book were written has been a particularly ideologically driven time. In his book on ideology and discourse, James Gee (1996) wryly states, "To many people, ideology is what other people have when they perversely insist on taking the 'wrong' viewpoint on an issue. Our own viewpoint, on the other

hand, always seems to us simply to be 'right'" (p. 1). Gee points out
that in contemporary discourse, the word "ideological" is frequently
used to cast aspersions on the viewpoints of one's opponent, implying
that he or she is an ideologue who operates within a closed system
of ideas and values and is completely unwilling to entertain opposing points of view. In reality, however, the term, "ideological" may
be used simply to refer to the fact that any given position or stance
about a social practice, such as teacher education, is based on some
set of cultural ideas, beliefs, principles, and values, rather than to
make an evaluative comment about a particular set of ideas and
values. Similarly Timar and Tyack (1997) suggest that ideology—or
shared belief systems—has enormous power in shaping social institutions by building common cultural meanings and thus influencing
public expectations as well as policy and practice. Throughout their
analysis of the shift in school governance from the common school
emphasis on training moral citizens to the current view of education
as a consumer good, Timar and Tyack focus on the influence of what
they term, "the invisible hand of ideology" (p. 1).

Conceptualizing teacher education as ideological practice means
assuming that it is neither ideologically neutral nor value free, but is
instead rooted in the cultural ideas, ideals, and beliefs about teachers,
learners, schooling, society, and progress shared by particular groups.
It follows from this that an integral part of analyzing the events and
issues of teacher education is uncovering the value systems and cultural ideals behind them as well as identifying the groups and alliances
that share those values and ideals.

As noted in the Preface to this book, my intention in editorializing teacher education was to be both scholarly and opinionated, in
the sense of the long tradition of academic editorials. The contradiction in those twin goals notwithstanding, it was my hope both to
draw on and create scholarly analyses of current issues and events in
teacher education while at the same time taking a position on some
of the most important issues and, on some occasions, even sounding
a call to action about the directions of the field that I saw as seriously
flawed or wrong-headed. In doing so, I work in the tradition of
educational historian and policy analyst Larry Cuban, who in 1992
asked what the responsibility of scholars was to speak out against
policies they believed to be seriously "flawed in both logic and evidence, and ultimately, hostile to [their] vision for students" (p. 6).
Cuban characterized the momentum building in the late 1980s for

national tests and curriculum as a train rushing down a track. He asked whether scholars should accommodate what appeared by then almost to be political reality—by helping to build better track for the train in the form of, say, better tests—or, whether they should use their "expertise, evidence, and freedom" (p. 6) to try publicly to slow down the train by speaking out to lay and professional audiences in order to influence the policy debate. Cuban suggested that either choice (building better track or slowing down the train) was reasonable for a scholar, although he himself preferred slowing the train.

Following Cuban and others, then, one of my intentions in editorializing teacher education has been to suggest that in our roles as teacher education scholars and practitioners, we must also be public intellectuals, using our expertise, our evidence, and our freedom to challenge policies and practices that do not serve the interests of school students and try to lead the way in other directions that are more productive and more democratic. The strategy of simultaneously working against and within the system is paramount here. That is, it is essential both that teacher education scholars and practitioners offer critique in whatever public realms they have influence and access at the same time that they continue to do the work of teacher education within the boundaries of current policy and practice.

TEACHER EDUCATION AND POLITICS: TWO ANALYTIC FRAMEWORKS

As noted above, one of the major aspects of the "new teacher education" is that it is constructed as a public policy problem. Defining teacher education as a matter of public policy means focusing on the parameters of teacher education (e.g., teacher testing requirements, rules about 4- or 5-year programs, subject matter regulations, alternate route options) that institutional, state, or federal policymakers can control with the assumption that if and when the "right" policies are in place, they will solve simultaneously the problems of teacher quality and teacher supply. Increasingly, as part of the new teacher education, scientific research has been deemed the appropriate and desirable basis for identifying the right policies and practices, although as several of the editorials in this book suggest, this litmus test for policy is selective and may be more rhetorical than real. Nonetheless, the idea that solid evidence should drive policy and practice is in keeping with the larger evidence-based practice movement in the United States, the United Kingdom, and elsewhere. Although this has been challenged (e.g. Erickson, 2005; Lather, 2004; Trinder & Reynolds, 2000), it remains the prevailing view.

This section provides two analytic frameworks for understanding the politics of teacher education, one for understanding the politics of teacher education policy and the other for understanding the politics of teacher education practice. While closely related and thoroughly consistent, these two frameworks are also somewhat different from one another, the first taking a more macro view of public policy making and the other offering a more micro view of the politics of teacher education practice.

The Politics of Policy

With the passing of the No Child Left Behind legislation (P.L. 107–110, 2002), the federal government took an unprecedented stride into educational matters previously left to the states and/ or to higher education and professional organizations. In addition, competing agendas for educational reform, including the reform of teacher education, have grown increasingly publicized and politicized over the last several years. Arguably, there have never before been such blistering media commentaries and such highly politicized battles about teacher preparation policy as those that have dominated the public discourse and fueled legislative reforms at the state and federal levels during the last five to seven years—precisely the same time as the period during which all of the editorials in this book were written. During this time, the accountability movement—and with it a proliferation of high-stakes tests of students as well as their teachers—has come to dominate the educational agenda. At the same time, there has been considerable growth of private schools, charter schools, and for-profit school corporations, and in teacher education there has been growth of alternate routes, community college programs, on-line certification and degree opportunities, and for-profit teacher preparation centers. These have raised new questions about what it means to educate all learners for "the public good."

Some of the current debates about teacher education policy may be explained as turf battles, some as rhetorical maneuvering or political symbolism, and some even as ongoing challenges to an unjust system. Taken together, however, these debates point to the fact that policy making regarding teacher preparation is fundamentally a political enterprise, which must be analyzed and understood as such and that social institutions within a democracy are necessarily the sites of political disagreement. This book is based on the premise that education and, as part of that larger enterprise, teaching and teacher education are fundamentally and inevitably political. One goal of this collection of editorials, then, is not to politicize teaching and teacher education but to acknowledge, as fully and completely as possible, that they are already politicized (Bruner, 1996) and that analyses that leave out the political origins and implications of teacher education policy and practice are, at best, incomplete, and at worst, naïve and misleading.

In several of the editorials in this book, I draw on Deborah Stone's theory of public policy, elaborated in *Policy Paradox: The Art of Political Decision Making* (1997), to characterize developments and trends in teacher education policy. Stone suggests that, in the main, contemporary public policy analysis rejects politics, claiming instead to be about "rational analysis" and "disparag[ing] politics as an unfortunate obstacle to good policy" (p. x). In contrast Stone offers a model of policy analysis that accepts politics as not only an inevitable part of policy making but also a "creative and valued feature of social existence" (p. x). The crux of Stone's theory is the contrast she draws between a market model of society and with it a "rational" view of public policy making, on one hand, and a "polis" or political community model of society and also a "political" view of public policy making, on the other.

Stone's market model of society posits a collection of individuals with relatively stable individual preferences who weigh alternatives on the basis of deliberate and rational calculation. With a market model, policy making is part of what Stone calls the "rationality project," which is intended to take the politics out of policy. From this perspective, rational public policy making is based on a process wherein objectives are identified, a range of alternative actions to meet those objectives is identified, choices are evaluated on the basis of predictions (usually econometric) about their impact, and then the "right" choice is selected. From this perspective, individual people have individual interests, and they trade or exchange things with others in order to maximize their own well-being, which prompts resourcefulness and creativity. On the other hand, from the perspective of what Stone characterizes as the political community model of society, people live in a "web of dependencies, loyalties, and associations where they envision and fight for a public interest as well as their individual interests" (p. x). With a political community model, policy making is understood to depend on the ways in which people are psychologically and materially connected to and dependent upon each other. From this perspective, public policy making is understood to be influenced not so much by strictly rational choices but also by people's emotional bonds, their affiliations with social groups, and the shared meanings that connect them to others. From this perspective, policy making is seen as a struggle over ideas and over how the terms of policy debates are established. From this perspective, the focus is not simply on individuals, but on communities— both political communities (groups who live under the same structures and rules) and cultural communities (groups who share culture); here it is assumed that part of what motivates people is collective will and effort.

Stone (1997) suggests that the chief conflict in society is how to reconcile individual interests with public interests since there is never complete agreement about what the public interest is. With a market model, it is assumed that the market decides—that is, it is assumed that given a fair initial distribution of resources, the public interest is—by definition—the natural side effect of the accumulation of individuals pursuing their self interests. Competition is the key: what is best for a collection of individuals is by definition what is best for society, and choices are made on the basis of complete and accurate information. With a political model, however, it is assumed that cooperation and alliance building are as important as competition and that providing for the public good—not just private goods— is part of what motivates groups of individuals. Policy making is understood as problem solving, and groups are the key, including how groups are formed, split, and re-formed to get at public purposes. Far different from the assumptions underlying the purely rational view of policy making implicit in the market model, the political community model assumes that policy making is in part a function of interpretation, values, and passion—how people interpret information (which is always incomplete), who provides the information in the first place and what loyalties and affiliations are attached to that information, and which information is distributed and/or withheld (strategically or otherwise). Stone suggests that in the market model, change is assumed to come about as a function of exchange. In the political model, however, change is assumed to occur through the "interaction of mutually defining ideas and alliances." From Stone's perspective, then, policy making is not so much about how people use power to influence policy decisions, but how they use ideas to garner political support for their own views and their own ways of defining the questions that count at the same time that they work to challenge the viewpoints and defining questions and thus decrease the political influence of their opponents.

In many of the editorials in this book, where policy matters are described, I have worked from a perspective that is akin to Stone's. Using Stone's and other related ideas, I have analyzed how various groups with competing ideas about how to reform teacher preparation have struggled to control the enterprise by controlling the ideas and frameworks used to debate teacher education and to make policy about it. As a number of the editorials in this book suggest, it is often the case that although the values and priorities underlying policy debates are paramount, these are not explicitly debated. This means that an important goal of the critical discourse—in various forms, including editorials—is to uncover and unpack the politics of policy, or the ways that individuals and groups with differing policy positions forward and bolster their own views at the same time that they position and undermine opposing views.

The Politics of Practice

In discussions about the curriculum of teacher education and the nature of teacher education pedagogy, a distinction is sometimes made between a "political" kind of teacher education practice and some other kind of teacher education practice that is not political. For example, some teacher education scholars and practitioners suggest that focusing on social justice or equity in teacher education is "too political," while, in contrast, focusing on content and pedagogical knowledge is both more important and also more "neutral" when it comes to politics. Let us put aside for the moment the false dichotomy between social justice and equity, on one hand, and subject matter and pedagogy, on the other, since the former takes as a starting point the idea that all teachers must be well prepared in subject matter and pedagogy in order to teach all children to high standards. Disagreements about this dichotomy notwithstanding, the very existence of discussions about whether one kind of teacher education practice is "too political" in comparison with some other "nonpolitical" kind presumes that there is a choice in teacher education practice between politics and no politics, and that it is possible to engage in the practice of teacher education without being political (or, to concede a point at the outset, at least without being very political).

The premise of this book is quite the opposite. The premise here is that all teacher education practice (and by "practice," I mean a whole range of program and program-like matters, including decisions about the content and focus of the curriculum, the pedagogy developed, the assessment strategies employed, the arrangements regarding program structures and fieldwork experiences, and the ways candidates are selected and recruited into the field) is political in that it involves choices about what is included and what is left out, whose viewpoints and interests are served and whose may not be, which aspects of teaching and schooling are made problematic and which are taken for granted, and what assumptions are made—whether spoken or unspoken—about the purposes of teaching and schooling in a democratic society.

The editorials in this book are grounded in a conceptual framework for understanding the politics of teacher education practice based on critical questions (Cochran-Smith, 1998, 2003). The premise of the framework is that any particular teacher preparation program or practice (whether collegiate or otherwise) takes a stance on key issues or questions, which are then mediated by institutional, community and regulatory policies that are somewhat more external to practice. The key issues of practice can be framed in terms of eight critical questions: the diversity question; the ideology or social justice question; the knowledge question; the teacher learning question; the practice question; the outcomes question; the recruitment/selection question; and the coherence question. There are "answers" to these eight questions—either explicit or implicit—in any and all teacher education practice. How these questions are answered is, essentially, the politics of practice in that these answers involve choices and decisions based on values, priorities, ethics, beliefs, and ideals and in that these choices either help to maintain or challenge the status quo.

The "diversity question" has to do with how the increasingly diverse student population in American schools is constructed as a "problem" for teaching and teacher education and what are understood to be desirable "solutions" to this problem. Many critics of teacher education claim that historically, diversity has been constructed from a deficit perspective about the education of minority students, rather than regarded as a valuable resource to be extended and preserved. With the problem of diversity regarded as a deficit, it has also been historically assumed that the "inevitable" solution to the problem is assimilation, wherein differences are expected largely to disappear, and a "one size fits all" approach to curriculum, instruction, and assessment is assumed to equate with equity for all. The "ideology or social justice question," is closely related to the diversity question. It has to do with ideas, ideals, values, and assumptions about the purposes of schooling, the social and economic history of the nation, and the role of public education in a democratic society. In particular, this has to do with what images of American society (from meritocratic to hegemonic) as well as what notions of social justice (from everybody achieving to higher standards to redistributing society's resources) are assumed in teacher education courses, fieldwork arrangements, and other aspects of practice. Theorists and researchers who are critical of traditional teacher education practice have argued that implicit within it is a meritocratic view of American schooling and assessment and an assimilationist view of the purposes of education. Often, of course, the ideological stance underlying teacher education practice is unstated, with continuation of the status quo more or less presumed either by design or by default.

The "knowledge question" has to do with the knowledge, interpretive frameworks, beliefs, and attitudes that are considered necessary to teach, particularly knowledge about subject matter, pedagogy, and culture. Many critics of traditional undergraduate teacher education programs have suggested that there is not enough focus on deep knowledge of subject matter and too much focus on pedagogy and education foundations. Meanwhile critics of alternate forms of practice suggest that subject matter knowledge is necessary but not sufficient for teaching and that there is too little focus on pedagogy, how people learn, and how schools work. Along other lines, those who emphasize multicultural teacher education and issues of educational equity suggest that teachers need to know not only about "the knowledge base" of teaching but also how to critique the knowledge base as well as have knowledge of culture and the role of culture in learning and also need to develop the beliefs and skills to teach diverse groups successfully and to join with others in larger social movements.

The "teacher learning question," which has to do with how, when, and where adults learn to teach, is closely related to the knowledge question, with the former focusing on what teachers need to know and the latter on how they come to know it. The teacher learning question has to do with how learning to teach is regarded in teacher education practice—for example, as a matter of being trained to exhibit particular classroom behaviors, or a matter of developing interpretive frameworks for practice through participation in inquiry communities, or a matter of learning on the job through trial-and-error experience. The "practice question" involves the competencies and pedagogical skills teachers are assumed to need to teach effectively and how these are accounted for in teacher education practice. Closely related to (and in a certain sense, a subset of) the teacher learning question, practice includes not only how teachers learn to perform in classrooms but also how teachers' roles as members of school communities, as school leaders, and as theorizers of practice are conceptualized and instantiated in practice. It also includes how teachers' responsibilities to families and students and to communities are understood.

The "outcomes question," which has emerged as central in the last decade, has to do with the expected consequences of teacher preparation as well as how, by whom, and for what purposes these outcomes are assessed. This is in keeping with the general shift in the field away from focusing primarily on curriculum- or program-oriented standards and toward emphasizing instead performance-based standards and the long-term impacts of teacher preparation on K-12 students' learning. At the same time there has been a general shift to an outcomes- rather than an input-based approach to teacher education, however, there has also been a strong theme of resistance to narrow conceptions of outcomes in some examples of practice and in much of the theoretical literature. Along these lines, some teacher education practice is explicitly designed to be "against the grain" (Cochran-Smith, 1990) of common practice by questioning the ways schooling has systematically failed to serve many students from diverse backgrounds.

The "recruitment/selection question" has to do with which candidates should be recruited and selected for America's teaching force. The answers to this question implicit in various teacher education programs and practices have to do with the value of diversifying the teaching force, the importance of recruiting teachers with outstanding academic backgrounds, and/or the importance of seeking teachers who are likely to remain in teaching over the long haul. Different answers to the recruitment/selection question depend on different assumptions about the role of experience in teaching quality and whether subject-matter knowledge trumps life experiences and commitments. Finally the "coherence question," which encompasses the other seven questions discussed so far, has to do with the degree to which the stances taken on the first seven issues are connected to and coherent with one another and with how particular issues, such as issues related to diversity and equity, are positioned within a program—centrally or marginally.

Taken together, the key questions described above constitute a framework for understanding the politics of teacher education practice. In many of the editorials in this book, I have focused on one or more of the key questions of teacher education practice—knowledge, learning, outcomes, and so on—to get at the very different values, ethics, and priorities that underlie differing teacher education practices and the larger political and professional agendas to which these views are attached. As a number of the editorials in this book suggest, there are deep complexities and multiple meanings involved in understanding teacher education practice as well as deep complexities in the politics of practice.

THE ISSUES THAT DEFINE, THE ISSUES THAT DIVIDE

During the period from 1999 to 2006 when the editorials in this book were written, many new policies, commission reports, empirical studies, research reviews, report cards, reform proposals, foundation initiatives, and position statements related to teacher quality and teacher preparation were produced and disseminated. A search of *Education Week*'s archives for this period, for example, yields more than 4,000 entries related to teacher education. More than a dozen new reviews and syntheses of the research on teacher preparation (along with rejoinders and responses to these) were published since 2001. In addition, major statements—even "manifestos"—about teacher preparation and quality were produced by professional organizations, blue-ribbon commissions, think tanks, and major foundations with various political and professional agendas. Also during this time period, new teacher education accreditation standards were announced from the major national accrediting body (National Council for the Accreditation of Teacher Education), and the authorization of a new accrediting agency (Teacher Education Accreditation Council) with its own standards was announced. There were new state-level certification and licensure regulations put into place in nearly every one of the 50 states. During this same time period, the landmark No Child Left Behind Act (NCLB) (P.L. 107–110, 2002) greatly expanded the role of the federal government in education and legislated controversial definitions of both "highly qualified teachers" and "scientifically based research" in education. These were buttressed by subsequent policy reports such as the Secretary of Education's (U.S. Department of Education, 2002, 2003, 2004, 2005) annual reports to Congress on teacher quality, the first of which appeared just a few months after NCLB, to reinforce its definition of highly qualified teachers and assert that current approaches to teacher preparation were failing to produce the teachers the nation needed.

To say that there was a steady stream of documents and materials related to teacher education during this time period would be an understatement—there was a deluge. The deluge of materials, documents, and policies coupled with new regional and state reform initiatives, research collaborations, and assessment systems as well as commentary and debate about all of these served as the grist for the editorials in this volume. Five broad topics recur across the editorials, while, at the same time, five major analytic threads or themes run through them. The major topics include : (1) the role of research, particularly scientific research and evidence, in the improvement of teacher preparation; (2) competing agendas for the reform of teacher education, particularly competition between the professionalization agenda and the deregulation agenda, with its roots in a market-based model of society; (3) teacher education accountability strategies and systems, both external and internal, especially with regard to the outcomes of teacher education and to teacher/pupil testing; (4) teacher quality, including how teacher quality is (or ought to be) defined, what characteristics of teachers are associated with desired educational outcomes, and how quality indicators are related to the selection and retention of teachers; and, (5) issues related to teaching and teacher education for social justice and social change, especially the attention (or lack thereof) to issues of multiculturalism and equity in standards and regulations regarding the preparation, certification, and licensure of teachers. Each of these topics is elaborated below.

The Role of Research and Scientific Evidence in Teacher Education

In a growing number of arenas, the "science of education" has been greatly elevated (National Research Council, 2005). Today's rich data sources, powerful analytical techniques, and increasingly sophisticated researchers are presumed to permit the verification of scientifically based practices and policies that will increase students' achievement, improve teaching and schools, and solve the problems involved in providing universal education to a large and diverse population. The elevation of science is reflected in the formation of the U.S. Department of Education's Institute of Education Sciences and the What Works Clearinghouse, which was created to provide a central reliable source of scientific evidence in education for use by policymakers, practitioners, and the general public. Emphasis on greater scientific rigor is intended to respond to the widespread perception that educational research has been generally low in quality with constantly contested results and little capacity to improve educational policy and practice. The notion of "scientifically based research" and its complement, "evidence-based education," along with the new agencies and partnerships created to foster them reflect renewed confidence in the power of science to solve social and educational problems.

Disagreements about what constitutes science are not new, nor is burgeoning faith in the ability of science to solve educational problems, although many critics have pointed out that science cannot resolve issues about the purposes of schools or the students they should serve. As Lagemann (2000) noted, educational research has always been "an elusive science," with debates as early as the 1890s about whether there could truly be a science of education. Like the period Lagemann described at the beginning of the 20th century, the beginning of the 21st is also a time in which "science is remaking conceptions of truth and knowledge" (p. 19) in education generally and in teacher education particularly. Several of the editorials in this book directly take up questions related to the role and function of research in teacher education, including how research is defined, how it is (or can be) related to policy and practice, and how it ought to be evaluated. In addition, the editorials identify new research initiatives in teacher education—several with innovative research collaborations and mixed methods research designs—that are intended to examine scientifically the impact of teacher preparation on pupil, teacher, and school outcomes. Several of the editorials also scrutinize the "the research base" for teacher education, dissecting debates about what the research shows, sorting out the differing uses of the term "research" in the discourse of the field, and comparing the state of research in teacher education to that of other professions.

Competing Agendas for Reform

Competing agendas for the reform of teacher education are quite different from one another in history and tradition, with some strategies to control teaching politically and others reflective of long-term struggles for professional autonomy and equity. The two major contemporary reform agendas in teacher education are generally referred to as the professionalization agenda and the deregulation agenda (Cochran-Smith & Fries, 2001, 2005; Zeichner, 2003). The former aims to make teaching and teacher education a profession with a research-based and formal body of knowledge that distinguishes professional educators from lay persons, has jurisdictional responsibility, and works from consistent standards for professional practice. The major goal is to ensure that all teachers are fully prepared and certified. The deregulation agenda, on the other hand, aims to eliminate most requirements for entry into the profession based on the assumption that these simply keep bright young people out of teaching and focus on social goals rather than pupils' achievement. Deregulation is consistent with other market-based approaches to reform and with the larger movement to privatize health, education, and other services.

Unpacking and critiquing these two agendas is a recurring topic in the editorials in this book. A number of the editorials are critical of the market-based approach to teaching and schooling, which is dependent upon a strong competitive environment. The assumption underlying this approach is that to improve teaching and quality of life for the public writ large, what schools need most is the freedom to recruit, hire, and keep all teachers who can raise pupils' test scores regardless of their credentials. The editorials argue instead that this approach fails to understand the nature of teaching and learning and the motivations of those who enter the field (and stay). Several of the editorials also try to sort out the contradictory conclusions about the research base for teacher education reached by advocates of these agendas. In addition, some of the editorials deal with the fact that there are other agendas for reform besides these two, including efforts to regulate teacher education by increasing federal and state control of teacher education's inputs and outcomes, on one hand, and to construct teacher education as a social justice project, on the other, which is considered as a separate topic below. Although these multiple agendas are contradictory in some ways, they are not mutually exclusive. The editorials in this book consider how the various reform agendas overlap and collide with one another, depending on state regulations and on how the agendas are positioned by opponents and proponents.

Accountability and Outcomes

It is crystal clear that the accountability movement now dominates the discourse about reforming education and improving the schools in the United States. The annual testing requirements put into place by NCLB along with its annual requirements concerning pupils' and schools' progress now drive many state- and school-level initiatives regarding curriculum scope and sequence, graduation and promotion policies, and practices related to test preparation. As part of this larger accountability movement, there is now a major focus on accountability strategies and systems in teacher education. Some of the press for accountability is from sources external to teacher education at the institutional or program level—state-level certification regulations, licensure requirements, accreditation criteria, professional standards, and national reform initiatives. It is important to acknowledge, however, that the press for accountability is not just outside-in. It is also inside-in, that is, internal to institutions and programs, with many teacher education practitioners themselves concerned about whether they are meeting their own objectives and commitments related to the preparation of teachers. That the press for accountability comes from sources both external and internal to teacher education is not surprising. Teacher educators are influenced by the same social forces as policymakers and accreditors, and the press for accountability is part of a larger clamor in American society for all of the professions—including higher education— to respond to the forces of the market and prove their worth to consumers.

A number of the editorials in this book focus on accountability in teacher education, particularly on emerging assessment systems and the ways practitioners and policymakers are defining and measuring the outcomes of teacher education. A recurring theme is that the outcomes of teacher education are being constructed too narrowly, with accountability defined as test scores alone. The editorials raise questions about the feasibility of accountability systems intended to trace the test scores of pupils back to the specific teacher preparation program or institution, given the many intervening variables, the critical influence of school culture and climate (not to mention resources), and the multiple goals and purposes of teacher education. Several editorials focus specifically on the question of evidence in teacher education, challenging the application to teacher education of the underlying theory of "evidence-based education" as a reform strategy and raising fundamental questions such as "evidence of what?" and "evidence for whose purposes?" that expose the politics of evidence.

Teacher Quality and Its Indicators

Nationwide there is an emerging consensus that teacher quality makes a significant difference in schoolchildren's learning and in overall school effectiveness. Politicians, policymakers, and researchers of all stripes increasingly use this term to emphasize that teachers are a critical influence (if not the single most important influence) on how, what, and how much students learn. NCLB cemented into law the assumption that teacher quality matters by guaranteeing that all schoolchildren have "highly qualified teachers" who receive "high-quality" professional development. However, education researchers, practitioners, and policymakers do not agree upon a single definition of "teacher quality."

Within the general guidelines mandated by NCLB, the states are defining teacher quality differently from one another and putting different policies into place. Some researchers define teacher quality as student achievement, while others define it as teacher qualifications. While these are not necessarily mutually exclusive from one another, they represent different relative emphases and they have quite different—and extremely important—implications for teacher education policy and practice.

A number of the editorials in this book focus directly on the question of teacher quality, sorting out differing definitions and the various groups—parents and the general public, politicians of varying stripes, researchers from different paradigmatic and methodological backgrounds, teacher education practitioners, and school-based educators—who work from those definitions. When teacher quality is defined as student achievement, the premise is that although there is measurable variation in effectiveness across teachers, this variation is not captured by the common indicators of quality, such as teachers' preparation, experience, and test scores, but is captured in pupils' performance. With this approach, the point is to identify major differences in student achievement gains that are linked to teachers and then suggest implications regarding incentives, school accountability systems, and policies regarding the placement of teachers and students. The second approach defines teacher quality in terms of teacher qualifications. The point is to determine which (if any) of the characteristics, attributes, and qualifications generally considered indicators of teacher quality are actually linked to student achievement or other outcomes, such as principal evaluations of teachers or teachers' sense of efficacy.

As the editorials in this book indicate, these issues of teacher quality are closely tied to the accountability and testing movements, discussed above, and to the increasing focus on pupils' achievement as the appropriate outcome of teaching and teacher education. They also have to do with how we conceptualize and establish teacher education policies and practices related to teacher recruitment, selection, and retention.

Teacher Education for Social Justice

Over the last two decades, conceptualizing teaching and teacher education in terms of social justice has been the central animating idea for some educational scholars and practitioners who connect their work to larger critical movements. Advocates of a social justice agenda want teachers to be professional educators as well as advocates for students and activists committed to diminishing the inequities of American society. They also seek teachers more likely to stay in hard-to-staff schools with large numbers of minority and poor students. The social justice agenda overlaps with but also bumps up against the other agendas for teacher education reform noted above.

In the spirit of editorials as both "opinionated and scholarly," as I noted above, there is no question that this collection of editorials takes a social justice perspective on teacher education. Many of my editorials explicitly raise questions about teacher education for equity, social change, and social justice, particularly with regard to what is being left out of the discourse of reform and what is silenced in discussions about teacher education at the highest levels of power and influence. As the editorials indicate, advocates of a social justice agenda worry that concerns about the achievement gap and concerns about preparing qualified teachers have been melded together and converged with policymakers' obsession with testing and account-ability. The result is that educational equity is increasingly being conceptualized as opportunities for all students to be held equally accountable to the same high-stakes tests, despite unequal resources and opportunities to learn. Teacher preparation is increasingly being conceptualized as a way to ensure that all teachers have the subject-matter knowledge and the technical skills to bring pupils' test scores to certain minimum thresholds. And preparing young people to live in a democratic society is increasingly being conceptualized as efficiently assimilating all school children into mainstream values, language, and knowledge perspectives so they can enter the nation's workforce, contribute to the economy, and preserve the place of the United States as the dominant power in a global society.

This collection takes quite a different tack about the purpose of teaching, schools, and teacher education. Of particular concern is the increasingly narrow focus of the new teacher education on pro-ducing the nation's workforce coupled with excessive attention to the tests used to compare it to other countries. The editorials raise questions about the role of teacher education in preparing teachers who know how to prepare future citizens to participate in a demo-cratic society. The argument here is that there is very little discussion in the teacher education discourse about the need for all teachers to have the knowledge, skills, and dispositions to teach toward the democratic ideal and even less discussion about the need to evaluate teacher education—at least in part—by their success at producing teachers who teach for democracy. These goals are being silenced or squeezed out of the discourse.

Common Analytic Threads

In addition to the five major topics just described, there are also a number of analytic threads that run across and through these topics and thus stitch this anthology of editorials together. These threads are stated below in the form of five tenets for understanding teacher education research, policy, and practice—tenets that both guide the analyses offered in the editorials and also serve as a potential guide for understanding teacher education policy and practice in a more general sense.

(1) There is danger—even grave danger—inherent in dichotomy, simplicity, and reductionism. Concomitantly, there is necessity—even pressing necessity—for complexity in how we understand teaching, learning, and schooling, how we construct teacher education policies and practices related to these, and how we study all of this. (2) Many contemporary issues in teacher education have deep historical roots. It is important to learn from and connect to the past by locating contemporary issues in the context of the perennial issues that have animated teacher education development, critique, and reform for more than a century. On the other hand, it is also important to understand that each time perennial issues reemerge, they are somewhat different and are threaded into the tapestry of changed and changing political, social, and economic times and thus have a different set of meanings and implications. (3) In teacher education, as in other arenas, how the questions of the field are framed and how its problems are posed define and limit the range and variation of possible answers and thus prefigure what is emphasized, included in, and omitted from the discussion. This means that to a great extent, whoever has control of the questions in teacher education also has control of the answers, or the operating agendas and issues that drive changes and developments in teacher education research, policy, and practice. Identifying the key questions and how they are being constructed is essential to understanding the field. (4) Beneath the surface of every aspect of teacher preparation policy and practice and every debate about reform and renewal are particular configurations of values, ideals, beliefs, and priorities as well as particular constellations of actors who do and do not share those values and who do and do not have power and influence over various groups of others. In short, beneath the surface of every aspect of teacher education policy and practice is politics. It is impossible to avoid politics, and thus it is impossible to understand policy and practice fully or to clarify the issues thoroughly without also uncovering and understanding the underlying values and politics. (5) What happens at the margins of teacher education helps to define the center and to delineate the boundaries of the field. This

means that in order to get a handle on teacher education policy, research, and practice, it is necessary but not sufficient to analyze and critique what topics, themes, and issues are emphasized in the discourse. It is also necessary to determine and critically analyze what is marginalized, left out, or silenced in the discourse.

The editorials in this book explore the five topics listed above and the many complex issues that accompany them—research, competing agendas, accountability, teacher quality, and social justice. This topical discussion is understitched by the analytic threads that run throughout the editorials—complexity, historicity, questions, values, and omissions. Taken together as a body of work over time, the editorials collected in this book suggest that in a very real sense these major topics and the threads with which they are stitched to one another are both defining and dividing the contemporary field of teacher education. In other words, how these five topics are conceptualized, played out, and described locally, regionally, and nationally are defining the contours of contemporary practice and policy in teacher education and, at the same time, sometimes dividing the field by separating those with contrasting or conflicting views.

REFERENCES

Bruner, J. (1996). *The culture of education.* Cambridge, MA: Harvard University Press.

Cochran-Smith, M. (1998). Teaching for social change: Toward a grounded theory of teacher education. In A. Hargreaves, A. Lieberman, M. Fullan, & D. Hopkins (Eds.), *The international handbook of educational change* (pp. 916–951). The Netherlands: Kluwer Academic Publications.

Cochran-Smith, M., & Lytle, S. L. (1990). Teacher research and research on teaching: The issues that divide. *Educational Researcher, 19*(2), 2–11.

Cochran-Smith, M. (2003). The multiple meanings of multicultural teacher education. *Teacher Education Quarterly.*

Cochran-Smith, M. (2005). The new teacher education: For better or for worse? *Educational Researcher, 34*(6), 3–17.

Cochran-Smith, M., & Fries, K. (2001). Sticks, stones, and ideology: The discourse of reform in teacher education. *Educational Researcher, 30*(8), 3–15.

Cochran-Smith, M., & Fries, K. (2005). Paradigms and politics: Researching teacher education in changing times. In M. Cochran-Smith &

K. Zeichner (Eds.), *Studying teacher education: The report of the AERA panel on research and teacher education.* Mahwah, NJ: Lawrence Erlbaum, Publishers.

Cuban, L. (1992). Managing dilemmas while building professional communities. *Educational Researcher, 21*(1), 4–12.

Earley, P. (2000). Finding the culprit: Federal policy and teacher education. *Educational Policy, 14*(1), 25–39.

Earley, P. (2004). *Title II reauthorization, challenges, and opportunities: White paper for the American Association of Colleges for Teacher Education.* Unpublished manuscript, George Mason University, Fairfax, Virginia.

Erickson, F. (2005). Arts, humanities and sciences in educational research and social engineering in federal education policy. *Teachers College Record, 107*(1), 4–9.

Gee, J. (1996). *Social linguistics and literacies: Ideology in discourses.* London: Taylor & Francis.

Ingersoll, R. (2004). Four myths about America's teacher quality problem. In M. Smylie & D. Miretzky (Eds.), *Developing the teacher workforce: The 103rd yearbook of the national society for the study of education* (pp. 1–33). Chicago: University of Chicago Press.

Lagemann, E. (2000). *An elusive science: The troubling history of education research.* Chicago, IL: University of Chicago Press.

Lather, P. (2004). This is your father's paradigm: Government intrusion and the case of qualitative research in education. *Qualitative Inquiry, 10*(1), 15–34.

National Research Council Current Projects. (2005). Teacher preparation programs in the United States. Retrieved October 14, 2005, from www4.nas.edu/webcr.nsf/5c50571a75df494485256a95007a091e/49ec f39f5d0deaba85257098004884c6?OpenDocument?

P.L. 107–110. (2002). No Child Left Behind Act: Reauthorization of the elementary and secondary act. Retrieved June, 2002, from http://www .ed.gov

Rice, J. K. (2003). *Teacher quality: Understanding the effectiveness of teacher attributes.* Washington: Economic Policy Institute.

Stone, D. (1997). *The policy paradox: The art of political decision making.* New York: W.W. Norton and Company.

Timar, T., & Tyack, D. (1997). *The invisible hand of ideology: Perspectives from the history of school governance.* Denver, CO: Education Commission of the States.

Trinder, L., & Reynolds, S. (Eds.). (2000). *Evidence-based practice, a critical appraisal.* London, UK: Blackwell Science.

U.S. Department of Education. (2002). *Meeting the highly qualified teachers challenge: The secretary's annual report on teacher quality.*

Washington, DC: U.S. Department of Education, Office of Postsecondary Eductation.

U.S. Department of Education. (2003). *Meeting the highly qualified teachers challenge: The secretary's second annual report on teacher quality.* Washington, DC: U.S. Department of Education, Office of Postsecondary Education.

U.S. Department of Education. (2004). *The secretary's third annual report on teacher quality.* Washington, DC: Office of Postsecondary Education.

U.S. Department of Education. (2005). *The secretary's fourth annual report on teacher quality: A highly qualified teacher in every classroom.* Washington, DC: U.S. Department of Education, Office of Postsecondary Education.

Zeichner, K. (2003). The adequacies and inadequacies of three current strategies to recruit, prepare, and retain the best teachers for all students. *Teachers College Record, 105*(3), 490–515.

1 Teacher Education at the Turn of the Century

Teacher education is under attack. There is no shortage of accounts of what is wrong with teaching, teachers, and teacher education in the media or even the display windows of popular bookstores. Education deans across the country are scrambling to mount challenges to new state regulations intended to curtail the role of education schools in the preparation of new and experienced teachers. In a number of states, schools of education have been informed that their state accreditation is in jeopardy if sufficient numbers of teachers do not pass licensure exams. And eligibility for federal grants related to teaching and teacher education will soon be linked to state "report cards" that aggregate the test scores of would-be teachers by teacher preparation institution and thus produce a passing or failing "grade" for each institution and state.

As we enter the 21st century, then, the future of teacher education is at best uncertain. The standards movement now dominates discussions about teaching and learning, curriculum, and assessment, as well as all aspects of teacher learning, teacher assessment, and teacher certification. There are also unanswered (and perhaps unanswerable) questions about what it means to educate teachers for "the public good" in the face of the increasing privatization of American education through private schools, charter schools, for-profit school corporations, and now even for-profit teacher education programs. Prompted by changes in the standards of accrediting

SOURCE: *Journal of Teacher Education,* Vol. 51, No. 3, May/June 2000, pp. 163-165.

agencies, teacher-education institutions nationwide are shifting from input- to output-based programs and struggling with questions about what it means to provide empirical evidence that teacher education is a "value-added" endeavor that can be linked to both student learning and school change.

The teacher education profession finds itself responding to the charges against it as well as the complex demands placed upon it. Increasingly, there are competing positions in the discourse, and there is no clear consensus about what teachers need to know, who should provide education for teachers, how teachers should be certified and licensed, and what role university-based teacher preparation should play in school improvement. Lack of consensus is not new. Critique and criticism from many different perspectives are healthy as long as they are done with integrity and as long as all parties are responsible with their rhetoric and their claims.

This special issue of *JTE* contains a rich collection of articles on teacher education at the turn of the century. Authored by some of the leaders in the field and by people who are differently positioned from one another, these articles debate and offer rational (and in many cases, much needed) critique of important issues in the future of teacher education. Despite their different approaches and perspectives, the articles in this collection begin with the premise that the teacher-education enterprise is (or can be) valuable, and that we need to enhance the professionalization of teachers to preserve public education and broad participation in a democratic society.

There is, of course, another debate about teacher education that is more publicized and politicized than debates that are related in some way to the professionalization of teaching and teacher education. Although occurring simultaneously, this other debate is played out more in the election rhetoric of politicians than in the discourse of teacher educators, more in the pages of local newspapers than in the journals related to teacher education, and more in the sound bytes of television coverage than in the symposia of professional conferences. This deeply politicized debate confounds and sometimes overrides differences in the ways that major questions about professional knowledge and practice, language and cultural differences, and professional learning contexts are being framed within the educational community. Politically motivated solutions to the supposed state of affairs sometimes supersede grounded positions on the practices of teacher education. With a few notable exceptions (particularly Linda

Darling-Hammond, David Berliner, and others inside the teacher-education community such as Jeannie Oakes, Lee Shulman, and Art Wise, whose focus includes policy issues), many of us in teacher education have been conspicuous as much by our absence from the political debate as by our occasional participation in it.

This is unfortunate but not so surprising. Political debates are very unlike the more deliberate, carefully sequenced, and admittedly equivocal arguments of academics. At their extremes, the political debates are broad-brushed and simplistic, fueled by well-organized national and state-level conservative initiatives committed not to the critique and improvement of teacher education but to dismantling it completely (e.g., Farkas, Johnson, & Duffett, 1997; Kanstoroom & Finn, 1999; Stotsky, 1999). Many of those inside the educational community find the political debate anti-intellectual and not grounded in the knowledge base on teaching and learning, intended as much to provoke as to illuminate. One recent commentator, for example, declares that the teacher education curriculum has changed over the years primarily through the addition of a "heavy dose" of multiculturalism that is more "touchy-feely self-awareness" (Schrag, 1999, p. 32) than anything else. Another claims that teacher educators have virtually emptied the pages of elementary school reading materials of their white middle class characters and instead inserted easier texts about minority characters, which has caused a decrease in children's reading and thinking abilities (Stotsky, 1999). Still another (Farkas, Johnson, & Duffett, 1997) denigrates teacher educators for their commitment to public education as an "almost sacred democratic institution" (p. 24) and concludes that this commitment is fundamentally out of touch with the views of "the public," whose priorities are discipline, basic skills, and good behavior.

Commentaries like these from the Public Agenda and the conservative Fordham Foundation are often interlinked with one another in ways that are not immediately apparent. The authors support their claims with pseudo research, rumor, and innuendo that virtually ignore historical and demographic facts and/or rely on extraordinarily suspect methods of data collection and analysis. They claim nonpartisanship and neutrality of purpose when their critiques are in actuality rooted in a deeply political conservative agenda for the privatization of American education and for a return to a mythological American past when all students were educated to high standards and shared the same values.

At the extreme, conservative groups like these begin with the premise that we need to dismantle teacher education institutions completely and break up the monopoly that schools of education have too long enjoyed. Not surprisingly, they support alternative routes to certification that circumvent almost completely schools and colleges of teacher education. Their construction of the complex questions related to teacher knowledge and teacher learning is deceivingly simple: What teachers need to know is subject matter, which they gain exclusively outside of schools of education. Everything else can be picked up on the job. This dismisses the whole knowledge base on teaching and learning.

For better or worse (and many of us inside teacher education would say, worse, much worse), the most conservative voices are those being heard the loudest and clearest in the media and in the state houses of this nation. As offensive as this kind of commentary might be to many of us, it does exist and it does—to a degree greater than most of us in teacher education would like to admit—shape the debate and chart the course of policy in teacher education.

Teaching and teacher education are unavoidably political enterprises and are, in that sense, value-laden and socially constructed. Over time, they both influence and are influenced by the histories, economies, and cultures of the societies in which they exist, particularly by competing views of the purposes of schools and schooling. Like it or not, more of us in teacher education and in the educational research and policy communities will need to engage in these public and political debates if we are to have a real voice in framing the questions that matter for the future of teacher education. It may well be that the future of teacher education depends as much on how we critique and enhance the professionalization of teaching within the educational community as it does on how we engage in the public debate about privatization, regulation, and deregulation.

REFERENCES

Farkas, S., Johnson, J., & Duffett, A. (1997). *Different drummers: How teachers of teachers view public education.* New York: Public Agenda.
Kanstoroom, M., & Finn, C. (1999, July). *Better teachers, better schools.* Washington, DC: The Thomas B. Fordham Foundation.

Schrag, P. (1999, July/August). Who will teach the teachers? *University Business*, 29-34.

Stotsky, S. (1999) *Losing our language: How multicultural classroom instruction has undermined our children's ability to read, write, and reason.* New York: Free Press.

2 Gambling on the Future

In nearly every state in the union, high-stakes tests are now required both for K-12 students and for teacher candidates seeking initial licensing. The tests are more than deserving of their name—in many states, the ultimate stake for students is graduation from high school, and the stake for teacher candidates is entry into the teaching profession. Numerous commentaries locate the high-stakes testing movement within the context of larger discussions about the need for improved instructional skills and more professional teacher licensing procedures, on one hand, and for higher learning standards and more public and standardized assessments of students, on the other. Unfortunately, many of the larger discussions about testing are also connected to the long history of criticisms of teachers as mediocre students, "semiskilled" workers, "less-than-literate" individuals, and members of a minor or "not quite" profession.

Although many states are embroiled in major controversies about high-stakes testing for students and teachers, Massachusetts—once regarded as a leader in terms of its support for K-12 and higher education—now seems to enjoy the dubious distinction as the state that has earned the greatest national and international negative publicity about high-stakes tests. Some events from Massachusetts make this point, including the following:

- In June 1999, some 20,000 Massachusetts teachers marched to the State House to protest what they referred to as "a year of teacher bashing," a year that began with dismal test scores for prospective teachers publicized worldwide (59% of initial

SOURCE: *Journal of Teacher Education,* Vol. 51, No. 4, September/October 2000, pp. 259-261.

test takers failed) and with the Massachusetts Speaker of the House referring to teachers and their teachers (i.e., teacher educators and schools of education) as "idiots" (Vigue & Daley, 1999).

- In May of 1999, hundreds of Massachusetts students, teachers, and parents protested the state's Massachusetts Comprehensive Assessment System (MCAS) exam, which by the year 2003 will be required for high school graduation. A petition with more than 7,000 signatures calling for repeal of the law that requires the test was carried to the governor's office by student protesters. Speakers at protest rallies across the state included spokespersons for the National Association for the Advancement of Colored People, lawyers from the American Civil Liberties Union, and parents and students from urban, suburban, and rural Massachusetts schools and school districts. Protesters publicly rejected the test, which African American and Hispanic students fail at higher rates than do White students. They argued that it unfairly "punishes students" in urban areas and those from low-income families. Young people carried signs with giant red slashes through the letters MCAS, and other students carried placards with the words "MCAS = MORE CHILDREN ARE SORTED" (Vaishnav, 2000). This ingenious (and, from my perspective, quite accurate) rendition of the MCAS acronym is not unlike some of those invented by angry adolescents who, near the beginning of the 16 testing sessions it would take to complete the test, told their counselors that "MCAS" really stood for "MASSACHUSETTS CONSPIRACY AGAINST STUDENTS" (D. Krause, personal communication, April 18, 2000).

- Also in May, the Massachusetts State Board of Education approved the testing of teachers who teach math in school districts where 30% or more of students fail the math portion of the MCAS test. This new regulation is one of the most recent in the country to mandate testing of veteran teachers. Based on test results, the failing teachers (of failing students) will be required to undergo additional training and professional development but will not be fired. Termination was to have been the result of test failures for veteran teachers in legislation brought forward the year before by Massachusetts

Governor Paul Cellucci. This was subsequently voted down by the legislature. Massachusetts teacher groups immediately decried the new regulation, calling the testing of veteran teachers "illegal [and] unnecessary" and predicting that it will "damage the quality of mathematics education in our schools by driving good teachers out of the profession" (Vigue, 2000a). The teachers union has vowed to bring a lawsuit against the new teacher testing regulation (Vigue, 2000b).

These news bulletins are provocative and alarming. Highly publicized and politicized, they hint at the complexity of circumstances and the atmosphere of intentional acrimony that surrounds high-stakes testing in many states. At the same time, they reveal the "quick-fix" solutions that are often called for by politicians and by some segments of the public.

Massachusetts's latest bright idea—requiring massive teacher testing and "retraining" as answers to the problems supposedly just revealed by student testing but in actuality long already known—is at best a weak and overly simplistic approach to an extraordinarily complicated problem. At worst, it is one more widely publicized example of the construction of teachers and teacher education as both the last great hope and the worst culprit in what ails American schools. As Massachusetts teacher groups point out, this kind of approach ignores many of the most important factors that influence students' abilities to do well on standardized achievement tests and penalizes teachers and students in the neediest school districts (Vigue, 2000a). Part of the teachers' point is that other things are not going to change simply because teachers "teach better" or because there is a mandated and more uniform curriculum. The dire circumstances of cities and poor rural areas will remain. Widespread poverty, curtailed social and economic services, the growth of a permanent underclass, severely diminished opportunities for employment and mobility, and staggering disparities between the circumstances of those with and without advantages will remain. What will also remain is the failure of the educational system to serve particular groups of students, due at least in part to a long history of institutionalized racism and to disparities in the allocation of resources to urban, suburban, and rural schools and schoolchildren. Disparities exist in resources including equipment, supplies, and physical facilities, as well as books, access to computer technology, class size, teacher expertise, and students' opportunities to learn, not to mention basic neighborhood safety. If we change only one part of this complicated situation—that is, if we can somehow get teachers to "teach better" so that more kids can pass state-mandated high-stakes tests—but all of these other factors remain, do we really anticipate that the problems of American education will be solved?

The name "high stakes" is well deserved as a descriptor for K-12 student tests that determine high school graduation and for tests of prospective teachers (and now veteran teachers) that permit or deny career choice and/or mandate additional training. Borrowed from gambling—particularly gambling on poker and other card games based partly on chance and partly on skill—the term is used to indicate the potential for both great losses and great wins when one makes the choice to play at the big-money table. Unfortunately, much of the heated debate about high-stakes tests assumes that, like the best of poker games, test results are based solely on the skill demonstrated in a fair game played at a table to which everybody has had the same invitation and at which everybody has the same chance of drawing a winning hand. Test takers caught in the high-stakes national testing movement have had no choice about whether they will play in the big-money game, a game that is rigged from the start in favor of teachers and students from suburban and other highly resourced schools and communities. The "gamble" of high-stakes tests is hardly the same for these students and teachers as the "gamble" for those from urban, low-income, and other underresourced areas.

This special-themed issue of *JTE* focuses on high-stakes testing of both K-12 students and prospective teachers. Not surprisingly, we received multiple submissions for this issue that dealt explicitly with high-stakes tests in Massachusetts, two of which appear in this volume. We also received many other manuscripts that focus on various aspects of student and teacher testing across the nation. We are pleased to introduce in this volume a new occasional feature called "Agora," which provides a forum for the exchange of ideas on cutting-edge issues related to practice, policy, and research in teacher education. Contributors to this issue offer a variety of views on high-stakes testing, including perspectives from law, special education, language and literacy, students' rights, federal policy, urban school administration, higher education, K-12 teaching, preservice education, bilingual education, and other areas. Taken together, these contributions attest to the enormous complexity of the high-stakes testing movement. They raise provocative questions and cautions about the directions we are taking as a profession, and they suggest different directions we might do better to consider.

REFERENCES

Vaishnav, A. (2000, May 16). Hundreds of parents, teachers, students rally against MCAS. *The Boston Globe*, p. B3.

Vigue, D. (2000a, May 23). Board may order some teacher tests. *The Boston Globe*, pp. A1, A11.

Vigue, D. (2000b, May 24). Competency test OK'd for math teachers; legal challenge vowed. *The Boston Globe*, pp. A1, A24.

Vigue, D., & Daley, B. (1999, June 17). 20,000 teachers on the march give State House a message. *The Boston Globe*, p. A1.

3 The Questions
That Drive Reform

An intriguing way to trace the recent history of teacher education reform is in terms of the major questions that have driven the field and the varying and sometimes competing ways these questions have been constructed, debated, and enacted in research, policy, and practice. Along these lines, a loosely chronological list of the major questions that have driven teacher education over the past 50 years might go something like this: the attributes question, the effectiveness question, the knowledge question, and the outcomes question in teacher education. Each of these questions both shaped and was shaped by the political climate, degree, and kind of public attention to K-12 schooling, perceived supply and demand of teachers, federal and state policies and funding programs, evolving perceptions of teacher education as a profession vis-à-vis colleges and universities as well as schools, and emerging and competing paradigms and programs of research on teaching, teacher learning, and teaching/learning/curriculum in the subject areas.

The attributes question, which was prominent from roughly the early 1950s through the 1960s, asked, "What are the attributes and qualities of good teachers, prospective teachers, and/or teacher education programs?" Explored through studies of the personal characteristics of teachers and teacher educators, versions of this question emphasized both attributes related to personal integrity and human sensitivity as well as attributes of the liberally educated and/or academically able person. A different version of the attributes

SOURCE: *Journal of Teacher Education,* Vol. 51, No. 5, November/December 2000, pp. 331-333.

question was central to critiques of teacher education programs and faculty, especially the degree to which they provided (or failed to provide) intellectually rigorous, discipline-based training for new and experienced teachers worthy of a place at the university. This version of the attributes question drove debates about the balance between professional and arts and sciences courses, the scholarship of teacher education students and faculty, and the organizational structures of programs.

The effectiveness question posed a different issue: "What are the teaching strategies and processes used by effective teachers, and what teacher education processes ensure that prospective teachers learn these strategies?" This question drove many of the reforms in teacher education during the late 1960s through the mid-1980s. Influenced by new studies of the "scientific basis of teaching," many teacher education programs developed systems for evaluating prospective teachers according to scientific objectives and stated performance criteria. Checklists and other forms of assessment attempted to align classroom teachers' practices with the criteria used by fieldwork supervisors and also with teacher education processes, programs, and language. Other questions that shaped this period arose at least partly in response to perceived flaws in the effectiveness question. New questions about the meanings of classroom and school events countered the effectiveness question and began to identify what was left out of discussions that focused primarily on effective teacher behaviors.

Prompted by, but also concurrent with, public concern about the quality of teaching and teacher education, the knowledge question animated the field from the early 1980s through the late 1990s: What should teachers know and be able to do? What should the knowledge base of teacher education be? At the heart of the knowledge question was the desire to professionalize teaching and teacher education by building a common knowledge base for the profession. Building on early research about teachers' thinking and on emerging knowledge about subject matter learning, the knowledge question moved the field away from what effective teachers do to what they know and how they construct new knowledge appropriate for differing local contexts, particularly for increasingly diverse learners.

Versions of the knowledge question identified and made distinctions among formal and practical knowledge, pedagogical content knowledge, case knowledge, knowledge in action, reflection on knowledge, culturally relevant knowledge, and local knowledge generated through teacher research and action research. The knowledge question drove major policies and program revisions in teacher education intended to ensure that the burgeoning codified knowledge base was at the center of the curriculum. Some versions of the knowledge question also prompted the development of new contexts for teacher learning, including school-university partnerships, professional development schools, and new forms of collaboration across the professional lifespan.

The major question that is currently driving reform in teacher education is what I have been referring to as "the outcomes question in teacher education" (Cochran-Smith, 2000; 2001). As we enter the 21st century, the outcomes, consequences, and results of teacher education have become critical topics in nearly all of the state and national policy debates with regard to teacher preparation and licensure as well as in the development of many of the privately and publicly funded research agendas related to teacher and student learning. If the major question that drove the field during the past 15 years was, What should teachers know and be able to do? then the driving question for the last 3 or 4 years has been, How will we know when (and if) teachers know and can do what they ought to know and be able to do? Fundamentally the outcomes question has to do with the connection the public has a right to expect among teacher learning, teaching practice, and student learning. It begins with the premise that the ultimate goal of teacher education is student learning and also assumes that there are certain measures that, depending on the unit of analysis, can be used to indicate the degree to which this outcome is or is not being achieved for teacher candidates, K-12 students, teacher education programs and institutions, and the education profession itself.

It is important to note, of course, that the list of questions I have offered above does not include the only questions that have driven reform in teacher education nor even what some people would consider the most important questions. There has not been complete consensus in teacher education at any point over the past half-century—nor is there now—with regard to which questions are the right ones to be asking. Rather, there have always been competing questions as well as questions that critique, play off of, and take on the major driving issues. It is also important to note that none of the questions I have loosely associated with particular time periods was settled during that period or disappeared from consideration after that time. Rather, many of the questions that drive the field during particular eras are periodically recycled, reemphasized, and rethreaded into the current intersection of research, practice, and policy in ways that may or may not appear to be different from their previous iterations. Old questions are never just "same ole" old questions, however. They are instead "new" old questions because they have a different import and a different set of implications when they are woven into the tapestry of a changed and changing political, social, and economic time.

Finally, and most important to note, is that each of the driving questions I have listed above is in some fundamental way a question about the priorities and goals of the profession (and even of the nation) and not simply a question of research or of policy in teacher education. James Hiebert (1999) makes a related point in a thoughtful essay about the relationships between mathematics research and National Council of Teachers of Mathematics standards. He suggests that the rightness or legitimacy of priorities and goals are questions of value and belief rather than questions of evidence that can suggest educational decisions based on varying levels of confidence. As he points out, values questions can never be settled solely by empirical means.

At certain times, reform in teacher education is driven more by questions of value than by empirical evidence. As we enter the 21st century, it may be one of those times. Although there is general agreement that the outcomes question is important, we do not have a consensus about how outcomes should be defined, measured, and used in policy and practice decisions. In fact, if we move beneath the surface of agreement that teacher learning, professional practice, and student learning should have something to do with each other, we uncover serious disagreements. If we attempt to describe the relationship between teacher learning and professional practice, attempt to explain what we mean by teacher learning and student learning, attempt to elaborate the theoretical bases and consequences of the kind of student learning we are trying to account for, or even attempt to define what we mean by *students* (which students? how many? all of them or some statistically significant portion of them?), we uncover differences, some of which represent striking discrepancies in values as well as deep political and philosophical divides. Notwithstanding the growing—and many say unprecedented—consensus about standards and outcomes measures for teaching and teacher education within the profession, it is important to acknowledge that there is considerable disagreement both within the profession and between the profession and its detractors with regard to how outcomes should be constructed and upon what grounds the outcomes question should be decided.

The question that is currently driving reform in teacher education—the outcomes question—is a complicated one. Its various iterations rest on differing sets of assumptions about what teachers and teacher candidates should know and be able to do, what K-12 students should know and be able to do, and what the ultimate purposes of schooling should be. Demonstrating that teacher education programs and procedures are accountable, effective, and/or value-added assumes answers to these complex and prior questions of values, goals, and priorities, questions that cannot be settled empirically. Perhaps we would do well as a profession to identify more clearly the questions of value and the diametrically different ideologies that underlie many of the current debates about the outcomes question in teacher education.

REFERENCES

Cochran-Smith, M. (2000). The future of teacher education: Framing the questions that matter. *Teaching Education, 11*(1), 13-24.

Cochran-Smith, M. (2001). The outcomes question in teacher education. *Teaching and Teacher Education, an International Journal of Research and Studies, 17*(5), 527-546.

Hiebert, J. (1999). Relationships between research and the NCTM standards. *Journal for Research in Mathematics Education, 30*(1), 3-19.

4 Learning to Teach Against the (New) Grain

For a number of years, some of us involved in teacher education have been writing about the importance of learning to teach for social justice, social change, and social responsibility. Although these terms are not synonymous, they have generally been used to signify the idea that one important role of the college/university is to help prepare teachers to challenge the inequities that are deeply embedded in systems of schooling and in society. Underlying most versions of this argument is the assumption that teaching and teacher education are fundamentally political activities and that it is impossible to teach in ways that are neither political nor value-laden. The point, then, is not that teaching should be politicized but rather, as Bruner (1996) has suggested about education in general, that we recognize "that it is already politicized and that its political side needs finally to be taken into account more explicitly, not simply as though it were 'public protest'" (p. 29).

Over the years, I have had the opportunity to contribute to the concept of teacher education for social change by suggesting that it is not enough for beginning teachers to learn the basic skills of managing classrooms and constructing well-crafted lessons for all students. I have argued that even for the newest teachers—even for prospective teachers at the very beginning of the professional lifespan—part of the task is teaching "against the grain" by collaborating closely with both university- and school-based mentors to

SOURCE: *Journal of Teacher Education,* Vol. 52, No. 1, January/February 2001, pp. 3-4.

develop critique, challenge common practices, and engage in inquiry intended to alter the life chances of children. More than a decade ago, I opened an article entitled "Learning to Teach Against the Grain" (Cochran-Smith, 1991) by drawing on Antonio Gramsci's essay condemning political and social indifference in pre–World War I Italy. Asserting that indifference is often a mainspring of history, Gramsci argued that action had to be everyone's responsibility and that each individual, no matter how apparently powerless, had to be accountable for the role he or she played or failed to play in the larger struggles of the day. A major goal of the project of teacher education for social change has been helping prospective teachers think deeply about and deliberately claim the role of educator as well as activist based on political consciousness and on ideological commitment to combating the inequities of American life.

Constructing actual preservice programs that provide the social, organizational, and intellectual contexts for learning to teach against the grain in the company of more experienced mentors has been a daunting challenge for teacher educators. And no small part of that challenge has been to clarify and wrestle with complex questions about the role the university ought to play in teacher education and the larger responsibility of teacher education to and for society. These questions have been intensified by the political climate that has evolved over the last several years. Animated by their twin commitments to privatization and deregulation, powerful conservative groups have asserted that colleges and universities ought to play virtually no role in teacher education other than to provide a basic liberal arts education. And in K-12 schools, where—regardless of political affiliation—raising students' scores on standardized tests has become the major and sometimes the only goal, teachers who work against the grain are hardly in demand. In fact, in school systems that are deeply entrenched in standardization and standardized testing as the mode of school reform, new teachers who are willing to work completely *with the grain* may well be the best prepared and the most in demand. Illustrations are plentiful on listservs, in the popular media, and in the political rhetoric of debates. Chicago's completely scripted lesson plans for each subject, each grade level, and each day of the school year, for example, are touted in *Time Magazine* as especially effective and appropriate for beginning teachers. A teacher in a midwestern state is reprimanded by her principal because she has actual books in her first-grade classroom.

The books, deemed inconsistent with the required and heavily prescribed phonics-based initial reading program, are taken as de facto evidence that the teacher is not following the program. In another state, a teacher is fired for publicly criticizing her school system's standardized testing program.

There is grave concern in many circles about the growing trend nationwide to prescribe teachers' and teacher educators' work and circumscribe their opportunities to make professional decisions, question common practices, and develop responsible critiques. In a recent article on redefining the role of schools of education, Dennis Thiessen (2000) quoted this frightening description of the dramatically curtailed role of universities in teacher education in England. "Teacher training has become painting by numbers or rather learning to teach by numbers; and moreover, institutions are to be checked to see whether they are painting carefully and accurately within the lines" (Wilkin, 1999, cited in Thiessen, 2000, p. 130). What does it mean to prepare teachers to teach for social justice, to work against the grain, and to teach to change the world in a society where standardization and prescription are being mistaken for higher standards? What is the college/university role in teacher education at a time when many states are taking unprecedented action to control the coursework, the subject matter, the time spent in schools, and every other aspect of teacher education? We are at a crossroads in this country concerning the role of the college/university in teacher education and the role of teacher education in society. We are chillingly close in some states to "learning to teach by numbers" at a time when more than ever we need teachers able and willing to teach against the (new) grain of standardized practices that treat teachers as interchangeable parts and—worse—reinscribe societal inequities.

The words of bell hooks about the transformative possibilities of teaching and the critical role of the academy are consistent with my points here about the importance of student teachers' learning to critique and learning to construct practices informed by critique:

> The classroom remains the most radical space of possibility in the academy. For years it has been a place where education has been undermined by teachers and students alike who seek to use it as a platform for opportunistic concerns rather than as a place to learn. . . . I add my voice to the collective call for renewal and rejuvenation in our teaching practices. Urging all of

us to open our minds and hearts so that we can know beyond the boundaries of what is acceptable, so that we can think and rethink, so that we can create new visions, I celebrate teaching that enables transgression—a movement against and beyond boundaries. It is that movement which makes education the practice of freedom. (hooks, 1994, p. 12)

By concluding my editorial with these words from bell hooks, I am not suggesting that the only relationship of teacher education to society is a critical one, nor that the only goal of preservice education is to prepare prospective teachers to teach against the grain. What I am suggesting is that genuine critique, which emerges out of the collaborations of college- and school-based educators working together to alter children's life chances, is vital to the future of public education in a democratic society.

REFERENCES

Bruner, J. (1996). *The culture of education.* Cambridge, MA: Harvard University Press.

Cochran-Smith, M. (1991). Learning to teach against the grain. *Harvard Educational Review, 61*(3), 279-310.

hooks, b. (1994). *Teaching to transgress: Education as the practice of freedom.* New York: Routledge.

Thiessen, D. (2000). Developing knowledge for preparing teachers: Redefining the role of schools of education. *Educational Policy, 14*(1), 129-144.

5 *Multicultural Education*

Solution or Problem
for American Schools?

There is widespread agreement that we need dramatic changes in the ways we do business in American schools. However, there is also enormous disagreement about how we got to where we are today, what changes we actually need, and what role multicultural education has played in the process.

From some points of view, the pressing concern is how to educate all children well, particularly how to teach children of color, children who are poor, and children from diverse groups, who have been disproportionately underserved by the educational system. In Geneva Gay's (2000) book *Culturally Responsive Teaching: Theory, Research, and Practice,* for example, the chapter on power pedagogy begins with these lines:

> Teaching is a contextual and situational process. As such, it is most effective when ecological factors . . . are included in its implementation. This basic fact is often ignored . . . especially if [students] are poor. Instead, they are taught from the middle class, Eurocentric frameworks that shape school practices. This attitude of "cultural blindness" stems from several sources. One of these is the notion that education has nothing to do with cultures and heritages. . . . [Another is that] education is an effective doorway of assimilation into mainstream society for people from diverse [groups]. . . . These students need to forget about being different and learn to adapt to U.S. society. (p. 21)

SOURCE: *Journal of Teacher Education,* Vol. 52, No. 2, March/April 2001, pp. 91-93.

Throughout her book, Gay argues that simply spotlighting the achievement gap or blaming the families or backgrounds of failing groups has not gotten us very far. She also asserts that acknowledging the long history of racism and cultural hegemony—although true—will not solve the problem. Instead, she argues for new paradigms of competent instructional action, such as culturally responsive teaching. Gay makes it clear, however, that even this is not sufficient. Rather, she points out that teachers must have "the moral courage and the will to stay the course in efforts to make the educational enterprise more multiculturally responsive, even in the face of the opposition that is surely to come from somewhere" (p. 210).

Of course we do not have to look far to locate opposition to viewpoints such as Gay's, nor do we have to search to identify the "somewhere" from which that opposition comes. Sandra Stotsky's (1999) book on multiculturalism provides a very different read on the changes we need in the schools. In direct counterpoint to Gay's (2000) book, Stotsky's book argues that multicultural education is a problem for American schools:

> Most of the recent changes in the content of [elementary school instructional reading materials] and in the teaching methods outlined in them have been introduced as part of an approach to curriculum development called multiculturalism. . . . Multiculturalism was proposed as the only approach that could broaden the horizons of American school children and inculcate respect for racial and ethnic minority groups. . . . [Most] were willing to accept the advice of the scholars and teacher educators who advocated a multicultural approach. . . . Some did so out of desperation for what was promised as a pedagogical magic bullet, others . . . believed such changes were necessary for social equality. (p. 7)

Stotsky's (1999) pinpointing of multicultural education as a problem is clear in the full title of her book: *Losing Our Language: How Multicultural Classroom Instruction Has Undermined Our Children's Ability to Read, Write, and Reason.* Here Stotsky suggests that the more subtle agenda of multiculturalism is anti-White, anti-capitalistic, and anti-intellectual. Linking multiculturalism to progressive education and whole language, Stotsky warns, "The fusion of the anti-intellectualism of the multiculturalists and the anti-teaching philosophy of whole language advocates is an educationally deadly combination in the elementary grades" (p. 269).

These strikingly different views of multicultural education are rooted in their fundamentally different assumptions. I mention just four here: what the past in American schools and society was like, what role "difference" plays in teaching and learning, what the fundamental purposes of schooling are, and what kind of scholarship provides trustworthy evidence for future directions.

Gay's book, which contributes to a much larger body of work on multiculturalism, is based on the assumption that "the past" of American schools advantaged those who were middle-class, English-speaking, and White European-American. At the same time, this past disenfranchised and disadvantaged students of color, for whom instructional practice and curriculum—particularly after desegregation—were not congruent with culture, language, interactional patterns, and teacher expectations. Along these lines is the assumption that difference is inevitable in American schools. Because all children learn best when curriculum and instruction are congruent with cultural and language background, schools need to capitalize on the richness of difference. From this perspective, the purpose of school is to prepare all children to be participants in a democratic society, and the purpose of teacher education is to prepare teachers in ways that are critical, culturally responsive, and potentially transformative.

On the other hand, Stotsky's book is based on the assumption that what would save our schools is a return to the past. The past is an idealized time when American values were uncontested, the hegemony of the canon was unchallenged, and academic standards for all were rigorous and unyielding. Along these lines, difference is taken to be divisive, something to be neutralized in the schools where all children come to learn to be citizens by reading the same books and learning the same lessons. From this perspective, the purpose of school is to prepare children to be responsible and civic-minded all-Americans who will take their places in the nation's workforce, and the purpose of teacher education is to prepare teachers in ways that are standardized, culturally neutral, and potentially restorative (of the past).

Finally, Gay's book—and much of the scholarly work that has been collected under the label "critical race theory" (Ladson-Billings, 1999)—assumes that trustworthy evidence about directions for

America's schools takes many forms. In addition to some of the work that emerges from traditional paradigms, trustworthy modes of inquiry include critical ethnography and other forms of critical qualitative research, narrative and biographical/autobiographical scholarship, and inquiry that combines advocacy with analysis, action with theoretical grounding, and politics with scholarship. Stotsky and her counterparts, on the other hand, insist that there is only one kind of trustworthy research. They give credence only to traditional research grounded in positivist assumptions, which provides "proof" and law-like generalizations that hold true across contexts and are assumed to be free of political, ideological, and advocacy agendas.

In the final analysis, these diametrically opposed assessments of multicultural education must be understood as the result of different epistemologies and different values, beliefs, and assumptions about who knows and who counts when we take the final tally in American schools. As teacher educators, many of us assume that there is more than one way to know and that everybody counts in schools—essential premises, I believe, if we support public education and the future of a pluralistic, democratic society. If we begin with these assumptions, then we cannot conclude, as Stotsky does, that the past was value free, that differences ought to be eradicated in schools, and that the purpose of schooling is to determine which children fit best into an economic system that perpetuates the advantages of those with particular racial, cultural, and linguistic profiles. Rather we must conclude, as Gay and her counterparts do, that the past was anything but neutral, that differences offer rich potential for teaching and learning experiences, and that the purpose of schooling—no matter how daunting that purpose may be—is to struggle with the tensions that will always exist around the twin goals of providing learning opportunities that are excellent and equitable for all, not some.

REFERENCES

Gay, G. (2000). *Culturally responsive teaching: Theory, research and practice*. New York: Teachers College Press.

Ladson-Billings, G. (1999). Preparing teachers for diverse student populations: A critical race theory perspective. In A. Iran-Nejad & D. Pearson

(Eds.), *Review of research in education* (Vol. 24, pp. 211-248). Washington, DC: AERA.

Stotsky, S. (1999). *Losing our language: How multicultural classroom instruction has undermined our children's ability to read, write, and reason.* New York: Free Press.

6 Higher Standards for Prospective Teachers

What's Missing From the Discourse?

The standards movement—and with it new outcomes-based performance assessments and high-stakes paper-and-pencil tests for teachers and students—will arguably have more influence on teaching and teacher education than any other contemporary agenda or innovation. Across the nation, colleges and universities are scrambling to provide evidence that teacher education is a value-added endeavor linked to student achievement, and in many places there is intense pressure to shift teacher education from an "inputs" to an "outputs" model.

Even the most ardent supporters of college- and university-based teacher preparation do not dispute that teacher education programs should be able to justify their value and that prospective teachers should be able to teach to high standards. But what's missing from the discourse of higher standards and more demonstrable outcomes? What's receiving little or no attention in the flurry to reinvent pre-service education? Michael Fullan's (1993) *Change Forces* suggests one direction:

> As we head toward the twenty-first century . . . teachers' capacities to deal with change, learn from it, and help students learn from it will be critical for the future development of societies.

SOURCE: *Journal of Teacher Education,* Vol. 52, No. 3, May/June 2001, pp. 179-181.

They are not now in a position to play this vital role. We need a new mindset to go deeper. (p. ix)

The way that teachers are trained, the way that schools are organized, the way that the educational hierarchy operates, and the way that education is treated by political decision-makers results in a system that is more likely to retain the status quo than to change. (p. 3)

Fullan (1993) insists it will take a new mindset to deal with what is an otherwise insurmountable problem—the contradiction of continuous change demanded by educational reform and innovation on one hand and an educational system that is fundamentally conservative on the other. Fullan argues that "change agentry" is essential to the future development of our society and that all prospective teachers must be prepared to be effective agents of change.

Preparing agents of change was decidedly not the focus of the old teacher preparation. John Goodlad's major study of how and where teachers were prepared for the nation's schools (Goodlad, 1990; Goodlad, Soder, & Sirotnik, 1990) indicated that almost no teacher education programs included preparing teachers for change as part of their purpose: "Somehow, the idea that we are our own best agents of change and the will to act have taken a second seat to quiescence" (Goodlad et al., 1990, p. 398). So, what about the new teacher education? Does the standards-driven teacher education of the new century emphasize the preparation of change agents and demand demonstrations that prospective teachers know how to deal with, contribute to, and learn from change? Unfortunately, there is very little in the discourse of higher standards and demonstrable outcomes along these lines.

The emerging view of the reflective and knowledgeable professional teacher (Yinger, 1999) includes few if any images of teachers as activists, as agents for social change, and/or as allies for social justice. There is little in the new standards that suggests that prospective teachers are expected to challenge the current arrangements of schools and critique those teaching methods that are increasingly promoted as best practices for all students. The discourse of higher standards emphasizes that new teachers be able to teach (and prove they can teach) in such ways that all children can learn. But, there is much less in this discourse about classroom practices and ways of relating to students that are responsive to and culturally relevant for some students but look decidedly different from those being claimed for all. There is little in the discourse about new teachers' learning to critique standards-based K-12 education and the high-stakes tests that have hijacked the standards agenda in many schools. And there is little emphasis on the importance of new teachers' learning to question whose interests are being served, whose needs are being met, and whose are not being met by "best" school arrangements including new curricula that emphasize test preparation above all else. Even if we accept the position that critique along these lines is indeed an essential part of what prospective teachers should know, there is almost nothing in the discourse of the new teacher education about preparing prospective teachers to negotiate the treacherous waters of proving themselves competent in first-time teaching positions while at the same time challenging some of the assumptions and actions that others take for granted.

The image of teachers as professionals who learn from practice and document the effect of their teaching on students' learning is a clear part of the discourse of the new teacher education. Experienced as well as prospective teachers are expected to function as reflective practitioners, work collaboratively in learning communities, and demonstrate that their teaching leads to increased student achievement. But, a narrow interpretation of higher standards—and one that is lurking beneath the surface of the discourse that heralds the paradigm shift in teacher education from "inputs to outputs"—threatens the idea of teaching for change. As teacher educators across the nation develop the comprehensive assessment systems now required by the National Council for Accreditation of Teacher Education and many states (see Wise & Leibbrand, 2001), an important challenge will be to eschew narrow views of teaching and learning, particularly linear views of teaching as instructional practice that leads directly to demonstrable student learning gains. It will be important not to leave out of this discourse a notion of teaching practice that extends beyond what teachers do within the boundaries of their classroom walls to include how they understand and theorize what they do as well as how they take on roles as members of communities, constructors of curricula, and school leaders.

What is needed and generally missing from the discourse so far are discussions of outcomes measures that—ironically—make teaching harder and more complicated for teacher candidates rather than easier and more straightforward. Such measures would recognize the inevitable complexity and uncertainty of teaching and learning and acknowledge the fact that there are often concurrent and competing claims to justice operating in the decisions prospective teachers must make from moment to moment, day to day. The new teacher education ought to make room for discussions about outcomes that demonstrate how teachers know when and what their students have learned as well as how they manage dilemmas and wrestle with multiple perspectives. Outcomes ought to include how prospective teachers open their practice to public critique and utilize their own and others' research to generate new questions as well as new analyses and actions. They ought to include how prospective teachers learn to be educators as well as activists by working in the company of mentors who are also engaged in larger movements for social change. This kind of discourse about standards and outcomes is essential if we are to prepare prospective teachers who—to conclude with Fullan's (1993) words—are "skilled change agents with moral purpose . . . [who] will make a difference in the lives of students from all backgrounds, and by so doing help produce greater capacity in society to cope with change from within" (p. 5).

REFERENCES

Fullan, M. (1993). *Change forces: Probing the depths of educational reform*. London: Falmer.

Goodlad, J. (1990). *Teachers for our nation's schools*. San Francisco: Jossey-Bass.

Goodlad, J., Soder, R., Sirotnik, K. (Eds.). (1990). *Places where teachers are taught*. San Francisco: Jossey-Bass.

Soder, R., & Sirotnik, K. (1990). Beyond reinventing the past: The politics of teacher education. In J. Goodlad, R. Soder, & K. Sirotnik (Eds.), *Places where teachers are taught* (pp. 385-411). San Francisco: Jossey-Bass.

Wise, A. E., & Leibbrand, J. A. (2001). Standards in the new millennium: Where we are, where we're headed. *Journal of Teacher Education, 52*(3), 244-254.

Yinger, R. (1999). The role of standards in teaching and teacher education. In G. Griffin (Ed.), *The education of teachers: The 98th yearbook of the NSSE* (pp. 85-113). Chicago: University of Chicago Press.

7 Reforming Teacher Education

Competing Agendas

In the media and in public policy discussions, there is intensified emphasis on the quality of public education and the nation's teaching force. Teacher preparation in particular has received enormous attention as part of highly publicized and politicized efforts to get tough about results and standards with concentrated pressure on the higher education institutions that prepare teachers either to get better at teaching or get out of the business. Current pressures on teacher education have bite as well as bark, with some of the teeth provided by new mandatory Title II reporting, which will affect eligibility for federal funding and result in a federal report card on the states and on teacher preparation institutions.

It is useful to note that there are at least three agendas driving reforms in teacher education at national and/or state levels: the professionalization agenda, the deregulation agenda, and what some people are calling the overregulation agenda. Although overlapping in certain ways—with the degree of overlap dependent in part on the regulations and professional relationships established by individual states—these three agendas are also competing and even contradictory in other ways.

The professionalization agenda for reforming teacher education is part of efforts during the past several decades to establish a

SOURCE: *Journal of Teacher Education*, Vol. 52, No. 4, September/October 2001, pp. 263-265.

professional knowledge base for teaching and teacher education and on efforts by the National Council for the Accreditation of Teacher Education, the National Board for Professional Teaching Standards (NBPTS), and the Interstate New Teacher Assessment and Support Consortium (INTASC) to professionalize teacher education. Particularly influential on the current professionalization agenda was the publication of *What Matters Most: Teaching for America's Future* (National Commission on Teaching and America's Future [NCTAF], 1996) and the materials and initiatives that followed it. Spearheaded by NCTAF and Linda Darling-Hammond, key professional organizations are now collaborating on a common national system of teacher preparation and development based on professional consensus and high standards for teacher preparation, initial teacher licensing, and board certification of experienced teachers.

Alongside the professionalization agenda, however, is the well-publicized and now well-known movement to deregulate teacher education by dismantling teacher education institutions to break up the "monopoly" that the profession has "too long enjoyed." Spearheaded by conservative political groups and foundations such as the Fordham Foundation and the Pioneer Institute, deregulationists assert that the requirements of teacher preparation programs and state licensing agencies present unnecessary hurdles that keep bright young people out of teaching and focus on social goals rather than academic achievement. Chester Finn's Fordham Foundation, which frames its agenda in explicit opposition to professionalization, advocates alternate routes into teaching and high-stakes, state-level teacher tests as the primary gatekeepers into the profession (Kanstoroom & Finn, 1999). Although some of these tests have been criticized for their poor technical quality, their inconsistency with teacher education curricula, and/or their lack of validity as predictors of either teaching practice or student achievement, tests are generally accepted as public evidence that teachers are (or are not) meeting high standards.

In addition to high-stakes tests, most states across the country now have additional new regulations intended to reform curricula, programs, and policies for teacher preparation at higher education institutions. In some states, new regulations are largely in sync with the professionalization agenda, focusing on performance-based assessments of teacher candidates that are linked to INTASC and NBPTS standards. In other states, however, new regulations represent unprecedented moves to establish external control of nearly every aspect of teacher preparation, including allowable arts and sciences majors, amount and content of education course work, quality and kind of subject matter preparation, and extent and type of fieldwork experiences that teacher candidates have in schools. Although some would argue that these initiatives are merely responsible state oversight of the public education enterprise, many education professionals and other critics regard prescriptive state control as "over-regulation" of teacher education (Thiessen, 2000). Ironically, state agendas that overregulate teacher education do not function in opposition only to the professionalization agenda—by prescribing teachers' and teacher educators' work and circumscribing their opportunities to make professional decisions, construct curriculum and programs, and develop innovative programs in keeping with the missions of their institutions (Apple, 2001; Cochran-Smith & Dudley-Marling, 2001). Rather, they also work in opposition to the deregulation agenda—by mandating tighter controls and establishing more hoops and hurdles for prospective teachers rather than opening up more entryways into teaching and allowing for free market reform, as the deregulationists advocate. Again ironically, in some states, there are simultaneous efforts by state education agencies to overregulate teaching programs at higher education institutions, for example, by limiting acceptable majors for certification and/or stipulating the number, content, and even titles of required courses; to deregulate teacher preparation, for example, by establishing (and even privileging) alternate routes into teaching that are wide open in terms of teacher candidates' academic backgrounds and other experiences; and to professionalize teacher education, for example, by establishing high standards that are consistent across accreditation, licensing, and certification.

Underlying these reform agendas are differing ideas about how to evaluate teacher education, including what the appropriate outcomes of teacher education ought to be, as well as differing ideas about teacher preparation programs and curricula. Those who advocate a professionalization agenda suggest that the appropriate outcomes of teacher education are both its long-term impact (concluding that teacher education matters more than any other factor in determining K-12 students' learning and school achievement) and performance-based assessments of new and experienced teachers. Professionalizationists are also concerned about high and consistent standards

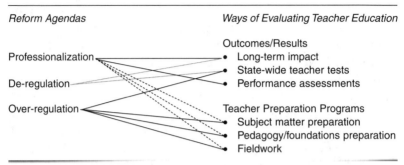

Reform Agendas   *Ways of Evaluating Teacher Education*

Figure 1   Reforming Teacher Education

for all aspects of teacher education programs, including arts and sciences preparation, subject matter knowledge, and education curriculum and fieldwork. Interestingly, those who advocate deregulation also regard long-term impact as an appropriate outcome of teacher education (although they conclude that it does not matter much at all in determining students' learning), as are scores on state-level teacher tests, which they see as the primary gatekeeper into the profession. State and federal policies intended to reform teacher education through over-regulation depend on high-stakes teacher tests as the most important outcome of teacher education but also want state control of the inputs of teacher education by prescribing multiple aspects of teacher preparation programs at higher education institutions. Figure 1 outlines some of the connections between the three reform agendas, on one hand, and the ways various constituencies are evaluating and assessing teacher preparation, on the other. This figure is intended to indicate some of the complexity inherent in the current press to reform teacher education and perhaps to explain why educators and teacher candidates feel confused and even intimidated at times by the competing agendas to which they must answer.

Finally, although all sorts of claims are being made in professional and political arenas about the potential of various agendas to improve teacher preparation and teacher quality, we actually know relatively little about the effects of these agendas. They are supported in varying ways and under different circumstances by the public, the media, political groups, external accreditation agencies, professional education organizations, state and federal government agencies, and administrators at higher education institutions. Together these agendas are placing intense and unprecedented demands on teacher preparation programs and on those responsible for teacher education. One of the most urgent demands is that teacher preparation programs, institutions, and organizations produce convincing empirical evidence of their effectiveness at enhancing teachers' learning, improving professional practice, and increasing students' learning. Although there are multiple debates about what it would mean to do so (see Cochran-Smith, 2001, for a much longer and more nuanced discussion about outcomes and the issues they entail), many teacher educators accept and even embrace the idea that we should be able to demonstrate—with solid evidence—that teacher education has positive effects on how teachers teach and on what and how much K-12 students learn. Many of us agree that as teacher educators, we should be working to get better at developing and presenting evidence that supports our work. But, we should also be demanding that policymakers, state education departments, accrediting agencies, economists, and critics alike produce documentation for their claims and that they demonstrate—with solid evidence— that the reform agendas they advocate for teacher education have positive effects on teacher quality, students' learning, and public education in and for a democratic society.

REFERENCES

Apple, M. (2001). Markets, standards, teaching, and teacher education. *Journal of Teacher Education, 52,* 182-195.

Cochran-Smith, M. (2001). Constructing outcomes in teacher education: Policy, practice, and pitfalls. *Educational Policy Analysis Archives, 9*(11) [Online]. Available: http://epaa.asu.edu/epaa/vol9.html/

Cochran-Smith, M., & Dudley-Marling, C. (2001). The flunk heard round the world. *Teaching Education, 12*(1), 49-63.

Kanstoroom, M., & Finn, C. (1999, July). *Better teachers, better schools.* Washington, DC: Fordham Foundation.

National Commission on Teaching and America's Future. (1996). *What matters most: Teaching for America's future.* New York: Columbia University, Teachers College.

Thiessen, D. (2000). Developing knowledge for preparing teachers: Redefining the role of schools of education. *Educational Policy, 14*(1), 129-144.

8 Desperately Seeking Solutions

One of the most persistent themes in the history of teacher education has been sharp public criticism coupled with ardent demands for improvement and change. Despite many reform initiatives over the years, however, it has been widely perceived that teacher education has been almost "impervious" to genuine reform (Fullan, 1998; Goodlad, 1990), failing to keep pace with the conditions of a changing society even when they threatened its very existence (Imig & Switzer, 1996). Perhaps it is the combination of a perceived historical failure to change coupled with the unprecedented intensity of current public attention that have prompted so many recent initiatives by prestigious national organizations and foundations that are related to teaching and teacher education, teachers' qualifications, and teacher quality. Although what follows is not a comprehensive list, the remainder of this editorial provides a brief description of some of the most visible current initiatives and reports that are directly related to teacher education; those recently completed are listed first, followed by those currently under way.

Center for the Study of Teaching and Policy Research Report on Teacher Preparation. Suzanne Wilson, Robert Floden, and Joan Ferrini-Mundy, Michigan State University (MSU), authored CTP's recent report, "Teacher Preparation Research: Current Knowledge, Gaps, and Recommendations," for the U.S. Department of Education/ the Office of Educational Research and Improvement (OERI). The

SOURCE: *Journal of Teacher Education,* Vol. 52, No. 5, November/December 2001, pp. 347-349.

authors examined more than 300 peer-reviewed research reports about subject matter preparation, pedagogical preparation, clinical training, policies for improving teacher education, and alternative certification. Drawing on the 57 studies that met rigorous criteria, the report concludes that the empirical research base for teacher education is thin. It recommends a new generation of research that looks across institutions, examines specific parts of teachers' preparation, and has stronger research designs. Executive summary and full report are available at: http://www.ctpweb.org.

Committee on Assessment and Teacher Quality Report. The National Research Council's Committee on Assessment and Teacher Quality recently issued "Testing Teacher Candidates: The Role of Licensure Tests in Improving Teacher Quality," edited by Karen Mitchell, David Robinson, Barbara Plake, and Kale Knolls. Chaired by David Robinson, the 19-member committee was impaneled by the National Academy of Sciences at the request of the U.S. Department of Education (DOE) to examine the appropriateness and technical quality of teacher licensure tests and the merits of such tests for holding states and higher education institutions accountable for the quality of teacher education. The report concludes that initial teacher licensure tests fall short of the intended policy goals for their use as accountability tools and as levers for improving teacher preparation and licensing programs. Complete report is available at http://www.nap.edu.

Educational Testing Service's Studies of Teacher Quality and Teacher Education. ETS's work on teacher quality and teacher education is not a single initiative but an emphasis in several of their centers. Along these lines, Harold Wenglinsky's study linking students' achievement in math and science with teacher qualifications, professional development and classroom practices, concludes that classroom practices matter most. His study on teaching teachers explores the links among the characteristics of teacher education institutions, their programs, and teacher effectiveness as measured by scores on licensure exams. Drew Gitomer, Andrew Latham, and Robert Ziomek's study on the academic quality of prospective teachers concludes that prospective teachers' academic ability varies widely by type of licensure sought. For information on these and other ETS studies, consult: http://www.ets.org.

AERA Consensus Panel on Teacher Education. The AERA Consensus Panel is an 18-month initiative intended to provide a synthesis of existing empirical and conceptual research related to the preparation of new teachers. Co-chaired by Marilyn Cochran-Smith and Ken Zeichner, the 17-member panel was convened partly in response to conflicting public claims about the research evidence for competing reform agendas. The work of the panel revolves around several controversial areas in teacher preparation: demographics, the components and pedagogy of teacher preparation, accountability systems, and the preparation of teachers for minority populations and for learners with special needs. Outcomes will include an edited volume, a special issue of this journal, and symposia at major conferences. For information, see Cochran-Smith & Zeichner (2005).

The Carnegie Foundation for the Advancement of Teaching Study of the Education of Teachers. Led by Carnegie President Lee Shulman, the Carnegie initiative is a 5-year study of the pedagogies of teacher education, which is part of a larger series of studies on preparation for the professions. A team of five university scholars is working with Carnegie staff within three strategic sites in teacher education, which have analogous practices in other professions: liberal arts and sciences, methods courses, and supervised field experiences. Cross-cutting these sites are key questions about pedagogies in teacher education, which are defined as decisions about what and how to teach and the assessment of what has been learned. The team is working on all aspects of the study at key sites with the assistance of local co-researchers. For more information, consult: http://www.carnegiefoundation.org.

Committee on Teacher Education of the National Academy of Education (CTE). Cochaired by Linda Darling-Hammond and John Bransford, CTE is a 2-year initiative designed to make curriculum recommendations to U.S. teacher preparation programs based on the knowledge teacher candidates need to become effective new teachers. The initiative is designed to be distinct from previous knowledge base projects in that it addresses curriculum issues directly and draws on both the individual and collective expertise of its members. The CTE initiative has a 28-member committee of diverse practitioners and researchers, a reading subcommittee chaired by Catherine Snow, and seven cooperating universities. Funded by OERI, the committee will meet six times over the 2-year period so that ongoing work can be combined with face-to-face discussions among CTE members. For more information, see Darling-Hammond (2005).

The Teacher Qualifications and the Quality of Teaching Study (TQQT). TQQT is a 3-year project conducted collaboratively by Mary Kennedy and Betsy Jane Becker (MSU). Funded by OERI, the project will synthesize research over the past 40 years that examines teacher qualifications (e.g. level of education, courses taken, major and minor areas of study, test scores, certification) in relation to quality of teaching practice (e.g. observations of teaching, artifacts from practice, pupil achievement). The synthesis—which will include qualitative and quantitative studies, multiple indicators of teaching quality; and multiple genres of research—will be used to develop a model of the complex relationships between teacher qualifications and teaching quality that accounts for confounding variables. For information, consult: http://www.msu.edu/user/mkennedy/publica tions/index.htm

Although some of these initiatives overlap in certain ways, they are not the same in intention and design or in organizational structure and authorship; several are intended to synthesize and critique existing research; several represent new research or new analyses of existing data bases; and some focus on the teacher education curriculum. Despite both differences and overlaps, it is interesting that all of these initiatives have emerged at roughly the same historical moment when teaching and teacher education are intensely publicized and politicized. Although "desperately seeking solutions" may be a catchy title for an editorial, none of these projects is either "desperate" in the sense of reckless and frantic or "seeking solutions" in the sense of attempting to dictate final and universally effective policies and practices. These initiatives do, however, share a sense of urgency about the need to improve teaching, teacher quality, and teacher education in order to address the problems (some might indeed say, "desperate" problems) of teaching and schooling in America. These initiatives also share a basic sense of confidence in what I have called elsewhere the "evidentiary warrant" in teacher education reform (Cochran-Smith & Fries, 2001), or the belief that rigorous and "unbiased" empirical research has the capacity to offer directions and guidelines about how to solve the problems of teacher preparation. Although important, this approach de-emphasizes the ideological, political, and moral aspects of teaching and teacher education, areas that may also need to be debated further. (Future *JTE* editorials will explore these issues in more detail.)

REFERENCES

Cochran-Smith, M. & Fries, M. K. (2001). Sticks, stones and ideology: The discourse of reform in teacher education. *Educational Researcher, 30*(8), 3-15.

Cochran-Smith, M. & Zeichner, K. (2005). *Studying teacher education: The report of the AERA panel on research and teacher education.* Washington, D.C: AERA.

Darling-Hammond, L. (2005). *Preparing teachers for a changing world: What teachers should learn and be able to do.* San Franciso: Jossey-Bass.

Fullan, M. (1998). *The meaning of educational change: A quarter century of learning.* In A. Hargreaves, A. Lieberman, M. Fullan, & D. Hopkins (Eds.), *The international handbook of educational change* (pp. 214-228). Boston: Kluwer.

Goodlad, J. (1990). *Teachers for our nation's schools.* San Francisco: Jossey-Bass.

Imig, D., & Switzer, T. (1996). Changing teacher education programs: Restructuring collegiate-based teacher education. In J. Sikula, T. Buttery, & E. Guyton (Eds.), *Handbook of research on teacher education* (2nd ed., pp. 213-226). New York: Macmillan.

9 *Teacher Education, Ideology, and Napoleon*

In an essay on medical practice, Vivian Ota Wang (2000) questioned what she called the "fallacy of neutral universalism." She argued that there are both overt and covert values underlying all medical practices and that these must be exposed and scrutinized if we are to understand the attitudes and actions of medical practitioners. She asserted,

> Western science fundamentally influences the character, methods, practices, ethos, ethics, and ideology of medicine and has nurtured a medical paradigm that is based on the fragile infrastructure of universality and neutrality ... [these] are the primary sources used to justify the expectations and behavior of medical professionals, their patients, and society. (pp. 148-149)

Wang's point that medical practice is never neutral, but is instead value-laden and ideological, is similar to Michael Apple's arguments about educational practice. In the preface to the second edition of *Ideology and Curriculum*, for example, Apple (1990) argued,

> Discussions about what does, can, and should go on in classrooms are not the logical equivalent of conversations about the weather. They are fundamentally about the hopes, dreams, fears, and realities—the very lives—of millions of children, parents, and

SOURCE: *Journal of Teacher Education*, Vol. 53, No. 1, January/February 2002, pp. 3-5.

teachers. . . . Until we take seriously the extent to which education is caught up in the real world of shifting and unequal power relations, we will be living in a world divorced from reality. The theories, policies, and practices involved in education are *not* technical. They are inherently ethical and political, and they ultimately involve—once this is recognized—intensely personal choices. (p. viii)

These arguments by Wang and Apple are consistent with the larger position that all social practice—whether in law, medicine, criminal justice, social service, or education—is value-laden and ideological rather than neutral and apolitical. Once the ideological basis of social practice is acknowledged, then it stands to reason that debates about how to reform practice—including educational practice—need to address openly the difficult choices and trade-offs that all choices about values and ideology entail.

In recent debates about how to reform teacher education, however, the trend has been in the opposite direction. Rather than debate the ideals, commitments, and values that are (or ought to be) the basis of improvements in teacher education, reformers have implied or asserted that their positions were neutral, apolitical, and value free, based solely on empirical evidence and not embedded within or related to particular agendas that are both political and ideological. At the same time, it has become more and more common to use the term *ideological* to cast aspersions on, undermine, and ultimately dismiss positions that compete with one's own.

James Gee (1996) made an intriguing argument along these lines in his volume on social linguistics and literacies, which was subtitled *Ideology in Discourses*. Gee pointed out that what he labeled "Napoleon's move" was a significant moment in the history of the term *ideology*, a move that has become a classic rhetorical strategy for attacking views one does not like.[1] Gee explained,

The Enlightenment philosophers had derived their views of what laws and governments ought to look like on the basis of a social theory of the mind, knowledge, and human beings. In attacking these philosophers, Napoleon used "ideology" as a term of abuse for a social policy which was in part or in whole derived from a social theory in a conscious way. Napoleon disliked the Enlightenment philosophers' social theory and its conclusions because they conflicted with his interests and his pursuit of power. Rather than arguing against this theory by arguing for a rival theory of his own, he castigates it as abstract, impractical, and fanatical. In its place he substitutes, not another theory, but "knowledge of the human heart and . . . the lessons of history . . . " which it just so happens Napoleon is in a position to know better than others and which just happens to support his policies. (p. 3)

As Gee pointed out, this move has been used ever since Napoleon to attack and dismiss social theories that conflict with one's own position and to suggest that one's opponent is an ideologue, operating within a closed system and unwilling to consider other points of view. This strategy is evident in many debates about current reform policies for teacher education.

One of the most provocative applications of Napoleon's move to dismiss a position *because* it was ideological occurred recently in an evaluation of teacher education programs in Colorado, as reported in the news media in the Denver area (e.g., Curtin, 2001; Langeland, 2001). As is true in many states, Colorado now has new and tighter regulations for teacher preparation, and all teacher education programs were required to be recertified by June 2001 or else be shut down. As this June deadline approached, Denver newspaper accounts revealed that a report by the conservative "watchdog" organization the National Association of Scholars (NAS) had been commissioned by the Colorado Commission on Higher Education to aid in their evaluations.[2] The report's conclusions about teacher education at the University of Colorado at Boulder (CU) made headlines across the state. Note that Napoleon's move is front and center in this critique. The report concluded:

There are problems here that are so significant that a mere "revision" is unlikely to correct them. Nothing short of a miraculous transformation can reverse the patently overt ideological proselytizing that goes on in the name of teacher education at CU. More than any other reviewed institution, CU's teacher education programs are the most politically correct and stridently committed to the social justice model. (Curtin, 2001)

The NAS report asserted explicitly that teacher education programs should be based on "objective" standards and "core knowledge" *rather than ideology*. The Colorado brouhaha over this excoriating critique had partly to do with the fact that the existence of the NAS document was denied until newspapers uncovered it. My point in this editorial, however, is that the NAS critique used ideology as a damning pejorative in and of itself to discredit and dismiss the work of certain teacher education institutions.

It is not surprising that there are many debates currently about what evidence actually exists for various reform approaches in teacher education. As my most recent editorial in this journal pointed out, there are a number of major initiatives under way nationwide to sort out competing claims about teacher education and teacher quality and to establish rigorous and objective analyses of the empirical evidence in these areas. There is no question that these efforts are important and that we must carefully scrutinize the evidence that seems to support competing claims about how best to reform teacher education. It is only common sense, after all, to want educational policies based on empirical evidence and facts rather than ideology, if we mean *ideology* in Napoleon's sense of a closed system of ideas put forward by ideologues who are preoccupied with idle theory rather than with data and real experience. But Napoleon's is not the only meaning of this term.

What I want to suggest here is that the most important questions about how to reform teacher education and provide quality teachers for America's schools will not be resolved *solely* by evaluating the evidence, although these efforts are critically important. It is also important that we debate and sort out the various ideological and political aspects of reform agendas. Unless underlying ideals, ideologies, and values (about, for example, the purposes of schooling, the knowledge that is most worthwhile for the next generation, and the meaning of a democratic society) are debated *along with* the "evidence," we will make little progress in understanding the politics of teacher education and the complexities of the various reform agendas that are in competition with one another.

NOTES

1. This point about ideology in the discourse of reform in teacher education draws on a larger argument made in Cochran-Smith and Fries (2001).

2. This is not to imply that it is only educational reformers whom many would label "conservative" who use Napoleon's move to critique the positions of others. This discourse strategy has been used by many critics

who represent a variety of viewpoints about teacher education and educational reform more generally. Examples are included in Cochran-Smith and Fries (2001).

REFERENCES

Apple, M. W. (1990). *Ideology and curriculum* (2nd ed.). New York: Routledge.

Cochran-Smith, M., & Fries, M. K. (2001). Sticks, stones and ideology: The discourse of reform in teacher education. *Educational Researcher, 30*(8).

Curtin, D. (2001, February 3). Report blasts teacher prep: CU, Metro State called too liberal. *Denver Post*, pp. 1B, 3B.

Gee, J. (1996). *Social linguistics and literacies: Ideology in discourses.* London: Taylor & Francis.

Langeland, T. (2001, February 2). *Report raises eyebrows: Study of teacher education kept under wraps.* Retrieved from http://co001.campusmotor .com/shell_story_news.html

Wang, V. O. (2000). The house of God: The fallacy of neutral universalism in medicine. In R. T. Carter (Ed.), *Addressing cultural issues in organizations: Beyond the corporate context.* Thousand Oaks, CA: Sage.

10 What's Preparation Got to Do With It?

Williams v. State of California is the lawsuit brought in April 2000 by the American Civil Liberties Union (ACLU) on behalf of public school children in 18 California school districts. According to the *ACLU Southern California Docket*, the suit charges that children who attend schools that lack "such basic and necessary learning tools as books, trained teachers, and seats for students" are deprived of fundamental educational opportunities and also that the state of California has failed to fulfill its constitutional obligation to provide "at least the bare essentials" for the education of all students. In addition, the suit challenges the "conditions of the schools for having a racially discriminatory effect on these children, most of whom are children of color" (see Natriello, 2004a; 2004b).

These conditions include lack of basic resources (e.g., outdated, defaced, or nonexistent textbooks; little or no access to computers; little or no school supplies; no library access), inadequate instruction (e.g., as few as 13% of teachers with "full teaching credentials," frequent use of substitute teachers, consistently unstaffed vacancies), over-crowding (e.g., makeshift and jammed classrooms with inadequate seats, multitrack schedules that limit course length and continuous study), and poor and/or unsanitary conditions (e.g., filthy, broken, or unavailable toilet facilities; rat infestations; leaking roofs; broken windows; and other dangers). Using data from the California Department of Education (DOE), the suit points out that

SOURCE: *Journal of Teacher Education*, Vol. 53, No. 2, March/April 2002, pp. 99-101.

in the plaintiffs' schools, children of color make up 96.4% of the student population, compared with 59% across the state.

The plaintiffs are seeking a judgment that would require the DOE to establish a systematic process for identifying and remedying substandard conditions. Meanwhile, Governor Gray Davis and the State of California claimed that public school conditions are the obligation of local school districts, not the state, and have counter-sued the 18 school districts named in the lawsuit. However, the California Supreme Court granted a motion in October for class certification in the case, which means that the suit can be expanded to include all children in substandard California public schools (not just students at the 18 originally named schools), suggesting that the court sees the problem as a statewide issue requiring statewide solutions (Smith, 2001). This latest decision has raised considerably the stakes involved in the case because any relief granted to the plaintiffs will now apply to every California school with substandard conditions.

For teacher education, a striking and important aspect of this lawsuit is its assumption that access to fully prepared, qualified teachers is not only essential to a good education but is also a major divide in the experiences of schoolchildren from advantaged and disadvantaged socioeconomic and racial groups. This assumption is, of course, quite consistent with the agenda to professionalize teaching and teacher education, best represented in the now widely quoted first report of the National Commission on Teaching and America's Future (NCTAF), *What Matters Most* (1996):

> This report offers what we believe is the single most important strategy for achieving America's educational goals: A blueprint for recruiting, preparing, and supporting excellent teachers in all of America's schools . . . (p. 3)

> Tens of thousands of people not educated for these demands have been unable to make a successful transition into the new economy. . . . Those who succeed and those who fail are increasingly divided by their opportunities to learn . . . (p. 11)

From this perspective, equal access to good teachers with rich opportunities for all students to learn is the best path to a citizenry educated for democracy.

The California lawsuit takes as a given the premise that well-qualified teachers are fully prepared and fully licensed teachers. As we now know all too well, however, what teacher preparation has to do with being a well-qualified and competent teacher is a highly contested issue, one that is apparently open to endless debates about what the evidence shows, what the existing data mean, and what the implications are for public policy.

The latest round of debates on this question that the California lawsuit takes for granted is found in the juxtaposition of *Teacher Certification Reconsidered: Stumbling for Quality*, a report sponsored by the Abell Foundation (2001a), whose self-stated mission is improving the quality of life in Baltimore and Maryland; and *The Research and Rhetoric on Teacher Certification: A Response to "Teacher Certification Reconsidered"* (Darling-Hammond, 2001), sponsored by NCTAF. The major conclusion of the Abell Foundation report, authored by the foundation's senior policy analyst, Kate Walsh, is captured in the caption for the Executive Summary:

> Maryland's requirement that individuals must complete a prescribed body of coursework before teaching in a public school is deeply misguided. This process, known as teacher certification, is neither an efficient nor an effective means by which to ensure a competent teaching force. Worse, it is often counterproductive. (p. iii)

Walsh directly challenges the claim that taking the certification coursework required by college and university programs is the most appropriate way to prepare teachers by exposing the "deficiencies" that characterize the research that supports teacher education:

> The academic research attempting to link teacher certification with student achievement is astonishingly deficient.
>
> To reach this conclusion, we reviewed every published study or paper—along with many unpublished dissertations—cited by prominent national advocates of teacher certification. . . . To our knowledge there has been no comparable effort by analysts to drill systematically down through these layers of evidence in order to determine what value lies at the core. (Abell Foundation, 2001a, p. iii)

According to Walsh, research that supports the efficacy of teacher preparation is selective, outdated, padded, technically unsound, and heavily reliant on nonstandardized measures, whereas a reliable body of research by economists and social scientists indicates that teacher effectiveness is not correlated with teacher preparation but with teachers' verbal ability. Walsh concludes that teacher certification in Maryland should be deregulated, that the state DOE should be held accountable for teachers' average tested verbal ability, and that responsibility for teacher qualifications should be devolved to school districts.

NCTAF's response to the Abell Foundation report, written by Linda Darling-Hammond (2001), opens by both repudiating the findings of the report and exposing its underlying local and larger political agendas:

> In a stunning exercise in misrepresentation, Kate Walsh has written a paper for the Abell Foundation that purports to prove that there is "no credible research that supports the use of teacher certification as a regulatory barrier to teaching.". . . Her agenda is to argue against reforms that would . . . bring qualified teachers to inner city schools. . . . A related agenda is to argue against Maryland's efforts . . . to expand incentives for improving the supply of certified teachers. . . . A final agenda is to rekindle support for the Resident Teacher Program in Baltimore, a program that has been a revolving door of under-prepared teachers. (p. 1)

Darling-Hammond (2001) argues that Walsh's characterization of educational research as "flawed, sloppy, aged and sometimes academically dishonest" (Abell Foundation, 2001a, p. 13) is in fact a better description of Walsh's own report. Darling-Hammond asserts,

> Walsh's paper, which is littered with dozens of inaccuracies, misstatements, and misrepresentations, sheds little light on them or their implications for the research base on teacher education and certification. (p. 3)

Nearly two thirds of Darling-Hammond's 62-page response is devoted to challenging the claims and representations of the Walsh report.

As this issue of *JTE* went to press, the Abell Foundation (2001b) had just released Walsh's rejoinder to Darling-Hammond, a detailed rebuttal supplemented with economic analyses. The Abell rejoinder and any re-rejoinder that may follow from NCTAF or other groups will certainly not be the last word in this debate. By now, it has become nearly impossible—even for those who specialize in research methodologies—to sort out the conflicting research evidence about teacher preparation without undertaking an independent, time-consuming, and massive synthesis of the literature.[1]

This editorial, its title borrowed from the question Tina Turner belted out not so long ago, is intended to spotlight two issues that are currently haunting teacher education. The first is the more obvious: What's teacher preparation got to do with teaching quality and with schoolchildren's educational experiences? This question is at the heart of the recent Walsh and Darling-Hammond papers and the ongoing debate about research evidence. The second question is somewhat less obvious but is at least as important as the first and perhaps cuts closer to the bone of the debates. This second question ties the California lawsuit with which I began this editorial to the ongoing debate about research: What's teacher preparation got to do with equity, with access to educational opportunity, and with preparing all the citizens of a demographically diverse society to live in a democracy? The California lawsuit, the NCTAF/Darling-Hammond positions, and the larger professionalization agenda are unambiguous about this: Teacher preparation has a great deal to do with equity. Indeed, a birthright of all students is access to the bare essentials of a good education: basic materials, well-qualified teachers, healthful conditions, and schools with enough seats to go around. The debate will rage on, but it is surely time to ask, Would anyone want less for their own children? Why do some people argue for less for other people's children when all of us live in the strongest democracy and the richest country in the world? Is access to fully prepared teachers a birthright only of those children who live in school districts rich enough to attract them?

NOTE

1. There are several major synthesis projects under way along these lines; some of these are described in an editorial in the previous issue of *JTE* (Vol. 52, No. 5).

REFERENCES

The Abell Foundation. (2001a, October). *Teacher certification reconsidered: Stumbling for quality.* Baltimore: Author. Available from http://www.abell.org

The Abell Foundation. (2001b, November). *Teacher certification reconsidered: Stumbling for quality. A rejoinder.* Baltimore: Author. Available from http://www.abell.org

Darling-Hammond, L. (2001, October). *The research and rhetoric on teacher certification: A response to "Teacher certification reconsidered."* Available from the National Commission on Teaching and America's Future Web site: http://www.nctaf.org

National Commission on Teaching and America's Future. (1996, September). *What matters most: Teaching for America's future.* New York: Columbia University, Teachers College.

Natriello, G. (Ed.). (2004a). *Teachers college Record. 106*(10).

Natriello, G. (Ed.). (2004b). *Teachers college Record. 106*(11).

Smith, D. (2001, October 3). Judge rules ACLU may expand schools lawsuit. *Los Angeles Times.* Available from the *Los Angeles Times* Web site: http://pqasb.pqarchiver.com/latimes/search.html

11 What a Difference a Definition Makes

Highly Qualified Teachers, Scientific Research, and Teacher Education

O n January 8, 2002, President Bush signed into law the reauthorization of the Elementary and Secondary Education Act (ESEA), which *The Washington Post* referred to as the "broadest rewriting of federal education policy in decades" and "Washington's top bipartisan achievement of 2001" (Milbank, 2002). In other news stories and editorials, the bill has been referred to as a triumph—the culmination of exhaustive efforts by both houses of Congress and concessions from both political parties (Robelen, 2002). Called the "No Child Left Behind Act," the bill pays homage to Bush's campaign focus on education (Broder, 2001).

The revised ESEA significantly increases both the federal role in precollegiate education and the overall amount of federal dollars earmarked for this purpose. The bill, which directly targets poor students and struggling schools by shifting funding formulas, requires mandatory annual testing of students from third through eighth grade and makes schools accountable by tracking test results, reporting to parents, and disaggregating results by race, gender, and other factors.

Although the bill's supporters claim it represents an unprecedented consensus, it has also raised concerns. A September letter

---

SOURCE: *Journal of Teacher Education,* Vol. 53, No. 3, May/June 2002, pp. 187-189.

from the National Conference of State Legislatures to Congress, for example, called the bill "an egregious example of a top-down, one-size-fits-all federal reform" (*Education Week*, 2001), sharply questioning that annual statewide testing in multiple subjects is necessary for an effective state accountability system. Others are concerned that the heavy-handed emphasis on testing will lead to manipulation of the system and narrowing of the curriculum. Commenting that the bill ought to be called the "No Child Left Untested Act," Robert Schaeffer of FairTest argued that mandatory testing will not show schools where to invest resources but will, on the contrary, take money away from initiatives not directly tested and will penalize (not help) struggling students (Toppo, 2002). Policy analysts have raised questions about the bill as a lever for state education reform, pointing out that although a number of states are still not in compliance with 1994 ESEA requirements, Title I funds have never been withheld from a state for noncompliance (Robelen, 2001). Other concerns include the bill's imbalance between mandates and funding and its inadequate attention to special education as well as the possibility of stigmatizing poor and minority students, the incapacity of the testing industry to keep up with the mandatory testing program, and the new layers of federal regulations that are likely to duplicate state efforts.

Of particular interest to the teacher education community is the bill's provision that every state ensure that all teachers are "highly qualified" and are "receiving high-quality professional development" (Section 1119). Highly qualified teachers are defined as those who have obtained full state certification (including through alternate routes) or have passed a state teacher licensing exam (Section 9101). It is worth noting that this provision of the bill implies that college- and university-based teacher education is neither the sole nor the required mode of preparation for teaching, cementing into this new federal legislation the legitimacy of current alternate routes that bypass traditional collegiate preparation in more than 40 states (Zeichner & Shulte, 2001). According to ESEA definitions, high-quality professional development may involve partnerships with higher education institutions that give teachers the opportunity to work with experienced teachers and college faculty but must, by definition, improve teachers' subject matter knowledge, align with state standards, and improve teachers' understanding of instructional strategies "based on scientifically based research" (Section

9101). Again this definition leaves ambiguous (and perhaps makes superfluous) the role of colleges and universities in the preparation of highly qualified teachers at the same time that it elevates scientifically based research.

According to ESEA, scientific research is the application of "rigorous, systematic, and objective procedures to obtain reliable and valid knowledge by employing systematic methods of observation or experimentation" (Section 9101). ESEA's scientific educational research

> involves rigorous data analyses that are adequate to test the stated hypotheses and justify the general conclusions drawn . . . [and] is evaluated using experimental or quasi-experimental designs in which individuals, entities, programs, or activities are assigned to different conditions and with appropriate controls to evaluate the effects of the condition of interest, with a preference for random-assignment experiments, or other designs to the extent that those designs contain within-condition or across-condition controls. (Section 9101)

It would be an understatement to say that the revised ESEA prefers educational research that utilizes randomized experiments and related designs. Indeed, the new bill virtually mandates this approach, which will have far-reaching consequences for what is funded and thus what will happen in K-12 schools as well as in colleges and universities.

It is instructive—and troubling—to contrast the definition of educational research used in the new ESEA with that put forward in the National Research Council's (NRC's) (2001) recent report *Scientific Inquiry in Education*. Chaired by Richard Shavelson, the NRC committee was charged by the U.S. Department of Education to "review and synthesize literature on the science and practice of scientific educational research" (p. 15) and make recommendations about how to support high-quality science. This charge to the committee was motivated, in part, by the widespread perception that the results of educational research have been low quality, constantly contested, and incapable of producing knowledge that improves educational policy and practice.

The NRC (2001) report states explicitly that it is not a particular design that makes research scientific:

The design of a study (e.g. randomized experiment, ethnographic case study) does not make the study scientific. A wide variety of legitimate scientific designs are available for education research. They range from randomized experiments . . . to in-depth case studies . . . to neurocognitive investigations. . . . To be scientific, the design must allow direct, empirical investigation of an important question, account for the context in which the study is carried out, align with a conceptual framework, reflect careful and thorough reasoning, and disclose results to encourage debate in the scientific community. (p. 4)

The report cautions that this does not mean anything goes in education research, and it also acknowledges that the degree to which knowledge has accumulated in the physical and social sciences far exceeds the degree to which it has accumulated in educational research. Nonetheless, the NRC report makes it clear that "there is no one method or process that unambiguously defines science" (p. 16). It is disturbing, then, that the federal government has certified a definition of research that is inconsistent with the definition put forward in the NRC report, which arguably represents the mainstream view of the community of educational researchers.[1] The ESEA definition of scientific research seems intended to preclude many research designs long accepted in the community of educational scholars, including in-depth case studies, ethnographic studies, multiple-methods studies, and some survey and interview designs.

Operating from a more inclusive perspective, the NRC (2001) report argues that certain designs are more appropriate than others to address certain questions under particular conditions and concludes that "in order to generate a rich source of scientific knowledge in education that is refined and revised over time, different types of inquiries and methods are required" (p. 70). On the other hand, ESEA's definition of research implies that there is only one valid question in education (What works? in the sense of teaching or teacher education strategies that lead directly to increases in scores on standardized tests) and only one scientifically rigorous and valid approach to answering that question (randomized experiments or quasi experiments that contain within-condition or across-conditions controls). This narrow view of the "right" question to ask in educational research is problematic on a number of grounds. History has already told us that this question leaves out many important subquestions: For whom is some particular strategy or policy working (or not working)? Under what conditions does a strategy work or not work? What does it really mean to say something "works" (or does not work) in the first place? Who decides? The single-minded and limited question, What works? does not get us very far in improving the learning opportunities of all students and does not go very far toward explaining why some children have historically been "left behind" by the educational system. ESEA's definition of scientific research, which forecloses rather than enhances possibilities, seems curiously at odds with the spirit of scientific inquiry in the first place and with the assumption that a healthy research community—just like a healthy democracy—depends on open debate, alternative viewpoints, and multiple perspectives.

JTE Special Issue: Evidence and Inquiry in Teacher Education

This special issue of *JTE* is intended to examine some of the research that currently exists in the field and also raise important questions. This issue has an unusual format with two longer pieces, the first by Suzanne M. Wilson, Robert E. Floden, and Joan Ferrini-Mundy, based on their longer synthesis of the research on teacher preparation, and the second by Susan Florio-Ruane, who argues for a broadening of research questions and approaches in teacher education. These two articles are followed by nine shorter articles about evidence and inquiry in teacher education by scholars with different perspectives and different connections to teacher education. Each of the authors was invited to read the two longer articles and then use them as jumping-off points for their own contributions to this issue. In the spirit of open debate and inquiry, the editors of *JTE* hope that this issue will contribute to current discussions about research and evidence in teacher education.

Note

1. It is important to note that some educational researchers will find the National Research Council's (2001) characterization of research cautious and conservative, although more forward looking than the Elementary and Secondary Education Act's (ESEA's). Others in the educational

research community will undoubtedly quarrel with the NRC's definition of scientific research, which rejects versions of both positivism and postmodernism.

REFERENCES

Broder, D. S. (2001, December 17). Long road to reform, negotiators forge education legislation. *The Washington Post*, p. A01.

Milbank, D. (2002, January 9). With fanfare, Bush signs education bill. *The Washington Post*, p. A03.

National Research Council. (2001). *Scientific inquiry in education.* Washington, DC: National Academy Press.

Robelen, E. W. (2001, November 28). States sluggish on execution of 1994 ESEA. *Education Week, 21*(13), 126, 27.

Robelen, E. W. (2002, January 9). ESEA to boost federal role in education. *Education Week, 21*(16), 13, 28, 29.

State group: ESEA bills "seriously flawed." (2001, October 10). *Education Week, 21*(6), 31.

Toppo, G. (2002, January 7). Bush to sign education bill, but the debate over required testing goes on [Electronic version]. *The Associated Press.*

Zeichner, K., & Shulte, A. (2001). What we know and don't know from peer-reviewed research about alternative teacher certification programs. *Journal of Teacher Education, 52*(4), 266-282.

12 The Research Base for Teacher Education

Metaphors We Live (and Die?) By

O ne of the most pressing issues in teacher education today is the vigorous controversy among policymakers and others about whether or not there is a research base that justifies particular practices related to the preparation, certification, recruitment, retention, and entry routes of teachers. What people mean when they talk about "the research base" and/or "the evidence" for teacher education, however, is not always made explicit, and in fact, there are a number of different images or metaphors for "research" that are prevalent in the discourse.

In *Metaphors We Live By*, Lakoff and Johnson (1980) suggested that images and metaphors are not at all the trivial bits of everyday language that some people believe them to be, but they are instead powerful forces in the construction and maintenance of the world views by which we live (and die). They suggested that,

> Metaphor is for most people a device of the poetic imagination and the rhetorical flourish—a matter of extraordinary rather than ordinary language . . . We have found, on the contrary, that metaphor is pervasive in everyday life. . . . If we are right in suggesting that our conceptual systems are largely metaphorical, then the way we think, what we experience, and what we do everyday is very much a matter of metaphor. (p. 3)

SOURCE: *Journal of Teacher Education,* Vol. 53, No. 4, September/October 2002, pp. 283-285.

Lakoff and Johnson argued further that metaphors guide future actions which, in turn, fit the initial metaphors and thus make experience coherent. There are several distinct guiding metaphors for research underlying current discussions about the research base for teacher education.

Research as weapon. In some of the most highly politicized discourse, research has been used as a weapon in the battle between professionalization and deregulation reform agendas for teacher education. The weapon metaphor calls to mind images of fighting, attacks and counterattacks, winners, losers, and casualties; it also suggests the absence of compromise and consensus building. When research is a weapon, the battle is about whether or not there is solid research evidence that teacher preparation and certification are positively correlated with K-12 students' achievement. Waged through publicly disseminated syntheses of previous research, the battle has grown increasingly fierce and in some instances ad hominem—with some critiques seemingly intended more to discredit opposing researchers than to debate research findings. The best examples of research as weapon are the *Teachers College Record* exchange between Linda Darling-Hammond (2000) and Dale Ballou/Michael Podgursky (2000); the report-rejoinder-rebuttal between the National Commission on Teaching and America's Future (Darling-Hammond, 2001) and the Abell Foundation (2001a; 2001b); and the excoriating critiques of researchers in favor of professionalization that have been published in Chester Finn's new magazine, *Education Next.* When research is a weapon, it is not farfetched to suggest that the battle is about life and death for collegiate teacher preparation and also—ultimately—about whose children have the right to fully licensed teachers.

Research as report card. Research is also portrayed as a mechanism for the public grading of teacher-preparation institutions and states. The report card metaphor conveys images of oversight and supervision—teacher and child, passing and failing, and reports filled with A's, B's, F's and a required parent's signature. The obvious example here is the federal Title II Report Card, which provides annual information for every state and teacher-preparation institution about the performance on teacher tests of all candidates certified by that state.

The ostensible purpose is to guide consumers' choices in the teacher-preparation marketplace. When Secretary of Education Rod Paige announced the report card web site, he stated, "Our goal is to assure that all teaching programs are working to train our future teachers in the most effective methods according to evidence-based research" (http://www.title2.org). Despite the fact that the National Research Council (2000) concluded that tests are inadequate measures of teacher education quality and ineffective levers for reform, the Title II report card conveys powerful images about the need for close and continuous oversight of teacher education by outside agencies.

Research as warranty. A third conversation about the research base has to do with whether particular policies contribute to desired teacher education outcomes, including increases in teachers' knowledge, performance, attitudes, and retention in the profession as well as students' learning. The warranty metaphor carries images of cash-back guarantees for items purchased and other consumer assurances that money expended will pay off in the long run. In some of the recent teacher education discourse, research is used as the warranty for the degree of confidence government agencies and/or collegiate institutions should have that particular teacher preparation policies will yield results commensurate with the human and fiscal resources expended. There are a number of clear illustrations of research as warranty, including the Office of Educational Research and Improvement (OERI)-funded synthesis of teacher preparation research (Wilson, Floden, & Ferrini-Mundy, 2001), the Education Commission of the States' secondary analysis of the same studies with a policy emphasis (Lauer, 2001), and the in-progress work of the American Educational Research Association Consensus Panel on Teacher Education (Cochran-Smith & Zeichner, 2002).

Research as foundation. In many academic conversations, research is regarded as the foundation for teacher preparation, a metaphor that conjures up images of pouring cement, laying brickwork, and building scaffolding for other structures. The foundation metaphor does not focus directly on the impacts of teacher preparation as the first three do. Rather, it is assumed first that there is a body of knowledge based on cutting-edge empirical research in various academic disciplines that is relevant to teaching, learning, and schooling, and second, that when teachers know and act on this knowledge, schooling is more effective. Recent illustrations include the in-progress work of the

National Academy of Education's Committee on Teacher Education (Darling-Hammond, 2002) as well as multiple efforts to develop a knowledge base about culturally appropriate K-12 curriculum and pedagogy (e.g., Gay, 2000; Irvine & Armento, 2001; Ladson Billings, 1995; Villegas & Lucas, 2001). The targeted audience for these efforts is the teacher preparation community (and to a lesser extent, policymakers), and the goal is to determine minimal expectations for what all new teachers should know before they enter classrooms.

Research as stance. The stance metaphor suggests that effective educators take a research perspective on their work—carefully observing, challenging underlying assumptions and beliefs, posing questions, collecting and analyzing data, and continuously reinventing practice to improve students' learning. This metaphor calls to mind body postures, particularly the positioning of the feet as in sports or dance, but also political or philosophical positions and their consistency/inconsistency over time. Research as stance has to do with the position teachers take toward knowledge, its relationships to practice, and the purposes of education. Unlike previous examples, those that illustrate stance are local teacher preparation programs and projects where educators learn together in communities by engaging in action research, teacher research, and other forms of practitioner inquiry (e.g., Cochran-Smith & Lytle, 1993; Hammer, 1999; Lampert & Ball, 1998; Noffke, 1995). The assumption here is that knowledge evolves rapidly in modern society and that educators need to know how to deal with change, learn from practice, and engage in evidence-based problem solving.

In the current climate of intense debate about the research base for teacher education, it is useful to sort out which metaphors are operating in which conversations and who the major speakers are and what their larger agendas entail. Debates by policymakers about teacher preparation report cards in a "get tough" accountability climate, for example, are quite different from conversations among teacher educators about how to engender an inquiry stance linking coursework and field experiences for student teachers. Both of these, of course, are different from conversations among institutional administrators about the warrant for fiscal decisions to establish professional development schools or new school partnerships. It is also important to examine the underlying assumptions that operate in various conversations. Different conclusions about the research base for teacher education are often dependent on different assumptions in the first place about teaching, learning, and schooling, even though these are seldom made explicit. Finally, it is important to acknowledge that questions about how to prepare teachers can never be answered solely on the basis of research evidence. These questions also have to do with ideas, ideals, values, and beliefs about teaching and learning, the resources available to communities, and the purposes of education in a democratic society. Ultimately, we will need to debate values and beliefs as well as the "research-based evidence" if we are to make progress in our thinking about how to prepare new teachers.

References

Abell Foundation. (2001a). *Teacher certification reconsidered: Stumbling for quality*. Baltimore: The Abell Foundation.

Abell Foundation. (2001b). *Teacher certification reconsidered: Stumbling for quality: A rejoinder*. Baltimore: The Abell Foundation.

Ballou, D., & Podgursky, M. (2000). Reforming teacher preparation and licensing: What is the evidence? *Teachers College Record, 102*(1), 5-27.

Cochran-Smith, M., & Lytle, S. (1993). *Inside/Outside: Teacher research and knowledge*. New York: Teachers College Press.

Cochran-Smith, M., & Zeichner, K. (2002, April). *The AERA Consensus Panel on Teacher Education: A Progress Report*. Paper presented at the annual meeting of the American Educational Research Association, New Orleans, LA.

Darling-Hammond, L. (2000). Reforming teacher preparation and licensing: Debating the evidence. *Teachers College Record, 102*(1), 28-56.

Darling-Hammond, L. (2002, April). *Formulating recommendations for teacher preparation: The National Academy of Education Project*. Paper presented at the annual meeting of the American Educational Research Association, New Orleans, LA.

Gay, G. (2000). *Culturally responsive teaching: Theory, research and practice*. New York: Teachers College Press.

Hammer, D. (1999). Teacher inquiry. In J. Minstrell & E. van Zee (Eds.), *Teaching and learning in an inquiry-based science classroom*. Washington, DC: American Association for the Advancement of Science.

Irvine, J. J., & Armento, B. J. (2001). *Culturally responsive teaching: Lesson planning for elementary and middle grades*. Boston: McGraw-Hill.

Ladson-Billings, G. (1995). Toward a theory of culturally relevant pedagogy. *American Educational Research Journal, 32*(3), 465-491.

Lakoff, G., & Johnson, M. (1980). *Metaphors we live by.* Chicago: University of Chicago Press.

Lampert, M., & Ball, D. (1998). *Teaching, multimedia, and mathematics: Investigations of real practice.* New York: Teachers College Press.

National Research Council. (2000). *Tests and teaching quality.* Washington, DC: National Academy Press.

Noffke, S. (1995). Action research and democratic schooling: Problems and potentials. In S. Noffke & R. B. Stevenson (Eds.), *Educational action research: Becoming practically critical.* New York: Teachers College Press.

Wilson, S., Floden, R., & Ferrini-Mundy, J. (2001). *Teacher preparation research: Current knowledge, gaps, and recommendations.* Washington, DC: Center for the Study of Teaching and Policy.

13 Reporting on Teacher Quality

The Politics of Politics

S ecretary of Education Rod Paige's report to Congress on the status of teacher quality in the nation, *Meeting the Highly Qualified Teachers Challenge*, was released to the public in early June 2002 (U.S. Department of Education, 2002). This is the first of the annual reports on teacher quality that are now required as per the reauthorization of Title II of the Higher Education Act (HEA) in 1998, which also requires states to report annually on the quality of teacher preparation programs, which in turn depends on institutional reporting to states on the qualifications of all teacher candidates recommended for certification.

Although the report is worth a thorough read, its conclusion is perfectly captured by its heading, "A Broken System," in the executive summary: "Schools of education and formal teacher training programs are failing to produce the types of highly qualified teachers that the No Child Left Behind Act demands" (U.S. Department of Education, 2002, p. viii). The report argues that states' academic standards for teachers are low, whereas the barriers that keep out qualified prospective teachers who have not completed collegiate teacher preparation are high. The report concludes that states must transform certification requirements, "basing their programs on rigorous academic content, eliminating cumbersome requirements not based on scientific evidence, and doing more to attract highly

SOURCE: *Journal of Teacher Education*, Vol. 53, No. 5, November/December 2002, pp. 379-382.

qualified candidates from a variety of fields" (U.S. Department of Education, 2002, p. viii). The report also argues that alternate route programs are the "model" option for fixing the broken system which, if widely implemented, would solve the teacher quality and teacher supply problems simultaneously.

There are a number of ways to respond to the secretary's report, some more visceral than others. I suggest in this editorial that four critiques are essential: an empirical critique, a conceptual critique, a social justice critique, and a political critique.

An Empirical Critique

The secretary's report is clear in its conclusions about what does and does not count in high-quality teaching: "In summary, we have found that rigorous research indicates that verbal ability and content knowledge are the most important attributes of highly qualified teachers. In addition there is little evidence that education school coursework leads to improved student achievement" (U.S. Department of Education, 2002, p. 19).

One major problem with the secretary's report is that many of its conclusions differ fundamentally from those of other reviews of research on teacher preparation, including the recent, widely circulated synthesis of research on teacher preparation by Wilson, Floden, and Ferrini-Mundy (2001), which was funded by the U.S. Department of Education through the Center for Teaching and Policy at the University of Washington and summarized in the previous issue of *JTE* (Wilson, Floden, & Ferrini-Mundy, 2002). Heap (2002) explicitly notes the discrepancy between the secretary's report and the Wilson synthesis. Heap points out that unlike the secretary's report, the Wilson synthesis concludes that: the often-claimed link between college study of subject matter and teaching quality is not so clear; there is evidence that teacher education *does* contribute to teaching quality; and, alternate route studies are inconclusive because of completely inconsistent definitions of *traditional* and *alternative*. The secretary's report also makes no mention of other syntheses and empirical studies (although published in reputable peer-reviewed journals) that conclude that there *are* teacher qualifications (in addition to subject matter knowledge and verbal ability) that are related to student achievement. These qualifications include: knowledge of teaching and learning gained through teacher preparation courses and experiences, teaching experience, and teacher certification status (e.g., Darling-Hammond, 2000a, 2000b, 2001). Instead of a careful weighing of the empirical evidence, then, the secretary's report references only 1 of the 57 rigorous empirical studies in the Wilson synthesis. Otherwise it cites private agency literature and foundation reports not published in peer-reviewed journals or similarly vetted by the research community, a direct conflict with the established procedures of scientific research in education (National Research Council, 2001).

A CONCEPTUAL CRITIQUE

Putting aside for a moment the empirical issues, the secretary's report is based on a very limited conceptualization of teaching, learning, and education. The report depends on three assumptions: quality teaching is a college-educated person with high verbal ability who transmits knowledge; learning is a compliant student who receives information and demonstrates it on a standardized test; and, education is a set of structural arrangements that make these effective and cost-efficient.

These notions are not so much incorrect as they are severely impoverished. There is certainly some evidence that teachers' content knowledge and verbal ability account for some of the variance in students' achievement. However, decades of research on teaching (e.g., Richardson, 2001; Wittrock, 1986) confirm that this is a much too simplistic way to conceptualize teaching in the first place. Teaching involves much more than transmitting information. It includes representing complex knowledge in accessible ways, asking good questions, forming relationships with students and parents, collaborating with other professionals, interpreting multiple data sources, meeting the needs of students with widely varying abilities and backgrounds, and both posing and solving problems of practice. Likewise, learning is not just receiving information. The science of learning shows that learning is a process of developing usable knowledge (not just isolated facts) by building on previous knowledge and experience, understanding and organizing information in a conceptual framework, and monitoring progress toward learning goals (National Research Council, 2000).

Along these same lines, education is not simply about test scores and monetary investments. Education also has to do with preparing citizens to live in a democracy, engage in satisfying work, and function as lifelong learners who can cope with the challenges of a rapidly changing global society. A report intended to provide "a wealth of new information on teacher quality in the U.S." (U.S. Department of Education, 2002, p. iii), as the secretary's report is intended to do, would be better served by the richest available conceptions of teaching, learning, and education rather than the most impoverished.

A SOCIAL JUSTICE CRITIQUE

The secretary's report is critical of the use of "waivers" and other emergency or temporary suspensions of normal certification requirements that allow unqualified people to take teaching positions. The report is closely aligned with the No Child Left Behind Act (NCLBA), which—as the secretary's report applauds—will not permit these "waivers and loopholes" (U.S. Department of Education, 2002, p. 34) as of the 2005-06 school year.

To its credit, the secretary's report notes that "high-poverty school districts [are] more likely to employ teachers on waivers than more affluent districts" (U.S. Department of Education, 2002, p. 34). However, one of the greatest failings of the secretary's report is that it does not frame the disparities between the qualifications of teachers in high- and low-poverty schools as a major social issue facing the nation, as others have done (e.g., Darling-Hammond & Sclan, 1996; Oakes, Franke, Quartz, & Rogers, 2002). Instead, the secretary's report uses the states' information on waivers to highlight and apply its definition of "highly qualified teachers," which is drawn directly from the *NCLBA*.

Based on the assumption that quality teaching depends almost solely on content knowledge (a conclusion already highly suspect on both empirical and conceptual grounds, as noted above), the report defines a highly qualified teacher as one "who has obtained full State certification as a teacher (including certification obtained through alternative routes to certification) or passed the State teacher licensing examination, and holds a license to teach in such State" (U.S. Department of Education, 2002, p. 4). Although the import of this definition may not be immediately appreciated, it is critical. To a great extent (depending on individual states' alternative route requirements), what this new definition of "highly qualified teachers" has the potential to do is instantaneously transform unqualified teachers into qualified ones. For example, a teacher who is "unqualified" because of no experience in the classroom, no courses in pedagogy, no knowledge of cultural differences, no study of how people learn, no knowledge of human development, and so on, may with the stroke of the pen that institutionalized the new federal definition be instantaneously transformed into a "highly qualified teacher," provided he or she has passed a state teacher test.

This is nothing more than sleight of hand regarding issues of social justice, as is borne out in the remainder of the secretary's report. Just three paragraphs after referring to the shortage of qualified teachers in high-poverty schools as part of the "crippling cost of the conventional teacher certification and compensation system" (U.S. Department of Education, 2002, p. 34), the message changes dramatically. The report reassures readers that

> The news on waivers is not necessarily entirely bad. Almost 50 percent of teachers on waivers . . . possess a major in their subject areas or have passed the state's content exams. . . . Under a streamlined certification system . . . these teachers would be considered highly qualified. (U.S. Department of Education, 2002, p. 34)

At best, this comparison obfuscates the acute and chronic problem of unequal distribution of resources to high-poverty schools. At worst, it defines the problem away, reducing the disparities in teacher qualifications between low- and high-poverty schools by as much as half simply by changing a definition. This ignores the very real possibility that unless financial and other incentives are provided for teachers in high-need areas, we will end up with a two-tiered educational system wherein the least well-prepared teachers and paraprofessionals teach the students in the most need.

A POLITICAL CRITIQUE

As indicated throughout this editorial, the secretary's report reads more like a partisan position paper than a careful analysis of new state and institutional data. Placing the language of the secretary's report side by side with the language of the "manifesto" of Chester Finn's Fordham Foundation (Kanstoroom & Finn, 1999), an organization widely known for its strident positions on market-based educational reform and the deregulation of teacher education, is particularly telling. Secretary Paige's report, which purportedly analyzes new national patterns based on the Title II reporting, frames the problem (and the solution) to teacher quality issues in almost exactly the same way and uses some of the exact language as Fordham's manifesto, which was signed by William Bennett, E. D. Hirsch, Diane Ravitch, James Peyser, and others in 1999.

The politics of the report, especially its political position on market-based educational reform, is further reflected in its structure and proportions. There is heavy emphasis on the "streamlined" alternate route system that would purportedly shift authority to local principals and let the market decide whether teacher "training" is worthwhile. However, this recommendation goes far beyond the scope of the report required by Congress, and there is absolutely no evidence that this approach would create a strong and effective teaching force.

There have been criticisms that Title II state reports paint too rosy a picture of teacher preparation and that some states are "gameing the system" by making certification tests an admissions rather than an exit requirement and, thus, reporting 100% pass rates on the tests. The Education Trust warns us to interpret this and other results "with caution" and claims that many state reports are misleading if not dishonest (Huang, Yi, & Haycock, 2002). There may indeed be some inconsistent and misleading information from some states, although there are quite defensible reasons for certain results and omissions in many of the reports.

In the final analysis, however, the secretary's report ignores empirical evidence that contradicts its recommendations even though published in peer-reviewed journals, works from an under-conceptualized view of teaching and learning, addresses problems of social justice by tinkering with definitions instead of redistributing resources, and presents a partisan position rather than the thoughtful guidelines needed for policies that have an impact on all citizens. In short, politics trumps everything else in the secretary's report on teaching quality. Surely this is not what Congress had in mind when it incorporated the Title II teacher quality reporting system into its reauthorization of the Higher Education Act (HEA).

ACKNOWLEDGMENTS

The positions expressed in this editorial are entirely the responsibility of the editor. However, I would like to acknowledge the very thoughtful and helpful feedback of *JTE* Associate Editors Curt Dudley-Marling, Larry Ludlow, and David Scanlon, as well as comments from Drew Gitomer, James Heap, Jeannie Oakes, and Karen Zumwalt.

REFERENCES

Darling-Hammond, L. (2000a). Reforming teacher preparation and licensing: Debating the evidence. *Teachers College Record, 102*(1), 28-56.

Darling-Hammond, L. (2000b). Teacher quality and student achievement: A review of state policy evidence. *Education Policy Analysis Archives, 8*(1).

Darling-Hammond, L. (2001, October). *The research and rhetoric on teacher certification: A response to "Teacher certification reconsidered."* New York: National Commission on Teaching and America's Future. Available from http://www.nctaf.org

Darling-Hammond, L., & Sclan, E. M. (1996). Who teaches and why? In J. Sikula (Ed.), *Handbook of research on teacher education* (pp. 67-101). New York: Macmillan.

Heap, J. (2002, June). *The DOE secretary's report: Meeting the highly qualified teachers challenge* (Internal Memo to the Governor's Commission on Teaching Success). Athens, Ohio: Governor's Commission on Teaching Success.

Huang, S., Yi, Y., & Haycock, K. (2002, June). *Interpret with caution: The first state Title II reports on the quality of teacher preparation.* Washington, DC: The Education Trust.

Kanstoroom, M., & Finn, C. (1999, July). *Better teachers, better schools.* Washington, DC: Thomas B. Fordham Foundation.

National Research Council. (2000). *How people learn.* Washington, DC: National Academy Press.

National Research Council. (2001). *Scientific inquiry in education.* Washington, DC: National Academy Press.

Oakes, J., Franke, M., Quartz, K., & Rogers, J. (2002). Research for high quality urban teaching: Defining it, developing it, assessing it. *Journal of Teacher Education, 53*, 228-234.

Richardson, V. (Ed.). (2001). *Handbook of research on teaching* (4th ed.). Washington, DC: American Educational Research Association.

U.S. Department of Education. (2002, June). *Meeting the highly qualified teachers challenge: The secretary's annual report on teacher quality.* Washington, DC: U.S. Department of Education, Office of Post Secondary Education.

Wilson, S., Floden, R., & Ferrini-Mundy, J. (2001). *Teacher preparation research: Current knowledge, gaps, and recommendations, A research report prepared for the U.S. Department of Education.* Seattle: University of Washington: Center for the Study of Teaching and Policy.

Wilson, S., Floden, R., & Ferrini-Mundy, J. (2002). Teacher preparation research: An insider's view from the outside. *Journal of Teacher Education, 53,* 190-204.

Wittrock, M. C. (Ed.). (1986). *Handbook of research on teaching* (3rd ed.). New York: Macmillan.

14 The Unforgiving Complexity of Teaching

Avoiding Simplicity in the Age of Accountability

The current unprecedented emphasis on teaching quality emerged from the standards and accountability movement of the 1990s. From the beginning, the issue of "teaching quality" was framed as part of the larger movement to make schools, school districts, and teachers more responsible and accountable for students' learning.

As a policy matter, a political priority, and in public opinion polls, teaching quality and teacher accountability are now inextricably tied. For example, the most recent Hart-Teeter poll, commissioned by the Educational Testing Service (Hart & Teeter, 2002), is entitled "A National Priority: Americans Speak on Teacher Quality." This bipartisan public opinion survey found that even since September 11, improving education is a top priority for American adults, with only family values and fighting terrorism ranked higher. The link between teaching quality and teaching accountability is crystal clear in the poll's highlights:

- *The public strongly supports standards and accountability.* Although Americans support measures to raise teacher quality, they continue to insist on reforms that raise standards and accountability for both students and teachers.

SOURCE: *Journal of Teacher Education,* Vol. 54, No. 1, January/February 2003, pp. 3-5.

- *All groups recognize that the quality of teaching determines the quality of education.* Americans want more and better teachers in the nation's schools. . . . Nine in ten (91%) adults support offering more training programs so teachers can continue to learn and become better teachers. (Hart & Teeter, 2002, p. 2)

The poll also indicates that Americans are willing to pay higher taxes for better teachers—including improved working conditions, higher salaries, and ongoing professional development—as long as these are linked to greater accountability. Along these lines, more than 73% of adults surveyed favored testing student achievement and holding teachers and schools responsible for their scores, and 70% wanted teachers tested on subject knowledge and skills.

There is little debate in the education community about the assertion that quality of teaching and teacher preparation ought to be defined (at least in part) in terms of student learning. Few question the idea that the public has a right to expect that how teachers are prepared has something to do with what they know, how they teach, and what and how much their students learn. There are also few who question the assertion that higher education institutions ought to take some of the responsibility for these connections. Increasingly, however, the accountability bottom line—higher scores on standardized student achievement tests—is the singular focus of state and federal policies related to teaching quality and teacher preparation and a major focus of external funders and professional accrediting agencies that deal with teacher preparation. Increasingly, teaching quality and students' learning are *equated with* high-stakes test scores. It is this simplistic equating that is problematic rather than the larger notion of accountability itself.

The reauthorization of the Elementary and Secondary Education Act (ESEA) in 2001 established an unprecedented and greatly enlarged federal role in educational matters previously considered the purview of the states and/or of the educational community. ESEA legislates mandatory annual statewide testing of K-12 students in multiple subject areas and requires that schools hire only "highly qualified" teachers, certified through traditional or alternate routes and with passing scores on state teacher certification tests. As Richard Elmore (2002) rightly points out, ESEA also cements into law the equating of teaching quality and student learning with scores on high-stakes tests:

The federal government further mandates a single definition of adequate yearly progress, the amount by which schools must increase their test scores in order to avoid some sort of sanction . . . the law sets a single target date by which all students must exceed a state-defined proficiency level. . . . Thus the federal government is now accelerating the worst trend of the current accountability movement: that performance-based accountability has come to mean testing alone. (p. 35)

Policies intended to improve teaching quality can only be as good as the underlying conceptions of teaching, learning, and schooling on which they are based. Unfortunately, as a number of critics (including myself) have argued (Cochran-Smith, 2001; Earley, 2000; Engel, 2000), many current policies and policy recommendations share narrow—and some would say impoverished—notions of teaching and learning that do not account for the complexities that are at the heart of the educational enterprise in a democratic society.

Oddly enough, a book about writing—Anne Lamott's (1994) *Bird by Bird: Some Instructions on Writing and Life*—is helpful along these lines. In her chapter on the "moral point of view," Lamott advises writers to avoid simple oppositions in their development of plots and characters:

I used to think that paired opposites were a given, that love was the opposite of hate, right the opposite of wrong. But now I think we sometimes buy into these concepts because it is so much easier to embrace absolutes than to suffer reality. [Now] I don't think anything is the opposite of love. *Reality is unforgivingly complex* [emphasis added]. (p. 104)

Lamott admonishes writers not to avoid the intense complexity of real life but to embrace it and write with passion about its biggest questions.

Although in a different way, Lamott's advice about how to write applies equally well to how we need to conceptualize teaching quality if we are ultimately to understand, assess, and improve it. *Teaching is unforgivingly complex*. It is not simply good or bad, right or wrong, working or failing. Although absolutes and dichotomies such as these are popular in the headlines and in campaign slogans, they are limited in their usefulness. They tacitly assume there is consensus across our diverse society about the purposes of schooling and what it means to be engaged in the process of becoming an educated person as well as consensus about whose knowledge and values are of most worth and what counts as evidence of the effectiveness of teaching and learning. They ignore almost completely the nuances of "good" (or "bad") teaching of real students collected in actual classrooms in the context of particular times and places. They mistake reductionism for clarity, myopia for insight. And, as Elmore (2002) suggests, they "utterly fail" (p. 35) to appreciate the institutional realities and complexities of accountability in various schools and school districts as well as in particular states.

As teachers—and teacher educators—we must be held accountable for our work. But measures of this work cannot be determined by narrow conceptions of teaching quality and student learning that focus exclusively on test scores and ignore the incredible complexity of teaching and learning and the institutional realities inherent in the accountability context. Part of what we need in teacher education right now are efforts to be responsible and responsive to the concerns of the public, to acknowledge the exigencies of public policy, and to preserve complexity in the press for accountability. Such efforts need to transcend rhetoric and clearly demonstrate that we are taking responsibility for examining our programs in order to assess and ultimately strengthen the performance of our graduates and their students in K-12 schools.

One such initiative is the Ohio Partnership for Accountability (OPA), which is a consortium of Ohio's 51 teacher preparation institutions, the Ohio Department of Education, and the Ohio Board of Regents (Ohio Accountability Project, 2002). The 5-year project combines three studies to examine the relationships among features of teacher preparation, school students' performances on standardized tests as well as their broader learning, and multiple systems of accountability. OPA relies on a mixed-methods approach, combining K-12 student data based on value-added assessment techniques, prospective teacher data intended to identify differing configurations of their teacher preparation experiences, and experienced teacher data about classroom discourse patterns and instructional practices that are linked with both the development of higher order thinking processes and teacher effectiveness as measured by value-added techniques.

The significance and strength of this project is not simply that it links three distinct but interrelated studies in order to preserve the complexity of teaching quality, teacher preparation, student learning, and multiple accountability contexts, although this is certainly a central and critical feature of its design. The worth of the project is also derived from its success (so far) in bringing to the table (a) a multi-institutional research team with interests in many aspects of teaching quality and teacher preparation and with expertise in multiple research methods, (b) an advisory board that includes representatives from all of the relevant Ohio stake holders, and (c) a national external review panel that quite intentionally includes those with diverse methodological and ideological positions.

The Ohio initiative is not the perfect research study nor the perfect accountability project that asks all of the significant questions about the exceedingly important issues of teaching quality and teacher preparation. Of course, no project ever is or ever could be. But this project, which is still in the planning stages, represents the kind of effort it will take for institutions to be accountable while honoring complexity. Einstein is reported to have said that everything should be as simple as possible—but no simpler. The position in this editorial is not that the teacher education community should avoid simplicity merely because we prefer the elegance and sophistication of more complex models. Rather, we must avoid what is too simple—isomorphic equations between teaching quality and test scores and between student learning and test scores—because they are grossly inadequate to the task of understanding (and ultimately improving) teaching and learning in a diverse but democratic society in the 21st century.

REFERENCES

Cochran-Smith, M. (2001). The outcomes question in teacher education. *Teaching and Teacher Education, 17*(5), 527-546.

Earley, P. (2000). Finding the culprit: Federal policy and teacher education. *Educational Policy, 14*(1), 25-39.

Elmore, R. F. (2002). Testing trap. *Harvard Magazine, 105*(1), 35.

Engel, M. (2000). *The struggle for control of public education: Market ideology vs. democratic values.* Philadelphia: Temple University Press.

Hart, P. D., & Teeter, R. M. (2002). *A national priority: Americans speak on teacher quality.* Princeton, NJ: Educational Testing Service.

Lamott, A. (1994). *Bird by bird: Some instructions on writing and life.* New York: Anchor Books.

Ohio Accountability Project. (2002, September 23). *Teacher education and student achievement in complex contexts of accountability.* Dayton: Ohio Partnership for Accountability.

15 Teaching Quality Matters

For almost a decade now, teaching and teacher education have been pivotal issues in state and national elections and legislation. In addition, there have been dozens of reports, surveys, blue-ribbon panels, research syntheses, professional initiatives, and new empirical studies examining the presumed relationships among teacher qualifications, teacher preparation, teaching performance, and educational outcomes. In short, it has become commonplace to presume that matters of teaching quality figure largely in the ultimate improvement of education.

Despite this convergence of attention, it is important to note that there is often more than one question tangled up in debates about teaching quality. Three of the most important of these are: Does quality of teaching make a difference in students' learning and their lives? How do we define teaching quality? and How do we best recruit and prepare highly qualified teachers? In editorials for this journal and elsewhere, I have written extensively about the highly politicized debates that surround the third question regarding the preparation of highly qualified teachers. In this editorial, I touch briefly on whether or not teaching quality makes a difference and then concentrate on the issue of how we should define teaching quality.

DOES TEACHING QUALITY MAKE A DIFFERENCE?

On this first question, there is enormous consensus. The American public, the education profession, researchers, legal advocates, and

SOURCE: *Journal of Teacher Education,* Vol. 54, No. 2, March/April 2003, pp. 95-98.

policymakers all seem to agree that quality of teaching makes an important difference in students' learning, their achievement, and their life chances. In a recent public opinion poll on teacher quality (Hart & Teeter, 2002), for example, it was clear that although the public strongly favored educational reform tied to accountability, they also equated educational improvement with quality teaching and were not willing to lower hiring standards to solve the teacher shortage problem. Along similar lines, even among those who argue for diametrically opposed approaches to teacher preparation, there is apparent consensus that teaching quality is a critical influence on how and what students learn. The frequency of citations by researchers and policymakers of all stripes to William Sanders's conclusion that individual teachers are the single largest factor that adds value to student learning (Sanders & Horn, 1998) makes this point persuasively. Finally, legal advocates in several pending cases across the country have consistently asserted that access to highly qualified teachers is a birthright of all children (American Civil Liberties Union, 2000).

In short, despite different assumptions about the purposes of schooling, the nature of teaching as an enterprise, and appropriate ways to measure teaching effectiveness, there is enormous consensus that teaching quality makes a significant difference in learning and school effectiveness. The No Child Left Behind Act (NCLB) cemented this conclusion into law with its guarantee that all schoolchildren must have "highly qualified teachers."

How Do We Define Teaching Quality and Highly Qualified Teachers?

On this second question, there is much less consensus. For the public at large (again based on the Hart-Teeter poll), communication, teaching skills, and a teacher's ability to interest students—rather than content information—are most important. When asked to define quality teaching more specifically, 42% of respondents mentioned designing learning activities that inspired pupil interest, 31% said having enthusiasm, and 26% said having a caring attitude, although only 19% mentioned having a thorough understanding of the subject. When asked to name the biggest problem preparing teachers, 67% said that developing the skill to make material interesting and accessible was a greater problem than developing content area knowledge. The public's emphasis on know-how and relating to students makes an interesting comparison to other definitions of teaching quality.

NCLB requires that every state provide schoolchildren with "highly qualified teachers" who receive "high-quality professional development." Highly qualified teachers are defined as those with full state certification (including through alternate routes) or pass scores on state teacher exams. High-quality professional development is defined as that which improves subject matter knowledge, aligns with standards, and improves instructional strategies "based on scientifically based research." Recent comments by highly ranked Department of Education (DOE) leaders provide further indication of what the DOE expects from teachers. For example, Assistant Secretary for Elementary and Secondary Education Susan Neuman recently spoke to the Association of American Publishers. She urged reading publishers to simplify their textbooks by providing explicit instructions on what to teach, how to teach it, what sequence to follow, how many times to repeat each instruction, and how much time to spend on each sequence, rather than including what was characterized as a "confusing hodgepodge" of options that are too complicated for teachers (Manzo, 2002).

Urging publishers to simplify materials for teachers seems somewhat inconsistent with the idea that highly qualified teachers are bright, well-educated, and knowledgeable in subject matter, the traits emphasized in the secretary's annual report to Congress on teaching quality (U.S. Department of Education, 2002). In fact, the secretary's report states unequivocally that content knowledge and general verbal ability are the most important attributes of highly qualified teachers. It is puzzling, then, that teachers with solid subject matter knowledge and strong intellectual ability would need simplified teaching materials and explicit instructions about exactly how, how much, what, and when to teach. The best explanation for this inconsistency may be that the "highly qualified teacher" required by NCLB and being pushed in many states is a technician who faithfully implements the highly sequenced instructional techniques stipulated in government-approved texts and materials, which are based on the results of "scientific research" about what purportedly works best for all schoolchildren.

The highly qualified teacher as careful technician contrasts dramatically with the image of the highly qualified teacher forwarded by the professional organizations related to teaching, teacher education, accreditation, and advanced certification. From a professional perspective, the highly qualified teacher knows subject matter (what to teach) and pedagogy (how to teach) but also knows how to learn and how to make decisions informed by theory and research from many bodies of knowledge and also is informed by feedback from school and classroom evidence in particular contexts. Recent literacy research along these lines suggests that teachers' ability to exercise professional discretion is a major factor in student achievement (Allington & Johnston, 2001; Presley et al., 2001).

Although somewhat consistent with the public's emphasis on knowing how to teach and how to relate to students, a professional definition of quality teaching is quite different from the technical definition implicit in many of the policies and practices now being implemented by the DOE. The professional teacher is not confused by an array of options for instruction. Rather, the professional teacher routinely selects from a repertoire of teaching strategies those that are best suited to the needs of learners in the local context at the same time that he or she forms productive relationships with parents and community members. The professional definition of the highly qualified teacher assumes that teaching is a complex and somewhat uncertain process with knowledge constructed in the interactions of particular teachers, students, materials, texts, and prior experiences. This image of teaching contrasts sharply with the view underlying technical definitions wherein teaching is presumed to be a certain and linear process within which knowledge is transmitted more or less directly from teacher to student by following a fixed and scientifically predetermined sequence of instructions.

Teaching Quality Matters: Questions and Cautions

It should be clear from this necessarily abbreviated discussion that although there is great consensus *that* teaching quality matters, there is little consensus about most other matters related to teaching quality. As the debates continue, we need to know which of the teaching quality questions is on the table at any given time. Then, as teacher educators and as public intellectuals, we need to ask—and keep on asking—critical questions about the issues. We need to ask empirical questions about how much and what kind of documentation there is about teacher learning, student learning, professional practice, and access to educational opportunities that supports or challenges particular positions. We need to ask conceptual questions about the definitions of teaching and learning that are presumed within particular positions, especially whether these are in keeping with current knowledge about the science of learning, the complexity of teaching, and the role of cultures, language, and experience in schooling. Furthermore, we need to ask what it means to demand highly qualified teachers for all children but, at the same time, increasingly control and prescribe their work by stipulating precisely what techniques teachers are to employ as well as how, how often, and when. We need to ask experiential questions about which of the competing definitions of teaching quality are in keeping with our own experiences as learners and with the kinds of teachers and learning opportunities we want for our own children and grandchildren.

We also need to ask political questions about the larger agendas to which differing definitions of quality teaching are attached and about whose best interests these agendas serve and ignore. Perhaps most importantly, we need to question the assumed roles of teachers and teaching quality in school and societal change. Teachers are increasingly being constructed as the cure for not only all of the ills of an ailing educational system but also for the problems of a flawed society—poverty, unemployment, bureaucracy, cultural and linguistic hegemony, and a long history of institutional racism.

If teachers are being set up as the panacea for problems that have heretofore been intractable, what are the implications when students fail to learn? Who and what are let off the hook when teachers and teacher educators are held completely responsible? Whose interests are served by the explanation that teachers are the central answer to providing all schoolchildren with access to rich learning opportunities? We need to be cautious about the differing purposes of schooling in a democratic society that are implicit in differing definitions of teaching quality and highly qualified teachers. We need to ask whether—in varying definitions of highly qualified teachers—there are images of teachers with the knowledge and experience to prepare all citizens to live in, contribute to, critique, and learn from a democratic and incredibly diverse society. Finally, we need to ask what it means when a relentless focus on teachers' abilities to boost test scores easily overpowers concern about teachers' ability to exercise professional judgment, critique common practices that disadvantage certain groups of students, and work for social justice. We need to be sure these latter abilities are included in our definitions of highly qualified teachers.

References

Allington, R. L., & Johnston, P. (2001). Characteristics of exemplary fourth grade instruction. In C. Roller (Ed.), *Research on effective teaching*. Newark, DE: International Reading Association.

American Civil Liberties Union. (2000). *ACSL-Southern California docket: Williams et al. v. State of California et al., 2001*. Retrieved from http://www.aclu-sc.org/courts.

Hart, P. D., & Teeter, R. M. (2002). *A national priority: Americans speak on teacher quality*. Princeton, NJ: Educational Testing Service.

Manzo, K. K. (2002). Majority of states told to revise reading plans. *Education Week*, pp. 1-3.

Presley, M., Wharton-McDonald, R., Allington, R. L., Block, C. C., Morros, L., Tracey, D., et al. (2001). The nature of effective first-grade literacy instruction. *Scientific Studies in Reading, 5*, 35-58.

Sanders, W., & Horn, S. (1998). Research findings from the Tennessee Value-Added Assessment System (TVAAS) database: Implications for educational evaluation and research. *Journal of Personnel Evaluation in Education, 12*(3), 247-256.

U.S. Department of Education. (2002). *Meeting the highly qualified teachers challenge: The Secretary's annual report on teacher quality*. Washington, DC: Office of Postsecondary Education.

16 Assessing Assessment in Teacher Education

For almost a decade now, "the outcomes question" has been driving reform in teacher education (Cochran-Smith, 2001). Spurred by sharp criticisms that teacher education programs have not been held accountable for results and that there is little evidence that higher education-based teacher preparation is a fiscally sound and effective educational policy, many new efforts to assess and/or enhance the impact of teacher education have emerged. Although these often rest on strikingly different assumptions about what teachers and pupils should know and be able to do and about what the larger purposes of American schooling should be, all of these efforts assume that a defining goal of teacher education is student learning. They also assume that there are certain measures that can be used to assess the degree to which this outcome is or is not being achieved by teachers, K-12 pupils, teacher educators, higher education institutions, alternative programs, local and state policies, and the education profession itself.

This editorial provides a brief "assessment of assessment" in teacher education by outlining several recent efforts to analyze, document, or enhance the impact of collegiate teacher preparation on teaching, learning, and practice. To make the point that current assessment efforts are quite different from one another in form, content, and intention, I have included examples from the following three loosely defined groupings: empirical studies or reviews that

SOURCE: *Journal of Teacher Education,* Vol. 54, No. 3, May/June 2003, pp. 187-191.

assess the effectiveness of teacher education/teacher certification as a broad educational policy; national initiatives to make teacher preparation more assessment-based and evidence-driven by spearheading and linking local efforts along these lines; and regional efforts to assess the impact on attitudes, learning, and practices of naturally occurring variations among program components, structures, and arrangements to influence local program decisions but also inform larger policy controversies.

ASSESSING TEACHER EDUCATION/TEACHER CERTIFICATION AS EDUCATIONAL POLICIES

For some time now, there have been highly visible and highly contentious debates about whether or not there is an empirical warrant for collegiate teacher education and/or for state-regulated teacher certification as broad educational policies that add value to teaching quality and pupil learning outcomes. Two important studies have recently added to this debate.

Darling-Hammond and Youngs's (2002) review of existing research on "highly qualified teachers" was written as a direct response to Secretary of Education Rod Paige's report on teaching quality (U.S. Department of Education, 2002). The Darling-Hammond and Youngs article rejects the conclusions of the Secretary's report, claiming that it fails to meet its own standards for the use of scientific research in formulating public policy. The bulk of the Darling-Hammond and Youngs article is a repudiation of Paige's major propositions based on a thorough analysis that takes into account age of the studies included, sample size, research methods, levels of aggregation, and teacher retention. Not surprisingly, Darling-Hammond and Youngs reach conclusions that are diametrically opposed to Paige's. They conclude the Secretary's recommendations are not based on scientific evidence; there *is* evidence that teacher preparation contributes at least as much to effectiveness and retention as do verbal ability and content knowledge; and, although some of them are well designed, alternate entry paths that do not include the core aspects of teacher preparation lead to ineffective teachers who feel underprepared and leave teaching at high rates.

Like the Darling-Hammond and Youngs review, Laczko-Kerr and Berliner's (2002) recent study of the impact of certified and "under-certified" elementary school teachers on pupils' academic achievement also adds fuel to the fiery debate about teacher certification as educational policy. Laczko-Kerr and Berliner compared the achievement test scores of pupils taught by recently hired regularly certified teachers and by "under-qualified" teachers (emergency, temporary, and provisionally certified teachers, including a subset of "Teach for America" [TFA] teachers) in low-income school districts in Arizona. Based on an analysis of matched pairs of teachers, Laczko-Kerr and Berliner found both that the pupils of certified teachers scored substantially higher than the pupils of under-certified teachers and that the pupils of TFA teachers performed no better than the pupils of *other under-certified teachers*. Laczko-Kerr and Berliner conclude that educational policies that allow under-prepared teachers to teach, particularly those that place under-prepared teachers in low-income schools with children who are most in need of good teachers, are harmful and will only exacerbate current achievement gaps.

It is crystal clear that neither of these recent studies will be the last word about teacher education and teacher certification as broad educational policies. But perhaps they will help to sharpen the terms and conditions of the debate. If scientifically based research evidence is to be the gold standard by which all educational policies and practices are assessed (a proposition that is, itself, arguable on several important grounds), then researchers and critics alike will more and more stridently—and justifiably—demand that policymakers live by their own rules and provide convincing empirical evidence for the policies they enact that will shape schoolchildren's educational opportunities and their life chances.

Making Teacher Education More Assessment-Based and Evidence-Driven

It has been acknowledged for some time now that the strongest teacher education programs are those based on coherent conceptual frameworks, guided by current theory and research, and infused with the wisdom of practice. Until very recently, however, few of even the strongest teacher education programs across the country could be thought of as assessment-based or evidence-driven. Two intriguing national initiatives, although quite different from one another in scope and design, are along these lines.

Teachers for a New Era (TNE) is an initiative funded primarily by the Carnegie Corporation of America (headquartered in New York City) to change dramatically the way teacher education is understood and enacted at selected institutions across the nation. Highly visible because of the Carnegie imprimatur and substantial funding, the TNE initiative demands radical changes in organization, resource allocation, faculty evaluation criteria, and collaborative relationships. The first of TNE's three design principles ("respect for evidence") is especially relevant to the topic of this editorial. Respect for evidence means establishing a process wherein program decisions continuously draw upon research, and teacher effectiveness is defined in part in terms of pupil learning. Across the country, at the institutions connected to the Carnegie project, new initiatives are now underway to develop value-added tracking systems to assess the impact of program graduates on pupils' learning, to carry out design experiments to inform decisions about program components, and to assess systematically teacher candidates' and pupils' learning over the course of a given program and beyond it.

Project Delta is an initiative of the Carnegie Foundation for the Advancement of Teaching (located in Palo Alto, California) in partnership with a dozen or so teacher preparation programs across the nation. Delta has three central goals—to foster the capacity within teacher education programs themselves to assess progress and effectiveness, to shift accountability from external policy to internal practice, and to generate knowledge that can be used in both local programs and more broadly. The centerpiece of Delta is the development and use of a set of "low stakes–high yield" integrative assessment instruments that measure the growth of teacher candidates' knowledge and skill (primarily in content and pedagogy) by focusing on teachers' and pupils' learning. Core and locally developed assessments will be shared across and within institutions via nested learning communities and seminars. Ultimately, the point of Delta is to encourage data-driven local inquiries that inform local program decisions but also contribute knowledge to the field as a whole.

The intentions and scope of the Delta project are more modest and less prescriptive than those of TNE. Nonetheless, these two initiatives are not inconsistent with one another, and together they have enormous potential to change the ways we think about assessment in teacher education. Transforming teacher education into an enterprise that is grounded in research, revolves around continuous assessment of learning, and making decisions driven by evidence is nothing short of a culture shift in our field. Ultimately, however, the success of Carnegie-type initiatives will depend on sustainability, dissemination, and most importantly, convincing evidence that they make a difference in children's lives.

STUDYING REGIONAL VARIATIONS TO ASSESS LOCAL PRACTICE AND INFORM LARGER POLICIES

An important current development in teacher education assessment is the emergence of regional studies that take advantage of naturally occurring variations among program components, structures, and arrangements to inform local practice. Interestingly, however, these also have the potential to address larger issues and inform general policies in teacher education. These studies focus on the impact of teacher preparation elements and structural arrangements on teachers' attitudes, knowledge, and practices; teachers' and students' learning and learning opportunities; and, teachers' entry and retention in the profession. I mention just three regional examples along these lines, although there are many others.

In a previous editorial, I cited the Ohio Partnership for Accountability as an example of a project that attempted to account for the complexity of both teacher preparation and the accountability contexts in which it is embedded (Ohio Partnership for Accountability, 2002). The 5-year project combines three studies to examine the relationships among features of teacher preparation, school students' performances on standardized tests as well as their broader learning, and multiple systems of accountability. The goal of the project is to develop evidence about the features of Ohio teacher-preparation programs that have an impact on teachers' and students' learning to inform local program decisions as well as state and regional policies.

The "Massachusetts Teacher Preparation and Induction Study" (Maloy, Pine, & Seidman, 2002) was conducted by teacher educators and researchers at three Massachusetts institutions to examine the impact of professional development schools and other models on teacher preparation and teacher quality. In the first year of the study, a survey was used to gather information about teachers who had experienced the following three different kinds of teacher preparation:

school-university professional development school partnerships, university-based preparation without professional development school partnerships, and alternative certification preparation based on a fast-track summer program with mentoring during the year. Results indicate that all three models produce committed teachers, the fast-track model recruits an older and more experienced group of teachers, and the professional development school model produces teachers who feel more confident about using a variety of teaching methods, assign a much higher value to their preparation, and are more likely to assume leadership roles in the schools. Because each of the participating institutions offers both professional development school and nonprofessional development school programs, this study provides evidence that informs local decisions about program structures and arrangements. As the study continues longitudinally, it will continue to generate findings to be used in program decisions.

The "Western Oregon Longitudinal Study of Preparation Program Effects" (Schalock, Schalock, & Ayers, 2003) is being conducted by researchers at Western Oregon University who have been developing teacher work samples for years as a way to document teacher candidates' impact on pupils' learning. This longitudinal study, which is currently at the analysis stage, is intended to examine the impact of variations in teacher preparation on pupils' learning outcomes. The study is addressing the following two major questions: Do early career teachers vary in terms of thinking, dispositions, practices, and impact on student learning? And, can variations be attributed to differences in preparation programs, particularly with regard to alignment with Oregon's overall design for standards-based schools and teaching practices? The study draws on multiple data sources collected over the 3 years, including classroom surveys, self-rating instruments, in-class observations, interviews, teacher portfolios, student work samples, document collection, and demographic data. The study is intended to link aspects of teacher preparation with what actually happens in classrooms.

These three regional studies—from Ohio, Massachusetts, and Oregon—represent an emerging trend in teacher education assessment: efforts to capitalize on and study naturally occurring variations (e.g., different models of preparation at the same universities, teacher candidates with and without preparation aligned with state curriculum standards, different program structures and arrangements across institutions) in teacher preparation to produce evidence that can guide program design decisions. In each case, these studies are being conducted collaboratively by researchers closely linked with program design, and thus information is intended to feed directly back into program decisions, although it also has implications for larger policy and practice issues. These projects also contribute to what has thus far been a missing program of research in teacher education—research that connects teacher preparation to outcomes by examining some of the links among preparation, on the one hand, and teachers' learning, their professional practices, and their K-12 students' learning, on the other.

Assessing Assessment

It is certainly worth asking why the initiatives and debates mentioned above are newsworthy at this point in time. Why is it that assessment of outcomes is not already the driving force in teacher education program decisions? The state of professional education in other areas offers an interesting perspective. In business education or legal education, for example, we do not have empirical evidence that taking ethics courses has a strong impact on the practices or the client outcomes of MBAs and attorneys (and, in fact, we often have stunning anecdotal evidence to the contrary). And yet, there is strong professional consensus that studying ethics is critical to the business world and the legal system. Likewise, we do not have experimental evidence indicating that physicians who study anatomy or physiology have higher rates of patient survival than those who do not. Nonetheless, the lack of empirical evidence does not deter most of us from thinking not only that physicians ought to study these topics, but also that the value of their studying them is self-evident. Taking a lesson from other professions, then, it may well be that one of the reasons we do not have empirical evidence confirming that it is important for teachers to study how people learn or how to teach subject matter may well be that for most of the profession, these matters are self-evident.

Another reason there has been little large-scale or longitudinal research assessing the impact of the particular components of collegiate teacher preparation is that studies of this kind are complicated and expensive, and it is seldom possible—or professionally justifiable—to control for or manipulate the myriad of intervening variables. Research on teacher education has been marginalized and underfunded for decades. It now seems clear that we need well-developed impact studies that allow for comparisons of recruitment strategies as well as comparisons of the pedagogies, components, and practices of teacher education. However, how research problems are prioritized is always connected to economic and social conditions (Weiner, 2000). Research that measures impact on a large scale and over time requires funding, institutional infrastructure, and research skills in a variety of methods and approaches. It also requires the commitment to make these issues a priority and the will to work on this program of research over the long haul. At least until very recently, these conditions have been lacking.

Finally, it is important to acknowledge that the current press for outcomes and evidence in teacher education is not an isolated phenomenon. Rather, it reflects several larger trends in higher education and in society more generally. In specialized accreditation organizations, for example, the emphasis has generally shifted from inputs to outcomes measures (Dill, 1998). These developments are, in turn, part of a larger trend in higher education, what Graham, Lyman, and Trow (1998) refer to as an "increasing clamor to apply quantitative measures of academic outcomes to guarantee educational quality for consumers" (p. 7) at the higher education level. This trend may reflect a growing public distrust of higher education and a general lack of confidence that the world of academe is capable of solving real-world problems. It also reflects larger global trends to privatize education and other human services and to discipline these services in the ways of a market-based economy (Apple, 2001). In teacher education, this trend is being played out in the growing demand that university-based teacher education programs compete in the educational marketplace with the increasing array of streamlined alternate routes to certification, fast-track teacher recruitment projects, for-profit teacher preparation providers, and distance-based teacher training businesses.

REFERENCES

Apple, M. (2001). Markets, standards, teaching, and teacher education. *Journal of Teacher Education, 52*(3), 182-195.

Cochran-Smith, M. (2000). Editorial: The questions that drive reform. *Journal of Teacher Education, 51*(5), 331-333.

Cochran-Smith, M. (2001). The outcomes question in teacher education. *Teaching & Teacher Education, 17*(5), 527-546.

Darling-Hammond, L., & Youngs, P. (2002). Defining "highly qualified teachers": What does "scientifically based research" actually tell us? *Educational Researcher, 31*(9), 13-25.

Dill, W. (1998). Specialized accreditation: An idea whose time has come? Or gone? *Change*, pp. 18-25.

Graham, P., Lyman, R., & Trow, M. (1998). *Accountability of colleges and universities: An essay.* New York: Columbia University Press.

Laczko-Kerr, I., & Berliner, D. C. (2002). The effectiveness of "Teach for America" and other under-certified teachers on student academic achievement: A case of harmful public policy. *Education Policy Analysis Archives, 10*(37).

Maloy, R., Pine, G., & Seidman, I. (2002). *Massachusetts teacher preparation and induction study report on first year findings* (National Education Association Professional Development School Research Project Teacher Quality Study).

Ohio Partnership for Accountability. (2002). *Teacher education and student achievement in complex contexts of accountability.* Dayton, OH: Ohio Partnership for Accountability.

Schalock, D., Schalock, M., & Ayers, R. (2003, January). *Teacher preparation effects in the classroom: Findings from a 3-year longitudinal study.* Paper presented at the American Association of Colleges for Teacher Education, New Orleans.

U.S. Department of Education. (2002). *Meeting the highly qualified teachers challenge, The Secretary's annual report on teacher quality.* Washington, DC: Author, Office of Postsecondary Education.

Weiner, L. (2000). Research in the 90s: Implications for urban teacher preparation. *Review of Educational Research, 70*(3), 369-406.

17 Teacher Education's Bermuda Triangle

Dichotomy, Mythology, and Amnesia

L egend has it that there is a triangular area in the Atlantic Ocean, defined at its points by Puerto Rico, Bermuda, and Miami, into which countless people and more than 70 sea and air crafts have disappeared without a trace during the last half century. Dozens of theories have been offered to explain the so-called mysterious disappearances, some pure science fiction, others more scientific, and some focused on human error and bad luck.

Interestingly, neither the Coast Guard nor reputable scientists are persuaded by supernatural explanations for events in the area, nor do they even acknowledge that the number of disasters is unusual given the area's heavy traffic and its size and location (Rosenberg, 1974). Thus, at least officially, there are no inexplicable disappearances, no Bermuda Triangle, and no mystery to solve. As it turns out, the "mystery" of the Bermuda Triangle, which got its start as the lead story in a fiction magazine, has been popularized in articles, best-sellers, and television documentaries through what Robert Todd Carroll, author of "the skeptics' dictionary," calls "communal reinforcement among uncritical authors and a willing mass media to uncritically pass on speculation" (Carroll, 2002).

Teacher education may not have TV shows promoting speculation about it, but it does have its share of unfounded assumptions,

SOURCE: *Journal of Teacher Education,* Vol. 54, No. 4, September/October 2003, pp. 275-279.

assertions, and explanations that are circulated more or less uncritically by the media, by critics of teacher education, and sometimes by the profession itself. The defining points of "teacher education's Bermuda Triangle" are not the geography of Puerto Rico, Bermuda, and Miami but the intellectual landscape of dichotomy, mythology, and amnesia.

COLLEGE GRADS VERSUS ED SCHOOL GRADS: THE DANGER OF DICHOTOMIES

Many dichotomies are based on the mistaken assumption that the only alternative to a particular idea, concept, or position is its opposite or its absence. Although dichotomies are often rhetorically effective, they are rarely useful for sorting out complex issues. Instead they tend to reduce important differences to mere caricatures while obscuring equally important similarities and nuances.

The dichotomy most plaguing teacher education right now is the one between "college grads," on one hand, and "ed school grads," on the other. When this dichotomy is invoked, college grads—who are assumed to possess subject matter knowledge and verbal ability—are regarded as the most desirable teaching recruits. At the same time, ed school grads—who are assumed to be deficient in both of these areas—are regarded as least desirable. Although this dichotomy is reductionist, false in certain ways, and dangerous, it is being widely promoted by influential individuals and groups, including conservative foundations that advocate deregulation of teacher education and other market-based reforms; the U.S. Department of Education (DOE) (2002), which has proclaimed that subject matter knowledge and verbal ability are the only empirically certified attributes of highly effective teachers; and the American Board for the Certification of Teacher Excellence (2003), whose mission is to develop a new, low cost, and transportable teaching credential based on paper-and-pencil tests of subject matter and professional knowledge.

The main thing wrong with the dichotomy between college grads and ed school grads is that it's wrong. It suggests that people entering teaching have *either* learned subject matter knowledge *or* they have been prepared to teach in programs sponsored by schools, colleges, and departments of education and thus not learned subject matter. The implication, of course, is that collegiate-based teacher preparation has nothing to do with subject matter and, to the contrary, it wastes precious time on inanities such as pedagogy, educational foundations, or supervised fieldwork and community experiences. This false dichotomy ignores completely the fact that currently most of those who are prepared in collegiate programs have earned both full subject matter majors (e.g., English or mathematics, if they are planning to teach at the secondary level, or psychology or child development, if they are planning to teach at the elementary level) as well as education majors or minors. In fact, since the 1980s, almost all states have increased the academic requirements for teachers, including requirements in many states that they complete subject area majors as well as or instead of education majors.

Another part of what is wrong with the college grad versus ed school grad dichotomy is that it is misleading about the verbal ability (shorthand for academic ability or intelligence) of prospective teachers. The dichotomy insinuates that college grads are "the best and the brightest" while ed school grads are the dregs of the college population. This is not only insulting to the teaching profession but also inaccurate and inadequate to account for the complexities involved. In fact, as Zumwalt and Craig (2005) indicate, it has now been shown that early studies that concluded that prospective teachers had particularly low SAT scores were misleading in large part because they used high school students' intentions to identify the group going into teaching. More recent studies indicate that different ways of defining prospective teachers yield different conclusions about SAT scores. Defining prospective teachers at every successive point along the teacher pipeline (those intending to teach, actually entering a teacher preparation program, actually seeking licensure, etc.) yields higher SAT scores. At graduation, national studies now indicate that those seeking licensure in secondary content areas have SAT scores comparable to or higher than other college graduates whereas those seeking elementary school licensure have scores that are average for college students, although lower than average for college graduates (Gitomer & Latham, 2000). While this does not suggest that there is no need for teacher education programs to improve (indeed, there is ample room for improvement), it does suggest that the simple dichotomy between college grads and ed school grads is false and misleading.

ALTERNATE ROUTES AS MODEL POLICY: THE PROBLEM WITH MYTHOLOGY

The second vertex of teacher education's Bermuda Triangle is mythology. Myths play an important role in most cultures, encapsulating important beliefs, attitudes, and values held by a group or society. In everyday language, however, the word *myth* is often used to refer to someone or something whose existence is widely believed in but who is indeed fictitious.

Currently, a widely circulating myth about teacher education has to do with the effectiveness of alternate routes into teaching. The first annual report to Congress on teaching quality (U.S. Department of Education, 2002) by DOE Secretary Rod Paige went a long way toward propagating this myth. The report unequivocally concludes that states must radically transform teacher preparation systems, eliminating all requirements and policies that are not based on scientific evidence. At the same time, however, the report declares that alternate routes, specifically "Troops to Teachers" and "Teach for America," are the model policy option. Unfortunately, as Darling-Hammond and Youngs (2002) argue in their critique of the report, the report "fails to meet the DOE's own standards for the use of scientifically based research to formulate policy" (p. 13). Indeed, as a number of recent syntheses of the empirical research related to alternate routes corroborate (Allen, 2003; Wilson, Floden, & Ferrini-Mundy, 2001; Zeichner & Schulte, 2001), the conclusion that there is empirical evidence to support alternate routes is more myth than fact.

It is important to note two things about the syntheses cited above. All of them find that it is difficult to draw conclusions across the empirical research because of the lack of consistency about how "alternate" and "traditional" programs are defined. But the second point is even more important: None of the syntheses concludes that there is empirical evidence that alternate routes are the model policy option for teacher quality. The primary conclusion of the Office of Educational Research and Improvement (OERI) sponsored Wilson, Floden, and Ferrini-Mundy (2001) synthesis, for example, is that there is not a solid base for conclusions; they call for more research and more rigorous research. They tentatively allow that the few studies that do exist in this area seem to point to the following: Although certain alternate routes may attract a more diverse pool of teacher candidates, they have a mixed record for attracting the best and the brightest teachers and for teaching performance. Teachers from "high-quality" or "structured" alternate routes look similar to traditionally prepared teachers on some dimensions. Finally, they point out that although there is very little research in this area, "successful" alternate routes may have these labor- and resource-intensive features: high entrance requirements, extensive mentoring and pedagogical training, frequent evaluation and feedback, practice in teaching before full teaching responsibility, and high exit standards. (In other words, they look a lot like successful university-based teacher education programs, which are also labor and resource intensive.) In an article in this journal, Zeichner and Schulte (2001) reached conclusions quite similar to those of Wilson et al., but cautioned even more unambiguously that it would be "very risky . . . to use these studies to draw any conclusions about alternative teacher certification programs in general" (p. 279).

Sponsored by the Education Commission of the States and drawing heavily on the Wilson, Floden, and Ferrini-Mundy (2001) analyses, Allen's (2003) recent synthesis of the research about teacher preparation is intended specifically for policymakers at the state level. His report rates the degree of confidence policymakers should have in specific policies regarding teacher preparation (either *moderate support*, *limited support*, or *inconclusive findings*) based on the extent of empirical evidence for these. It is very important to note that only Allen's designation *moderate support* even comes close to the DOE definition of "scientifically based research." Allen's overall conclusion is that the research support for alternate routes is "not substantial." Indeed, not even one of the "modest conclusions" Allen allows receives even the *moderate support* designation! Nevertheless, he suggests there is *limited support* for two results: Some teachers prepared through alternate routes may ultimately be as effective as traditionally prepared teachers but may have more difficulties early on. And, for those entering teaching through alternate routes, short-term retention may be comparable to those in university programs but not long-term commitments.

Despite their different purposes, these major syntheses are quite consistent in their conclusions. There are no clear, compelling, and empirically strong conclusions that can be made about alternate routes into teaching at this time. What this suggests is that the claim that alternate routes are "model programs" is not much more than myth right now—widely believed by certain groups but not supported by evidence.

TEACHER PREPARATION AS TRAINING: THE TROUBLE WITH AMNESIA

The third of the vertices in teacher education's Bermuda Triangle is amnesia, the inability to remember and/or the loss of memory. From the quirkiest of perspectives, it is perhaps possible that amnesia is refreshing in certain ways, providing a clean slate or a new lease on life. However, amnesia surely creates more problems for its sufferers than it solves, rendering it difficult to make connections, learn from past mistakes, or benefit from what has gone before.

Like many areas in education, teacher education is often plagued by the lack of historical perspectives on present issues. Currently, teacher education is troubled by historical amnesia about conceptualizing teaching as a technical activity and, accordingly, conceptualizing teacher preparation as a training problem. The current agenda to produce "highly qualified teachers" works from the assumption that it is possible to establish through scientifically based research a set of certifiable classroom practices—"what works" in teaching—that teachers can be trained to use. This first assumption relies on a set of mutually dependent assumptions: Teaching is a technical activity, knowledge is static, good practice is universal, being prepared to teach is being trained to do what works, and pupil learning is equal to higher scores on high-stakes tests.

Although not exactly the same, this approach is certainly related to many of the developments in teacher education during the late 1960s through the mid-1980s. Influenced by new studies of the "scientific basis of teaching" and by empirical evidence about effective teaching strategies (Gage, 1972), many teacher preparation programs trained teachers to engage in specific classroom behaviors or competencies that had been correlated with gain scores in pupil achievement and developed systems for evaluating teachers according to scientific objectives and stated performance criteria. During the 1980s, in keeping with changes in how learning and cognition were coming to be understood more generally, the focus of teacher education shifted away from training and toward teacher thinking, teacher knowledge, and teacher learning. By the mid-to-late 1990s, however, there was still another shift—toward performance-based accountability, particularly assessments of the demonstrated outcomes teachers and programs produced (or not) in the learning of teachers and K-12 students. Currently, there is intense political pressure for teacher education to focus singularly (and some would say relentlessly) on K-12 students' and prospective teachers' scores on high-stakes tests.

My point here is not to elaborate on these developments in the history of teacher education but to reiterate that the tensions between regarding teaching as a technical or an intellectual activity and between regarding teacher preparation as training or a learning problem are not new issues in the early years of the 21st century. Although the tensions are certainly playing out differently now from the way they did during earlier times, these issues reflect a long history of tensions between what Borrowman (1956, 1965) called "the liberal and the technical" in the history of teacher education in America, and along related but somewhat different lines, what Dewey (1904) referred to in his discussion of the relationship between theoretical insight and practical activity as "laboratory" versus "apprenticeship" approaches to learning to teach.

It is important to note the complexity and deep roots of the issues involved so as not to contribute to the amnesiac renderings of teacher education that are often prominent in the policy and research literature. The fundamental tensions that drive teacher education emerge and reemerge periodically. Each time they do, they are threaded into and wound around the current intersections of educational and other kinds of research, practice, and policy. Thus, the tensions are both old and new. They are new in that they are woven into the tapestry of changed and changing political, social, and economic times and thus have a different set of implications each time they reemerge in prominence. But they are also old in that they represent enduring and deep disagreements in society about the purposes of schooling, the value of teaching, and the preparation of teachers.

In our complex political context, dichotomies, myths, and historical amnesia may turn out to be just as deadly for teacher education as whatever it is that happens in the Bermuda Triangle has been for seamen and airmen. One defense against these is more vigilant, critical, and public response to speculation—response that is based on evidence as well as careful analysis of underlying political agendas and ideological positions. Another is continued improvement and documentation of efforts that produce teachers who are academically and pedagogically knowledgeable as well as able to prepare pupils for democratic participation.

REFERENCES

Allen, M. (2003). *Eight questions on teacher preparation: What does the research say?* Denver, CO: Education Commission of the States.

American Board for the Certification of Teacher Excellence. (2003). *American Board for the Certification of Teacher Excellence: Promoting teacher quality—impacting student learning.* Available from http://www .abcte.org

Borrowman, M. (1956). *The liberal and technical in teacher education: A historical survey of American thought.* New York: Teachers College Press.

Borrowman, M. (1965). *Teacher education in America: A documentary history.* New York: Teachers College Press.

Carroll, R. (2002). *Bermuda (or Devil's) Triangle.* Retrieved May 7, 2003, from http://skepdic.com/bermuda.html

Darling-Hammond, L., & Youngs, P. (2002). Defining "highly qualified teachers": What does "scientifically based research" actually tell us? *Educational Researcher, 31*(9), 13-25.

Dewey, J. (1904). The relation of theory to practice in education. In C. McMurray (Ed.), *The third NSSE yearbook.* Chicago: University of Chicago Press.

Gage, N. (1972). *Teacher effectiveness and teacher education: The search for a scientific basis.* Palo Alto, CA: Pacific Books.

Gitomer, D., & Latham, A. (2000). Generalizations in teacher education: Seductive and misleading. *Journal of Teacher Education, 51*(3), 215-220.

Rosenberg, H. (1974). Exorcizing the Devil's Triangle. *Sealift, 6,* 11-15.

U.S. Department of Education. (2002). *Meeting the highly qualified teachers challenge: The Secretary's annual report on teacher quality.* Washington, DC: Author, Office of Postsecondary Education.

Wilson, S., Floden, R., & Ferrini-Mundy, J. (2001). *Teacher preparation research: Current knowledge, gaps, and recommendations.* Washington, DC: Center for the Study of Teaching and Policy.

Zeichner, K., & Schulte, A. (2001). What we know and don't know from peer-reviewed research about alternative teacher certification programs. *Journal of Teacher Education, 52*(4), 266-282.

Zumwalt, K., & Craig, B. C. (2005). Teachers' characteristics: Research on indicators of quality. In M. Cochran-Smith & K. Zeichner (Eds.), *Studying teacher education: The report of the AERA panel on research and teacher education.* Mahwah, NJ: Lawrence Erlbaum.

18 Sometimes It's <u>Not</u> About the Money

Teaching and Heart

The current press for market-based approaches to the reform of teacher education is part of the larger movement to privatize health, education, and many other public and consumer services. As proponents of privatization (whom I refer to here as "marketeers") often point out in articles and commentaries in outlets such as Chester Finn's *Education Next*,[1] the success of market-based approaches is entirely dependent upon competition and a strong competitive environment. A bold statement of the basics of market-based reforms appears in an *Education Next* commentary by Frederick Hess (2001), who explains why a market approach to reforming the schools has thus far not been successful.

Hess's article is replete with melodramatic mixed metaphors about schools and schooling—"straightjacketed" public schools with no "watchdog" shareholders, the need to allow competition to "bloom and thrive" by "shattering" constraints, and school systems "strangled" by politics and bureaucracy. Hess complains that the conditions that make the market work—investors looking for maximum financial returns, employees motivated by monetary incentives, and managers authorized to make immediate personnel decisions—are "almost nonexistent" (p. 1) in schools and other public or charitable efforts, "especially those devoted to tending the needs of children of the disadvantaged" (p. 3).

SOURCE: *Journal of Teacher Education*, Vol. 54, No. 5, November/December 2003, pp. 371-375.

From a market-based perspective, the Hess article (2001) claims that there are several key factors that keep competition from being a more effective tool for school reform. One of these is that "teachers are attracted to education for its child-centered, humanistic, and autonomous character" (p. 7)—a very unfortunate state of affairs, according to Hess, because it means they do not respond effectively to competition. To unleash the "market bulldozer" into school reform (the kind that compels businesses to "improve constantly— or be crushed") (p. 4), Hess asserts that there would have to be fundamental change in the culture of schools. Based on the premise that "competition is fundamentally about fear" and that the power of competition in education is that "people fear for their investments or their jobs" (p. 5), Hess offers a simple solution:

> The simplest way to strengthen competition is to make it more threatening. Public school employees who are concerned about losing their jobs, desirable assignments, or material rewards are much more likely to cooperate with efforts to respond to a competitive threat. (pp. 7-8)

In concluding, Hess speculates that the discipline of the market would work best in large chains of for-profit schools that would attract a new breed of teachers "who care more about individual rewards and material incentives" and who are motivated by being part of a system "more reliant on self-interest" (p. 9). Presumably this new breed of teachers would not be like those whom Hess criticizes earlier in his article—the kind who enter teaching because they are committed to children or for other idealistic reasons.

There are many possible critiques of Hess's (2001) article, not the least of which is to excoriate its patronizing tone about "the disadvantaged," which pairs public education with charity, and its utter failure to acknowledge the covenant to provide quality education to all participants in our society, which is a bedrock of a democracy. In this editorial, however, I want to concentrate on the exquisite and deeply disturbing irony of Hess's analysis of teachers and teaching—an analysis that is simultaneously so right and so wrong. Hess is absolutely right when he says that teachers are often attracted to the profession for reasons that are not about money or self-interested career advancement but are, instead, about children and what Hess calls "humanistic" reasons. The irony, of course, is that, at the same time that he is right about why many people go into teaching, Hess is dead wrong about the fundamental nature of the activity of teaching and about how to fix schools and schooling.

This themed issue of *JTE*, which begins with an essay by Parker Palmer, focuses on teaching from the heart. My editorial touches on three of the ways in which the heart—and not just the money—matters in teaching and teacher education. Along with this entire issue of *JTE*, my editorial is intended to bring to the foreground a view of teaching that contrasts markedly with the view that underlies a competitive, marketeer approach to reforming schools and teacher education.

TEACHING AS CARING

Contrary to what Hess and other marketeers may wish for, teachers are seldom centrally motivated by fear of losing their jobs or their material investments. More often, they are motivated by fear of losing their students—losing them to the abysses of poverty, joblessness, low expectations, boredom, peer pressure, disaffection, lost opportunity, substance abuse, alienation, family disintegration, and, particularly for those who are poor or marginalized, to the utter lack of prospects for the future. In the face of these daunting challenges of modern society, caring is, in fact, an integral part of teaching and learning. Teaching involves caring deeply about students as human beings and, at the same time, caring just as deeply that all students have rich opportunities to learn academically challenging material that will maximize their life chances. Rather than trying to restructure schools so teachers are motivated by fear and intimidation, as the marketeers want to do, a better response might be to strengthen and reward teachers' efforts to care about their students.

It is now generally acknowledged that teaching and learning are social and relational processes; that is, they occur within socially and culturally constructed contexts and depend to a great extent on the establishment of relationships between teachers and learners (Witherell & Noddings, 1991). Documented accounts of teachers like Marva Collins and Jaime Escalante, whose students succeed against all odds, along with empirical studies of successful teachers of students from groups that have traditionally been underserved or in some way marginalized by the educational system (e.g., Ballenger,

1998; Ladson-Billings, 1995) are especially instructive here. Although there are a number of consistent threads in these accounts, one of the most striking of these is that successful teachers of underserved groups care about their students. They demonstrate that they are connected to, rather than disengaged from or (worse) afraid of, their students as individuals and as members of groups and larger communities (Irvine, 1990). And they work with, not against, individuals, families, and communities by consciously seeking to avoid functioning as a wedge between students and their families (Cochran-Smith, 1997) and by carefully seeking to avoid conveying the message that to succeed is to escape from, ignore, or rise above their own communities or become exceptions to the groups of which they are members. Ladson-Billings (1995) referred to this constellation of dispositions in teaching as *the ethic of caring* and *the ethic of accountability.*

The marketeers want more teachers motivated by fear who will be compelled and threatened into doing a more profitable job of teaching. However, the ethic of caring about students and the ethic of accountability for the welfare of students and their communities come from the heart rather than the pocketbook. They come from deep beliefs about the importance and value of the life chances of all children, the morality of teaching, and the future of our democratic nation. Commitments like these cannot be forced, and they cannot be bought. But they can be informed, nurtured, and channeled into productive work in schools and communities.

TEACHING AS LEARNING

As noted above, the marketeers want to "unchain the bulldozer" (Hess, 2001, p. 7) of market reform on schools and schooling. To do so, according to Hess (2001) and others, we need more "bright, ambitious teaching aspirants" (p. 9) and an environment that is more welcoming of "entrepreneurial personalities" (p. 7). At the same time, however, Hess tells us we also need administrators who "compel their subordinates to act" (p. 6) and a school culture that eschews teachers' "love of autonomy" and their "insulation from supervision" (p. 9). Once again, Hess and the marketeers have it partly right but also completely wrong.

Contrary to what Hess (2001) may imply, unfettered autonomy is quite rare in public schools. Isolation, however, is not. In fact, isolation has been recognized for some time now as a problem in the teaching profession. It is also true, as analysts have pointed out for years, that teachers' academic ability is one of the factors that is related to students' achievement and that some of the most academically able teachers leave the profession after a relatively short time. Contrary to the position of the marketeers, however, the solution to these problems is *not* to hire bright teachers animated by self-interest and material rewards so that they can work for administrators who use intimidation to get them to comply with efforts to respond to competitive threats. (One wonders, by the way, why bright and ambitious teachers would want to enter a profession in which fear was the major motivation to do well and in which teachers had no autonomy to make professional decisions in the best interest of their students. Rather, it seems reasonable to assume that the workers most likely to do well in such an environment would be compliant technicians who follow rules closely, respond without question to new directives, and require close supervision to perform well.)

A different response to the challenge of recruiting academically able teachers into the profession and to diminishing isolation among teachers is to conceptualize teacher preparation and teacher development across the lifespan as a learning problem rather than a training problem (Cochran-Smith, 2004) and create the professional norms and school conditions that support teachers' learning over the long haul. When teacher development is understood as a learning problem, part of the goal is to recruit and support teachers who know subject matter but also know how to pose and solve the new problems that continuously emerge in classrooms and schools, who know how to provide rich learning opportunities for all of their students, and who know how to work together with other teachers in learning communities. In short, when teaching is rightly regarded as an intellectual activity and when it is acknowledged that teachers are motivated, at least in part, by love of learning, then it becomes clear that what is needed are more opportunities for teachers to work with others in learning communities; raise new questions about students, subject matter, assessments, equity, and access; and generate local knowledge through collaborative analysis and interpretation.

The contrasts between a learning approach to improving teaching and the approach of the marketeers are obvious. The discourse in learning communities is quite different from the usual supervisory discourse, which Hess wants to intensify. Supervision, in which one party is assumed to be the expert and the other the recipient in need of information, tends to focus on the technical rather than substantive or critical aspects of teaching. In contrast, when teacher development is understood not simply as the transmission of specific skills but also as the generation of local knowledge, there is a whole different set of possibilities.

Teaching to Change the World

I have been a teacher educator for more than 25 years and have now worked or consulted with teacher education programs and institutions that span the continent. Over these years, I have asked hundreds of would-be teachers why they wanted to teach. Never once—whether entering through a university-based program or an alternate route like Teach for America—did a prospective teacher say that he or she wanted to be part of an efficient organization with a strong profitability margin. To the contrary, the explanation I heard most often was that people became teachers because they wanted to make a difference, they wanted to change the world, or they wanted to help improve the human condition. Certainly this is a naive sentiment in some ways. A savior mentality uninformed by awareness of the stark inequities of American society and untempered with historical and political understanding is inappropriate and even undermining. And, of course, teachers *cannot* fix the problems of society by teaching better, nor can teachers alone, whether through individual or group efforts, alter the life chances of the children they teach, particularly if the larger issues of structural and institutional racism and inequity are not addressed. However, as many scholars have pointed out, although teachers cannot substitute for social movements aimed at the transformation of society's fundamental inequities, their work has the potential to contribute to those movements in essential ways.

Different words have been used to capture the passion of this kind of a commitment to teaching—teaching for social justice, teaching for social change, teaching for social responsibility, and teaching to change the world, among others. In general, all of these ideas are based on the assumption that it is impossible to teach in ways that are *not* value-laden and ideological. This assumption is not an argument for politicizing education, however. Rather, it is an argument for recognizing that it is already politicized and that this should be fully acknowledged as an inherent part of education (Bruner, 1996). Part of teaching to change the world, then, is intentionally claiming the role of educator as well as activist based on political consciousness and on ideological and heart-felt commitment to diminishing the inequities of American life.

What the marketeers do not get at all is that sometimes *it's really not* about the money. Sometimes it really is about service, about changing the world, and about deep-seated commitments to providing access for all children to fully prepared teachers, quality educational experiences that prepare them for meaningful work and further education, and decently resourced schools. Contrary to what Hess and the marketeers may conclude, what we *do not* need are more teachers who are prepared to be compliant and who are motivated by the fear of losing their jobs. What we *do not* need are school cultures where managers coerce their subordinates into behaving in ways that respond to market threats and competition. What we *do* need are more teachers who are fully prepared to teach and who are motivated to make rich learning opportunities a reality for all schoolchildren. What we *do* need are school cultures that sustain and support teachers' (and students') learning over the long haul at the same time that they link these to larger efforts to change the conditions of schooling. Part of this is greater understanding of the fact that teaching and learning cannot be reduced simply to the bottom lines of efficiency and profitability. At their very core, teaching and learning are matters of both head and heart, both reason and passion.

NOTE

1. Chester Finn is the senior editor of *Education Next*, which is an electronic magazine published by the Hoover Institute and sponsored by the Fordham Foundation, the Manhattan Institute, and others.

REFERENCES

Ballenger, C. (1998). *Teaching other people's children: Literacy and learning in a bilingual classroom.* New York: Teachers College Press.
Bruner, J. (1996). *The culture of education.* Cambridge, MA: Harvard University Press.

Cochran-Smith, M. (1997). Knowledge, skills, and experiences for teaching culturally diverse learners: A perspective for practicing teachers. In J. Irvine (Ed.), *Critical knowledge for diverse learners and teachers* (pp. 27-88). Washington, DC: American Association of Colleges for Teacher Education.

Cochran-Smith, M. (2004). *Walking the road: Race, diversity, and social justice in teacher education.* New York: Teachers College Press.

Hess, F. (2001). The work ahead. *Education Next.* Retrieved March 30, 2001, from http://www.educationnext.org/20014/7hess.html

Irvine, J. (1990). *Black students and school failure: Policies, practice, and prescriptions.* Westport, CT: Greenwood Press.

Ladson-Billings, G. (1995). Toward a theory of culturally relevant pedagogy. *American Educational Research Journal, 32*(3), 465-491.

Witherell, C., & Noddings, N. (Eds.). (1991). *Stories lives tell.* New York: Teachers College Press.

19 Taking Stock in 2004

Teacher Education in Dangerous Times

I n an article about culturally relevant approaches to teacher assessment published a few years ago, Ladson-Billings (1998) asserted that those were "dangerous times" for teachers of students of color because new evaluations of teacher competency that did not account for culture could actually perpetuate teaching practices that did not serve children of color and children living in poverty. Borrowing Ladson-Billings' language, this editorial suggests that these are dangerous times for teacher education. Taking stock as the new year begins, the editorial posits that three major developments are currently driving practice, policy, and research in teacher education: an intense focus on teacher quality; the emergence of "tightly-regulated deregulation" as a federally mandated reform agenda for teacher preparation; and the ascendance of science as the solution to educational problems.[1] Although none of these necessarily or alone makes this a dangerous time, their convergence is pushing us dangerously close to a technical view of teaching, a training model of teacher education, the isomorphic equating of learning with testing, and an educational system in which "winner takes all" in terms of opportunities, resources, and outcomes.

INTENSE FOCUS ON TEACHER QUALITY

Over the past several years, a new consensus has emerged that teacher quality is one of the most, if not *the* most, significant factor

SOURCE: *Journal of Teacher Education,* Vol. 55, No. 1, January/February 2004, pp. 3-7.

in students' achievement and educational improvement. In a certain sense, of course, this is good news, which simply affirms what most educators have believed for years: teachers' work is important in students' achievement and in their life chances. In another sense, however, this conclusion is problematic, even dangerous. When teacher quality is unequivocally identified as the primary factor that accounts for differences in student learning, some policymakers and citizens may infer that individual teachers alone are responsible for the successes and failures of the educational system despite the mitigation of social and cultural contexts, support provided for teachers' ongoing development, the historical failure of the system to serve particular groups, the disparate resources devoted to education across schools and school systems, and the match or mismatch of school and community expectations and values. Influenced by the new consensus about teacher quality, some constituencies may infer that "teachers teaching better" is the panacea for disparities in school achievement and thus conclude that everybody else is off the hook for addressing the structural inequalities and differential power relations that permeate our nation's schools.

There is another danger here as well. Although we now appear to have consensus about the importance of teacher quality, there is no parallel consensus about how to define it: how to conceptualize teacher quality in ways that account for the complexities of teaching and learning, how to identify which characteristics of teacher quality are linked with desirable educational outcomes, how to decide which educational outcomes are desirable in the first place, and how to recruit, prepare, and retain teachers who provide rich academic learning opportunities but also prepare their students for participation in a democracy. Absent opportunities for discussion about what could or should constitute our definitions of excellent teaching and teacher quality, these are being defined primarily in terms of test scores—K-12 students' test scores as well as prospective teachers' test scores. For example, Sanders's (1998; Sanders & Horn, 1998) value-added teacher assessment model, which is widely cited as the empirical basis for the teacher quality agenda, is explicitly designed to differentiate teachers by sorting them into quartiles according to the test scores of their pupils.

The equating of teacher quality with test scores is also apparent in the new transportable teacher test being developed by the American Board for the Certification of Teacher Excellence (ABCTE), which is funded by a $45 million grant from the Department of Education. The mission of ABCTE is to develop a new, low-cost, and transportable teaching credential based on paper-and-pencil tests of subject matter and professional knowledge, which can be used across states to indicate which teachers are "highly qualified" in keeping with the presumed conclusion that subject matter knowledge and verbal ability are the only empirically certified attributes of highly effective teachers (Paige, 2002; Whitehurst, 2002). The problems with test scores as the singular measure of teaching and learning are now well known—the power of test-score-driven systems to narrow the curriculum, the negative impact of teacher tests on the diversity of the teaching force, and the failure of test scores to assess other important educational goals, such as preparing students for civic engagement. These present grave dangers for teacher education.

Tightly Regulated Deregulation

Over the past two decades, professionalization and deregulation have competed with one another as agendas for the reform of teacher education. Taking stock in 2004 reveals that proponents of these two agendas continue to debate the evidence for their positions and argue about the goals of education. But there has been an important twist in the struggle to win the agenda, a twist that boosts deregulation by coupling it—ironically—with intensified regulation. Tighter regulation of teacher education is reflected in increased federal and state control of both the "inputs" of teacher preparation (e.g., number, kind, and content of courses and fieldwork experiences) and its "outputs" or "outcomes" (e.g., assessments of the impact of teacher preparation on teacher learning, professional practice, and K-12 students' learning). Along these lines, 42 states now require statewide assessments for prospective teachers, 32 states require tests in one or more subject areas, and all states must report annually to the federal government on the quality of preparation programs (U.S. Department of Education, 2003).[2]

At the federal level (and in some states), deregulation and regulation have become strange but intimate bedfellows, advocating seemingly contradictory but simultaneous efforts to deregulate *and* tightly regulate teacher preparation. This new agenda for the reform of teacher preparation is reflected in the Secretary of Education's first and second reports to Congress on teacher quality

(U.S. Department of Education, 2002, 2003). The reports themselves, which are required as per the reauthorization of Title II of the Higher Education Act, signal tighter federal control of teacher preparation because they are intended to analyze the results of mandatory annual state reporting on the quality of teacher preparation programs, which in turn depend on institutional reporting to states about the qualifications of all teacher candidates recommended for certification. At the same time, however, the reports overtly favor deregulation, particularly in the form of programs and entry routes that severely curtail or bypass altogether the roles of colleges and universities in teacher preparation. In the second report, for example, there are a number of "promising innovations" highlighted in the discussion about states' progress toward meeting the highly qualified teachers challenge. A few of these exemplars are innovative college- or university-based programs, but the vast majority are training programs for former military and technology workers, online teacher training packages, and other initiatives that feature very short initial training followed by immediate classroom responsibility with concurrent on-the-job and course training.

It is certainly worth pursuing a variety of approaches to teacher preparation, and the point of this editorial is *not* at all to defend the status quo. However, there are also dangers involved in the proliferation of alternate routes to teacher certification, not the least of which is the distinct possibility of a two-tiered educational system wherein the pupils most in need of fully qualified and fully licensed teachers are the least likely to get them (Darling-Hammond & Sclan, 1996; Oakes, Franke, Quartz, & Rogers, 2002). Notwithstanding this very real and important concern, which I have written about previously, I concentrate in this editorial on another danger—the utter lack of evidence that tightly regulated deregulation is a prudent, evidence-based, or cost-effective strategy for reforming teacher preparation. It is simply not the case, for example, that there is a robust body of evidence indicating that we can solve the problem of teacher supply simultaneously with the problem of teacher quality by implementing statewide or nationwide alternate routes into teaching. As a matter of fact, syntheses of the empirical research on alternate routes indicate that the evidence is skimpy and inconclusive, making policy recommendations nearly impossible (Allen, 2003; Wilson, Floden, & Ferrini-Mundy, 2001; Zeichner & Schulte, 2001).

A good example along these lines is Rice's (2003) recent economic analysis of the aspects of teacher background that can be translated into policy and practice. Rice's analysis was funded by the Washington-based Economic Policy Institute, a nonpartisan research organization aimed at enlarging public debate about how to achieve a fair and prosperous economy. Rice concludes that many dimensions of teacher characteristics—including preparation, experience, and test scores—are important. She cautions, however, that neither continuation of the status quo nor elimination of all credentialing requirements are likely to lead to improvement. Rather, she argues:

> The evidence indicates that neither an extreme centralized bureaucratization nor a complete deregulation of teacher requirements is a wise approach for improving teacher quality. . . . Education policymakers and administrators would be well served by recognizing the complexity of the issue and adopting multiple measures along many dimensions to support existing teachers and to attract and hire new, highly qualified teachers. The research suggests that investing in teachers can make a difference in student achievement. (p. vii)

Following Rice's line of reasoning, it may be that the worst danger we face with tightly regulated deregulation is that we get the worst of both worlds—wholesale support for alternate routes that do away with most teacher requirements and make entry into teaching wide open, on one hand, and centralized control that diminishes state- and local-level decisions about the preparation of teachers and greatly prescribes professional discretion and autonomy, on the other.

THE ASCENDANCE OF SCIENCE

The third force driving teacher education in 2004 is the dramatic rise in prominence of the "science of education" and/or "the scientific research base" for education. The rise of science is reflected in the formation of the U.S. Department of Education's Institute of Education Sciences (IES), which explicitly "reflect[s] the intent of the President and Congress to advance the field of education research, making it more rigorous in support of evidence-based education" (Institute of Education Sciences, 2003). Shortly after it was established, IES created the "What Works Clearinghouse" to provide a centralized and reliable source of scientifically verified information about the effects of policies, strategies, and practices in education. The independent research organizations that support the clearinghouse provide systematic syntheses of studies of the effects of trials of behavioral and educational interventions.

The notion of "scientifically based research" and its complement, "evidence-based education," along with the new agencies that foster them reflect renewed confidence in the power of science to solve problems related to teaching quality, teacher preparation, and effective schools. This confidence is imbued in the policies and the language of the No Child Left Behind Act of 2001 (NCLB) (P.L. 107-110), which equates rigorous scientific research with experimental or quasi-experimental designs. IES Director Whitehurst (2001) defined evidence-based educational practices as those involving the integration of "professional wisdom" and rigorous empirical evidence. He makes it clear, however, that educational decisions currently rely far too heavily on professional wisdom and far too lightly on empirical evidence, of which randomized trials are the "gold standard." The application to teacher education of new federal dicta regarding scientifically based research is reflected in Whitehurst's (2002) summary of the scientific evidence on teacher quality, which finds it unfortunate that experimental methods have not yet found their way to research on teacher training.

There are virtually no studies in teacher education that conform to the federal government's current demand for randomized experiments by demonstrating direct causal links from teacher preparation to educational outcomes defined as pupils' gain scores on high-stakes tests. This is the case for a whole variety of historical and fiscal reasons, one of which has to do with the nature of the teacher education enterprise itself. "Teacher preparation" and "teacher education" are neither monolithic nor unitary pursuits. Even in the face of tightly specified policies, teacher education is instantiated in ways that are highly local—embedded in the multiple and changing contexts of local institutions and regions and subject to the interpretations and social interactions of individuals and groups. Complexity and variation rather than uniformity between and among structures, organizational arrangements, program types, institutional categories, and preparation paths or routes are the rule rather than the exception in teacher education.

In a recent book on the use of randomized trials in educational research (Mosteller & Boruch, 2001), Weiss's chapter (2001) is entitled, "What to Do Until the Random Assigner Comes." In it, Weiss describes the difficulty of conducting randomized field trials to evaluate community programs because of the complex and diffuse nature of work in communities. If we substitute "teacher education" for Weiss's "community programs," her point is very useful here: "Random assignment has a spare beauty all its own, but the sprawling world of [teacher education] is inhospitable to it" (p. 222). Given the "sprawling world" of teacher education, it is problematic to limit empirical research only to causal studies that depend on randomized experiments or on quasi-experiments. Although these constitute one form of research that should inform teacher education, they are not the "gold standard." Particularly because the specification of causal relationships in teacher education is likely to remain difficult and problematic, it is important to pursue many kinds of questions, which by definition demand different research approaches.

Finally, although there are many empirical questions that are worth pursuing, there are also many important questions related to teacher education that cannot be answered scientifically. Some of the most contested issues in the history of education have to do with fundamental disagreements about who should be educated, for what aims and purposes, what should be taught, how it should be assessed, and who should decide. None of these are questions of science and evidence. All of them are questions of value. Education (and teacher education) are social institutions that pose moral, ethical, social, philosophical, and ideological questions. It is wrong headed—and dangerous—to treat these questions as if they were value neutral and ideology free and to portray research as having the capacity to resolve the issues on the basis of evidence alone.

This editorial has suggested that what's driving teacher education in 2004 are the intersections and collisions of three major trends: intense and singular attention to teacher quality as individual teacher effectiveness in raising test scores, the emergence of highly regulated deregulation as the federal agenda for reforming teacher preparation, and the ascendance of science as the presumed solution to most educational problems. Contrary to the beliefs of some observers, these issues did not emerge as new phenomena during the past few years, nor are current attacks of teacher education historically unprecedented in kind or intensity. Rather, these three trends represent current instantiations of perennially contested issues—the purposes of education in a democratic society, the role of teacher preparation in relation to those purposes, the knowledge and dispositions teachers need to teach well, the potential and limitations of a "science" of education, and the locus of public and/or professional authority and control of teacher preparation. As we begin 2004, these issues are converging within the larger context of an acutely conservative political climate, a widespread movement to apply the rules and discipline of the market to education and other human services, and the prevailing assumption that science, which is value-free, ought to be the basis of all policy and practice decisions. Together, these make 2004 a decidedly dangerous time.

NOTES

1. A number of these issues have been addressed in previous editorials in *JTE*, to which I direct interested readers. In this editorial, I concentrate on the convergence of these issues at this point in time and on the "dangers" this presents.

2. Some critics (Cochran-Smith, 2001; Thiessen, 2000) have referred to this array of new requirements as the "over-regulation" of teacher education.

REFERENCES

Allen, M. (2003). *Eight questions on teacher preparation: What does the research say?* Denver, CO: Education Commission of the States.

Cochran-Smith, M. (2001). Reforming teacher education: Competing agendas. *Journal of Teacher Education, 52*(4), 263-265.

Darling-Hammond, L., & Sclan, E. (1996). Who teaches and why. In J. Sikula (Ed.), *Handbook of research on teacher education* (pp. 67-101). New York: Simon & Schuster Macmillan.

Institute of Education Sciences. (2003). *Institute of Education Sciences.* Retrieved September 12, 2003, from www.ed.gov/about/offices/list/ies/index.html?svc=mr

Ladson-Billings, G. (1998). Teaching in dangerous times: Culturally relevant approaches to teacher assessment. *Journal of Negro Education, 67*(3), 255-267.

Mosteller, F., & Boruch, R. (2001). *Evidence matters, randomized trials in education research.* Washington, DC: Brookings Institution.

No Child Left Behind Act of 2001. (P.L. 107-110).

Oakes, J., Franke, M., Quartz, K., & Rogers, J. (2002). Research for high-quality urban teaching: Defining it, developing it, assessing it. *Journal of Teacher Education, 53*(3), 228-234.

Paige, R. (2002). *Secretary Paige releases state reports on teacher preparation.* Retrieved May, 2002, from www.title2.org

Rice, J. K. (2003). *Teacher quality: Understanding the effectiveness of teacher attributes.* Washington, DC: Economic Policy Institute.

Sanders, W. (1998). Value-added assessment. *The School Administrator,* pp. 24-27.

Sanders, W., & Horn, S. (1998). Research findings from the Tennessee Value-Added Assessment System (TVAAS) database: Implications for educational evaluation and research. *Journal of Personnel Evaluation in Education, 12*(3), 247-256.

Thiessen, D. (2000). Developing a knowledge for preparing teachers: Redefining the role of schools of education. *Educational Policy, 14,* 129-144.

U.S. Department of Education. (2002). *Meeting the highly qualified teachers challenge: The Secretary's annual report on teacher quality.* Washington, DC: U.S. Department of Education, Office of Postsecondary Education.

U.S. Department of Education. (2003). *Meeting the highly qualified teachers challenge: The Secretary's second annual report on teacher quality.* Washington, DC: U.S. Department of Education, Office of Postsecondary Education.

Weiss, C. (2001). What to do until the random assigner comes. In F. Mosteller & R. Boruch (Eds.), *Evidence matters, randomized trials in education research* (pp. 198-224). Washington, DC: Brookings Institution.

Whitehurst, G. (2001). *Evidence-based education (EBE).* Retrieved September 12, 2003, from www.ed.gov

Whitehurst, G. (2002). *Scientifically based research on teacher quality: Research on teacher preparation and professional development.* Paper presented at the White House Conference on Preparing Tomorrow's Teachers, Washington, DC.

Wilson, S., Floden, R., & Ferrini-Mundy, J. (2001). *Teacher preparation research: Current knowledge, gaps, and recommendations.* Washington, DC: Center for the Study of Teaching and Policy.

Zeichner, K., & Schulte, A. (2001). What we know and don't know from peer-reviewed research about alternative teacher certification programs. *Journal of Teacher Education, 52*(4), 266-282.

20 Ask a Different Question, Get a Different Answer

The Research Base for Teacher Education

Although the history of teacher education has been braided with the history of educational research for many years, research is currently playing a more prominent role than ever before. In fact, in many of the major 21st-century debates about teacher quality and teacher preparation, the central focus, at least on the surface, is research itself, particularly on whether there is a research base for teacher education.

This editorial serves two purposes. First, the editorial provides information about two recent research efforts related to teacher preparation: (a) a major review of what the research says about teacher preparation and its implications for policy published by the Education Commission of the States (ECS) and (b) the research-grounded recommendations for the teacher education curriculum made by the Committee on Teacher Education (CTE) of the National Academy of Education (NAE). These efforts are alike in that each uses research to substantiate and justify its arguments regarding teacher preparation. They are also alike in that each is sponsored by a highly visible organization with an influential voice in the educational community. Notwithstanding these similarities, the editorial also makes the point that although in a certain way both reports

SOURCE: *Journal of Teacher Education,* Vol. 55, No. 2, March/April 2004, pp. 111-115.

are designed to assess the research base for teacher preparation, they are actually addressing quite different questions and using research in very different ways. The editorial argues that explicitly identifying and acknowledging these differences is essential to making sense of their conclusions about research and teacher education, which otherwise may appear contradictory.

POLICIES AND PROMISES

In July 2003, ECS published the first in its planned series of reports on teaching quality. Authored by the program director of the ECS Teaching Quality Policy Center, Michael Allen, the report (Allen, 2003) draws heavily on a set of three related reports: Wilson, Floden, and Ferrini-Mundy's (2001) analysis of the knowledge and gaps in teacher preparation research; Wilson and Floden's (2003) addendum to their first report, based on additional research nominated by ECS; and Lauer's (2001) secondary analysis of the 2001 Wilson report with an emphasis on policy-related questions.

Synthesizing the results of 92 empirical studies judged rigorous and relevant in the Wilson reports (Wilson & Floden, 2003; Wilson et al., 2001), Allen's (2003) synthesis addresses eight questions about teacher preparation that are of particular interest to policymakers at the state and other levels, as well as to educators and researchers. These include questions about the contribution to new teachers' effectiveness of subject matter and pedagogical knowledge, field experiences, alternate routes, preparation for teaching in low-performing schools, stringent program requirements, and accreditation. In addition to answering each of the questions based on the available empirical evidence, the report also rates the degree of confidence policymakers should have in the answers (either strong support, moderate support, limited support, or inconclusive findings) based on the kind, quality, quantity, and consistency of the research. Highest marks are given to studies that shed light on the causal relationships the questions address, especially experimental and quasi-experimental studies or correlational studies using advanced statistical approaches.

Allen's (2003) answer to the central question posed in the title of the ECS report (*Eight Questions on Teacher Preparation: What Does the Research Say?*) can be summarized in two words: very little. In fact, Allen concludes that none of the answers he provides for the eight questions has strong empirical support, and only one conclusion (that solid subject-matter knowledge is important to effective teaching) receives even moderate support—and this only in mathematics, at the secondary school level. Allen finds limited empirical support for these conclusions: Knowing how to teach subject matter is important, preparation in pedagogy can contribute to effective teaching, alternate routes may lead to short-term retention and may produce teachers who are ultimately as effective as others but with more difficulty in the beginning years, and deliberate efforts to prepare teachers for low-performing schools may be helpful. He concludes that there is inconclusive or no research at all regarding the characteristics of effective alternate routes, the effectiveness of stringent entrance requirements, the impact of program accreditation, the contribution of field experiences to teacher effectiveness, and the impact of institutional warranties. In these many areas where the research is limited or inconclusive, Allen suggests that reliable policy recommendations are difficult.

To understand the ECS report, it is important to note that it is based on a recently emerging conception of teacher education as a policy problem, with research the warranty for its solution. By policy problem, I mean that in the ECS report, and in some similar recent reports, it is assumed that one important way policymakers can meet the challenges involved in providing a well-prepared teaching force is by manipulating those broad aspects of teacher preparation (e.g., teacher tests, subject-matter requirements, entry routes) that have solid research to support them. The kind of research support sought is empirical studies, preferably experimental studies or correlational studies with sophisticated statistical analyses, which indicate that certain aspects of teacher preparation do or do not have a systematic and positive impact on pupils' learning or on other outcomes.

This policy approach to teacher preparation has not been the norm during most of the long history of critique and calls for reform in teacher education. Rather, as Evertson, Hawley, and Zlotnik (1985) pointed out in the mid-1980s, "most proposals for teacher education reform [have been] unburdened by evidence that the suggested changes will make a difference in the quality of students preparing to teach in elementary and secondary schools" (p. 2). Times have changed. In fact, if the many syntheses of research regarding teacher education that have been disseminated between

2000 and 2003 are any indication,[1] then treating teacher education as a policy problem that requires a research warrant for possible solutions has now become the centerpiece in many of the most publicized and politicized debates about teacher quality and teacher preparation.

The conclusion of the ECS report—that most of the broad policy aspects of teacher preparation have little or no conclusive empirical evidence—is very important but not really surprising. As noted above, policy has not been the focus of most of the research related to teacher education until recently. There are many reasons for this, two of which I note here. First, as scholars and reviewers have repeatedly pointed out, research related to teacher preparation has been marginalized and underfunded for most of its history. In the face of limited resources, many modest and small-scale studies have been conducted, often in the context of one teacher-education course or one preparation program. Although these studies can be extremely valuable for theory-building and also for the enhancement of practice, they have little or no value when teacher education is conceptualized as a broad-scale policy problem because they are not intended to establish causal relationships and because generalizations about the broad parameters of teacher preparation are impossible to draw from them.

A second reason there has not been much large-scale policy research on teacher preparation is that over the past two decades, many researchers have concentrated on teachers' subject-matter knowledge, teachers' pedagogical knowledge and skill, teachers' thinking and classroom decision making, teachers' learning in the context of communities, and teachers' beliefs and attitudes. Very little of this research was designed to establish empirical linkages to pupils' learning, partly because teachers' knowledge, learning, and beliefs were assumed to be important outcomes of teacher preparation in and of themselves and partly because it was considered self-evident that teachers who knew more, taught better. As Allen (2003) points out, however, "intermediate outcomes" such as knowledge and beliefs are of little interest to policymakers unless there is solid evidence of their connections to pupil achievement.

The major point to keep in mind about the new ECS study is that the question it asks is, "What does the research say about the broad policy parameters of teacher preparation and about their impact on pupil learning or other desirable outcomes?" This is a question of critical importance to policymakers, to researchers, and to teacher educators. When this question is addressed, then it is possible and reasonable to conclude, as do Allen (2003) and several other major reviewers (e.g., Lauer, 2001; Rice, 2003; Wilson & Floden, 2003; Wilson et al., 2001), that there is little conclusive empirical evidence. Allen and the other reviewers just noted offer very thoughtful and forward-looking recommendations about what kinds of research are needed to address questions about the research base for teacher preparation that come from a policy perspective. It is important to keep in mind, however, that because there is not conclusive empirical evidence about the positive impact of particular aspects of teacher preparation (e.g., traditional routes, courses in pedagogy), this does not imply anything about the impact of the elimination of those aspects or the efficacy of alternative aspects. It is also important to keep in mind that policy questions are not the only important questions that can be asked about the research base for teacher education. As the following example suggests, asking a different question may produce a different answer.

BUILDING THE KNOWLEDGE BASE

A second major research effort related to teacher education is the forthcoming report of the CTE of the NAE, which is currently in its final stages of preparation and review (Darling-Hammond & Bransford, 2005). The CTE project, cochaired by Linda Darling-Hammond and John Bransford, draws on the work of a 28-member committee, which includes teachers, teacher educators, and researchers whose areas of expertise include teacher education, educational psychology, language and culture, and subject-matter areas in education such as English and mathematics education, with a separate subcommittee on reading chaired by Catherine Snow. In addition, the committee collaborates with liaisons from eight cooperative universities that contribute experience- and program-based feedback from their respective institutions.

The intent of the CTE report is to articulate the knowledge bases for teaching and to make research-grounded recommendations about how core knowledge for beginning teachers can be included in teacher education curricula and pedagogies. Based on the premise that teaching is a profession that serves democratic purposes, the report recommends that every preparation program should provide the contexts within which prospective teachers develop knowledge, skills, and dispositions about the following: learners and their development within social contexts; subject matter, including how pupils learn content-specific knowledge and which subject-specific pedagogies and curricula are appropriate to various educational purposes; and teaching, including how to create, use, and interpret effective and appropriate instructional, assessment, and management strategies.

The CTE report uses four kinds of evidence as the grounding for its recommendations about the teacher education curriculum. These include basic research on human learning and development, including language acquisition and social contexts; research on how specific teaching practices influence pupils' learning; research on the relationships among teacher preparation, teachers' practices, and pupils' learning; and research on what and how prospective teachers learn in particular contexts.

The CTE report suggests that there is a body of well-defined and significant research that ought to inform the preparation of every new teacher. The first two thirds of the report concentrates on the knowledge, skills, and commitments that all new teachers need to help their pupils succeed by presenting core concepts in eight domains: learning, development, language, social contexts and purposes of education, content knowledge and pedagogy, teaching diverse learners, assessment, and classroom management. For example, the chapter on learning outlines core concepts about human cognition, such as memory, transfer, and the community-centered aspects of learning environments, based on several decades of research in the learning sciences. The chapter also draws on studies exploring the implications of the learning research for organizing schools and classrooms to support pupils' learning as well as organizing teacher-preparation programs and courses to support prospective teachers' learning. The chapter on assessment provides a model of formative assessment that draws on research in the cognitive sciences as well as on research indicating that when teachers' formative assessment strategies are improved, pupil learning gains are greater. The last third of the report focuses on prospective teachers as learners, reviewing what is currently known about how teachers learn and including discussion of promising pedagogies and of the institutional contexts of teacher education.

To understand the CTE report, it is important to note that it continues efforts that have been made over the last 15 years or so to establish and codify the knowledge base for teaching and to make this knowledge base the centerpiece of the preservice curriculum. The CTE project builds on previous knowledge-base projects, particularly the two knowledge-base books produced by the American Association of Colleges for Teacher Education (Murray, 1996; Reynolds, 1989), two handbooks of research on teacher education sponsored by the Association of Teacher Educators (Houston, 1990; Sikula, Buttery, & Guyton, 1996), and several generations of handbooks of research on teaching in general or on subject-matter teaching, specifically. The CTE project also builds on major efforts such as the National Research Council's (2000) comprehensive synthesis of what is known about how people learn. Unlike the ECS report, the primary audience for which is policymakers, the primary audience for the CTE report is teacher educators themselves as well as researchers and policymakers who are interested in a knowledge base for teacher preparation, established through professional and scholarly consensus and grounded in research on teaching, learning, teacher education, and teachers' learning.

The CTE project is part of the larger agenda to reform and improve teacher preparation through professionalization. This agenda aims to make teacher education a profession on par with other professions by establishing an official and formal body of knowledge that distinguishes professional educators from lay persons and that ensures that teachers for all students are fully prepared and fully certified. As the CTE report explains, other professions, such as medicine and law, use a similar approach to establishing the curriculum—reviewing the related research, consulting with experts, and gathering information from practitioners about promising practices.

The major point to keep in mind about the CTE report is that the question it asks about the research base for teacher education is, what bodies of basic and applied research about human learning, development, teaching practices, and teacher learning should inform the preparation of teachers? When this question is asked, it is possible and accurate to conclude that there is a strong research base that ought to inform the preparation of every new teacher who enters a classroom.

DIFFERENT QUESTIONS, DIFFERENT ANSWERS

At first glance, it may appear that the CTE report, which concludes that there is a wealth of important research related to teacher education, directly contradicts the ECS report, which concludes that research has very little to say about teacher preparation. In fact, however, as I have tried to suggest throughout this editorial, the two reports have different purposes and audiences, they use research in quite different ways, and they ask two entirely different questions about the research base for teacher preparation. Although their conclusions about teacher education research are quite different, they are not contradictory.

Rather, the different questions about the research base that are asked in the first place lead to different answers, each of which is appropriate and each of which has important implications for policy and practice. These two different questions are based on different logics about the role of research in teacher preparation. As noted above, the ECS report defines teacher preparation as a broad policy issue and thus draws only on evidence related to the causal questions it poses. The report accurately concludes that there is little conclusive research in these areas. The CTE report, on the other hand, defines teacher preparation as a professional enterprise and, like other professions, raises questions about the basic and applied research that ought to serve as the foundation of the professional teacher education curriculum. The report concludes, also accurately, that there is a great deal of research along these lines. As debates about the research base for teacher preparation continue, it is important to keep in mind that different questions lead to different answers. It is worth sorting out what kind of question is being asked, how research is being used, and to what larger professional and political agendas these are attached.

NOTE

1. See Cochran-Smith and Fries (2005) for a detailed discussion of previous reviews that have treated teacher preparation as a policy problem. This chapter also includes a discussion of the major reviews published from 2000 to 2003 and an analysis of their differing conclusions about the policy issues related to teacher preparation.

REFERENCES

Allen, M. (2003). *Eight questions on teacher preparation: What does the research say?* Denver, CO: Education Commission of the States.

Cochran-Smith, M., & Fries, K. (2005). The AERA panel on research and teacher education: Context and goals. In M. Cochran–Smith & K. Zeichner (Eds.), *Studying teacher education: The report of the AERA panel on research and teacher education.* Mahwah, NJ: Lawrence Erlbaum.

Darling-Hammond, L., & Bransford, J. (Eds.). (2005). *Preparing teachers for a changing world* (Report of the Committee on Teacher Education of the National Academy of Education). San Francisco: Jossey Bass.

Evertson, C., Hawley, W., & Zlotnik, M. (1985). Making a difference in educational quality through teacher education. *Journal of Teacher Education, 36,* 2-10.

Houston, R. (Ed.). (1990). *Handbook of research on teacher education* (1st ed.). New York: Macmillan.

Lauer, P. (2001). *A secondary analysis of a review of teacher preparation research.* Denver, CO: Education Commission of the States.

Murray, F. (Ed.). (1996). *The teacher educator's handbook: Building a knowledge base for the preparation of teachers.* Washington, DC: American Association of Colleges for Teacher Education.

National Research Council. (2000). *How people learn.* Washington, DC: National Academy Press.

Reynolds, M. (Ed.). (1989). *Knowledge base for the beginning teacher.* Oxford, UK: Pergamon.

Rice, J. K. (2003). *Teacher quality: Understanding the effectiveness of teacher attributes.* Washington, DC: Economic Policy Institute.

Sikula, J., Buttery, T., & Guyton, E. (Eds.). (1996). *Handbook of research on teacher education* (2nd ed.). New York: Macmillan.

Wilson, S., & Floden, R. (2003). *Creating effective teachers: Concise answers for hard questions.* Washington, DC: American Association of Colleges for Teacher Education.

Wilson, S., Floden, R., & Ferrini-Mundy, J. (2001). *Teacher preparation research: Current knowledge, gaps, and recommendations.* Washington, DC: Center for the Study of Teaching and Policy.

21 The Report of the Teaching Commission

What's Really at Risk?

At the beginning of 2004, the New York City–based Teaching Commission, established and chaired by former IBM Chairman Louis V. Gerstner, released "Teaching at Risk: A Call to Action" (The Teaching Commission, 2004) on the status of teaching in America's schools. Supported by private donations, the 19-member blue-ribbon Teaching Commission was made up of prominent leaders from business, government, and education. Directly linked to the goals of the No Child Left Behind Act (NCLB) (P.L. 107-110, 2002), the purpose of "Teaching at Risk" was to create a sense of national urgency about recruiting and retaining "highly qualified teachers" and to propose a plan of action.

In the opening pages, Gerstner warns that the nation's role as a world leader is in jeopardy and that an educational system that does not promote quality teaching is part of the problem:

> The United States enters the 21st century as an undisputed world leader. Despite difficult challenges at home and abroad, we still have the world's strongest economy, and American business continues to inspire growth and development across the globe. But our nation is at a crossroads. We will not continue to lead if we persist in viewing teaching ... as a second-rate occupation. (pp. 9-10)

SOURCE: *Journal of Teacher Education,* Vol. 55, No. 3, May/June 2004, pp. 195-200.

The report asserts that despite two decades of reform, "academic achievement is still disappointing" (p. 12) and "overall test scores are still at about the levels they were in 1970" (p. 13). The report also notes that there continue to be large disparities between the academic achievement of poor and minority students and their peers.

The commission calls for four reforms. First, teachers' salaries would be made competitive with other professions with the potential of higher pay for those who increase pupils' achievement or teach in hard-to-staff subject areas and schools. Second, college and university presidents would be held accountable for revamping teacher preparation by raising admissions standards, recruiting stronger students, and ensuring that prospective teachers have knowledge of subject matter, scientifically based practices, and schools. Third, there would be drastic revisions of state licensing and certification, including more rigorous teacher tests and encouragement of "streamlined" certification programs. Fourth, school principals would provide scientifically based mentoring and professional development for all teachers and would have increased authority to hire and promote teachers who raise test scores and get rid of those who do not. The commission's action plan includes working with governors, state school officers, and university presidents on teacher quality goals and joining hands with the federal government to support the goals of NCLB.

AT RISK, REDUX

The report of the Teaching Commission reflects a recurring historical pattern of blue-ribbon critiques of teaching and teacher education based on the assertion that the nation is in danger of losing its global position (Cochran-Smith & Fries, 2005). The immediate past iteration was "A Nation at Risk" (National Commission on Excellence in Education, 1983), published when the country was in an economic depression and there was concern it was not keeping pace with the changing world economy. In the 20 years since "A Nation at Risk," there have been debates about whether there actually was a crisis in educational achievement at that time and whether teaching and school quality actually are the linchpins in the nation's ability to compete in the global economy (e.g., Berliner, Biddle, & Bell, 1995; Bracey, 2003; Cremin, 1991). In addition, there have been differing assessments of the legacy of the two decades of reforms set off by the report (see, for example, the range of viewpoints in Gordon, 2004).

Twenty years after "A Nation at Risk," its namesake, "Teaching at Risk" (The Teaching Commission, 2004), asserts that "the capacity of America's educational system to create a 21st-century workforce second to none in the world is a national security issue of the first order. As things stand, this country is forfeiting that capacity" (p. 20). Given the nation's current concerns, it is not surprising that the commission's report again frames teaching quality as a problem of global competitiveness and national security. However, some critics will no doubt suggest, as they have about earlier reports (e.g., Bracey, 1999; Cremin, 1991), that part of the reason the commission seeks to create a sense of urgency is to distract attention away from those actually responsible for the monetary, trade, and industrial policies that influence economic competitiveness and lay the blame instead on the schools. Other critics may point out, as they have in the past (e.g., Coeyman, 2003), that a certain sense of urgency is necessary to keep the public convinced that the federal government cannot afford to leave something as important as education to state and local governments.

The problem of teaching quality as well as most of the solutions recommended by the commission are couched in the logic and language of the marketplace. The report claims, for example, that the costs of a poorly educated public are enormous in terms of individual productivity and expenses resulting from employees who lack basic skills. Drawing on analyses prepared for the commission by economist Eric Hanushek, the report suggests that "significant improvements in education over a 20-year period could lead to as much as a 4 percent addition to the Gross Domestic Product" (p. 14). What is disheartening about the report is that there are no comments at all about what the recommended $30 billion annual investment in teacher quality over a 20-year period might add to things other than the gross domestic product—for example, the critical capacity of the American electorate, the level and quality of civic engagement in local and national arenas, or the opportunities of the populace to engage in meaningful work. In the commission's report, as in the blue-ribbon critiques that preceded it, it is crystal clear that the purpose of education is to produce the nation's workforce and maintain its position in the global economy. Other purposes of education in a democratic society are not emphasized.

It is unlikely that "Teaching at Risk" will be groundbreaking in the way that its predecessor was. The commission's report repeats the litany of obstacles to teacher excellence that the Secretary of

Education's reports to Congress on teacher quality and other statements from federal officials and conservative foundations have already made exceedingly familiar: "one-size fits all compensation, flawed teacher preparation, ineffective leadership, and poor working conditions" (The Teaching Commission, 2004, p. 15). The commission's plan for enhancing teacher quality relies primarily on reforms, which—with the important exception discussed below—are consistent with the deregulation agenda that has been forwarded for a number of years: opening up multiple alternate entry routes into teaching, raising test score cutoffs for teachers, recruiting and keeping teachers by rewarding pupils' test score gains, and giving principals the authority to operate like business managers.

The important exception to this set of market-based reforms is the commission's recommendation that the university role in teacher preparation be strengthened (not simply bypassed), with top university leaders taking responsibility for improving the preparation of teachers. The report suggests that more rigorous university preparation will be accomplished primarily through a stronger role for arts and sciences and more attention to scientifically based teaching practices. The report also calls for mechanisms to guard against "faddism," which has often been code for "progressive" educational theories as opposed to "the basics" of academic achievement. The commission wants universities held accountable for the teachers they prepare with federal funding contingent on public reporting of graduates' teacher test scores, grade point averages, entry into teaching, and pupils' achievement. Along these lines, the report calls for better assessments and mentions as "promising models" the new American Board for the Certification of Teacher Excellence test as well as new collaborations between Educational Testing Service (ETS) and National Council for the Accreditation of Teacher Education (NCATE) to establish a minimum passing score on the Praxis II test of subject matter. Interestingly, the report says virtually nothing about the performance-based professional assessments developed over many years by National Board for Professional Teaching Standards (NBPTS) or the outcomes-based standards and program assessments now in place through NCATE (Berry, 2004).

WHAT'S REALLY AT RISK?

The Teaching Commission's report raises a number of concerns, many of which I have written about in previous editorials. Here I concentrate on only two: the problem of equating teacher quality with test scores and compensating teachers on that basis, as well as the problem of assuming that teachers and teaching are the panacea for the ills of American education and society.

Paying for Test Score Gains

The commission's recommendation for higher teacher pay is a welcome idea. There is no question that many talented college graduates who might have considered teaching will continue to be attracted to professions with more potential for economic security and societal respect as long as teachers' pay is not competitive. The catch in the commission's approach, however, is that the proposed higher salaries are tied almost completely to test scores, which are treated as the synecdoche (Madaus, 1993) for pupil's learning, teacher quality, and accountability in general.

The report calls for a new "compact," wherein teachers get higher pay but agree to be evaluated and compensated on the basis of performance, specifically through value-added assessments. Putting aside for the moment the points that there are important aspects of pupils' learning not measured by standardized tests and that there are worthy educational goals in addition to academic learning, there are also major problems with making high-stakes decisions on the basis of value-added models (VAM) of teacher assessment. As the commission points out, the best known VAM is the one developed by William Sanders and colleagues (Rivers & Sanders, 2002; Sanders, 1998; Sanders & Horn, 1998) on the basis of pupils' achievement test data from Tennessee. Sanders's model analyzes pupils' improvement from year to year and estimates how much a given teacher has contributed to yearly gain by factoring in the gains that were predicted based on past performance. Thus, the model purportedly "controls" for differences in pupils' background and ability, school characteristics, and other variables often assumed to effect achievement. The commission urges all states to implement value-added systems in conjunction with upgrading testing programs in compliance with NCLB.

In an incisive commentary, Barnett Berry (2004) points out problems with these recommendations. Many states do not have in place the infrastructure capable of assembling and accurately assessing the linkages between student achievement and teacher performance, because these require that state departments of elementary and secondary education, state higher education departments, universities, and K-12 school districts all collect and analyze data together. Berry also rightly notes that recent critiques of the technical aspects of Sanders's model—even from some analysts who support market approaches to improving teaching—have revealed serious technical difficulties. These include the unreliability of pupil gain scores across subject matter areas (Ballou, 2002), inadequate controls for factors such as poverty and English language competence (Ballou, 2002), failure to account for between-teacher effects and prior student achievement (Kupermintz, 2003), problems resulting from not distinguishing between the impact of school and other context variables and the impact of the teacher (Kupermintz, 2003; McCaffrey, Lockwood, Koretz, & Hamilton, 2003), and multiple technical issues related to missing data, estimation error and uncertainty, and sampling error (McCaffrey et al., 2003). Despite the fact that VAM is heralded as a breakthrough in teacher accountability, many of the technical problems involved are the same ones statistical models intended to estimate teacher effects have always faced.

A major RAND report (McCaffrey et al., 2003), recently commissioned by the Carnegie Corporation to evaluate VAM, concludes that although the research base is limited, there is "evidence that teachers have discernable, differential effects on student achievement, and that these effects appear to persist into the future" (p. xiii). The RAND report recommends much more research on VAM, particularly on the impact of the sources of error associated with the model and the impact of school contexts, which are currently not adequately accounted for. Most relevant to the recommendations of the Teaching Commission, however, the RAND report concludes that VAM should not be used for high-stakes decisions. Although the authors allow that VAM would not necessarily be more harmful than other existing methods for test-based accountability, they conclude,

> The research base is currently insufficient to support the use of VAM for high-stakes decisions. We have identified numerous possible sources of error in teacher effects and any attempt to use VAM estimates for high-stakes decisions must be informed by an understanding of these potential errors. (p. xx)

The stakes associated with the decisions spelled out in the report of the commission include the hiring, compensating, and firing of teachers. Given that our democratic society depends for its existence on the preparation of a thoughtful citizenry—a task to be accomplished primarily by the schools—what stakes could be higher?

Teachers as Saviors

As noted throughout this editorial, the report of the commission is based on the assumption that teachers are the single most important determinant of educational quality. Although this point has been made before, analysts only sometimes recognize its inherent paradox: Teachers are simultaneously taken to be the potential saviors of the American educational system as well as the source of most of its problems.

This view of teachers is very clear in the report of the commission: "The moment is ripe to . . . break the cycle in which low-performing college students far too often become the teachers of low-performing students in public schools" (p. 10).[1] The solution to the persistent problems of American public education, according to the commission, is an "intense, sustained, and effective campaign to revamp our country's teaching force" (p. 14).

Here, the commission takes a particularly troubling perspective, coupling its arguments about general declines in the achievement of U.S. pupils with its conclusions about the remarkable impact of individual teachers based on research using VAM. Like many policymakers, the commission is particularly enamored by VAM because of its purported ability to estimate the effects of teachers and schools independent of the effects of noneducational variables such as family background and socioeconomic status. The report argues that "excellent teaching, which combines passion and art along with academic prowess, has the potential to be the great equalizer" (p. 12). Although the report notes that there are other obstacles to improving education, it comes dangerously close to suggesting that most of these can be assuaged, if not solved, by improving teacher quality:

Bolstering teacher quality is, of course, not the only challenge we face as we seek to strengthen public education. There are social problems, financial obstacles, and facilities issues, among other concerns. But the Teaching Commission believes that quality teachers are the critical factor in helping young people overcome the damaging effects of poverty, lack of parental guidance, and other challenges. (p. 14)

The power and the danger of the commission's conclusion, of course, is that if teacher quality, "the great equalizer," can mitigate the effects of poverty, lack of opportunity, and inequitable resource distribution—not to mention the long history of institutional racism—then there is no need to create public policies or programs to ameliorate them. Rather than programs that target the elimination of poverty and the redistribution of resources, only initiatives that enhance teacher quality would be necessary.

Along with many others, I have argued repeatedly that the dire circumstances of children living in poverty are not going to change because teachers teach better. Along these lines, Weiner (1993) has asserted that the challenges of urban teaching are the result of systemic deficiencies that individual teachers cannot alter—complex school bureaucracies, the isolation of schools from the communities they are supposed to serve, and the large numbers of students whose families have neither the resources nor the will to support school values. The same critiques can be made about those who imply that teacher quality is the panacea for what is wrong with American education and American society. By ignoring structural inequalities and differential power relations, the Teaching Commission and others with a singular focus on fixing society by enhancing teacher quality place enormous and unrealistic responsibility on individual teachers. At the same time, they seem to imply that there is no need for policies and programs intended to address the larger issues. This is what's really at risk.

NOTE

1. As spelled out in detail in a previous editorial (Cochran-Smith, 2003), this assertion about the academic credentials of prospective teachers is, at best, only partially correct, and at worst, grossly misleading.

REFERENCES

Ballou, D. (2002). *Sizing up test scores*. Retrieved February 23, 2004, from http://www.educationnext.org 20022/10.html

Berliner, D., Biddle, B., & Bell, J. (1995). *The manufactured crisis: Myths, fraud, and the attack on America's public schools*. Boulder, CO: Perseus.

Berry, B. (2004). *Making good on what matters most: A review of Teaching at Risk: A Call to Action*. Retrieved January 24, 2004, from www .teachingquality.org

Bracey, G. (1999, September 15). *The propaganda of "A Nation at Risk."* Retrieved from www.america-tomorrow.com/bracey/EDDRA

Bracey, G. (2003). *April foolishness: The 20th anniversary of A Nation at Risk*. Retrieved February 22, 2004, from www.pdkint.org/kappan/ k0304.html.

Cochran-Smith, M. (2003). Teacher education's Bermuda Triangle: Dichotomy, mythology and amnesia (Editorial). *Journal of Teacher Education, 54*(4), 275-279.

Cochran-Smith, M., & Fries, K. (2005). The AERA panel on research and teacher education: Context and goals. In M. Cochran-Smith & K. Zeichner (Eds.), *Studying teacher education: The report of the AERA panel on research and teacher education*. Mahwah, NJ: Lawrence Erlbaum.

Coeyman, M. (2003, April 22). Twenty years after "A Nation at Risk." *Christian Science Monitor*.

Cremin, L. (1991). *Popular education and its discontents*. New York: Harper Collins.

Gordon, D. (2004). *A nation reformed? Twenty years after A Nation at Risk*. Cambridge: Harvard University Press.

Kupermintz, H. (2003). Teacher effects and teacher effectiveness: A validity investigation of the Tennessee Value Added Assessment System. *Educational Evaluation and Policy Analysis, 3*, 287-298.

Madaus, G. (1993). National testing system: Manna from above? A historical perspective. *Educational Assessment, 1*, 9-26.

McCaffrey, D., Lockwood, J., Koretz, D., & Hamilton, L. (2003). *Evaluating value-added models for teacher accountability*. Santa Monica, CA: RAND.

National Commission on Excellence in Education. (1983). *A nation at risk: The imperative for educational reform*. Washington, DC: Government Printing Office.

P.L. 107-110. (2002). *No Child Left Behind Act: Reauthorization of the Elementary and Secondary Act*. Retrieved June, 2002, from www.ed.gov

Rivers, J., & Sanders, W. (2002). Teacher quality and equity in educational opportunity: Findings and policy implications. In L. Izumi & W. Evers (Eds.), *Teacher quality* (pp. 13-23). Palo Alto, CA: Hoover Institution.

Sanders, W. (1998). Value-added assessment. *The School Administrator*, pp. 24-27.

Sanders, W., & Horn, S. (1998). Research findings from the Tennessee Value-Added Assessment System (TVAAS) database: Implications for educational evaluation and research. *Journal of Personnel Evaluation in Education, 12*(3), 247-256.

The Teaching Commission. (2004). *Teaching at risk: A call to action*. New York: Author.

Weiner, L. (1993). *Preparing teachers for urban schools: Lessons from 30 years of school reform*. New York: Teachers College Press.

22 *The Problem of Teacher Education*

S ince the time teacher education emerged as an identifiable activity, there have been few periods when it was not being critiqued, studied, rethought, reformed, and, often, excoriated. The title of this editorial does not refer to the "problem of teacher education" in a pejorative sense, however. Rather, the phrase is intended to draw attention to teacher education as a problem in three senses—the problem or challenge every nation faces in providing well-prepared and effective teachers for its children; teacher education as a research problem, which involves a larger set of educational issues, questions, and conditions that define an important concern of the scholarly community; and teacher education as a problematic and contested enterprise, troubled by enduring and value-laden questions about the purposes and goals of education in a democratic society.

This editorial concentrates on teacher education over the last 50 years. It suggests that during that time, as a society and an educational community, we have conceptualized and defined the "problem of teacher education" in three quite different ways: as a training problem, a learning problem, and a policy problem.[1] The editorial concludes with concerns about the current emphasis.

TEACHER EDUCATION AS A TRAINING PROBLEM

During the period from roughly the late 1950s to the early 1980s, teacher education was defined primarily as a training problem. The

SOURCE: *Journal of Teacher Education,* Vol. 55, No. 4, September/October 2004, pp. 295-299.

essence of this approach was conceptualizing teacher education as a formal educational process intended to ensure that the behaviors of prospective teachers matched those of "effective" teachers. To do this, teacher educators were charged with training teacher candidates to display those behaviors that had been empirically certified through research on effective teaching. Underlying this way of defining teacher education was a technical view of teaching, a behavioral view of learning, and an understanding of science as the solution to educational problems. In a symposium on teacher education that helped to shape this emerging view, B. O. Smith (1971) made this clear: "Generally speaking, . . . teacher education attempts to answer the question of how the behavior of an individual in preparation for teaching can be made to conform to acceptable patterns" (p. 2).

What was "acceptable" had to do with research. When teacher education was constructed as a training problem, the point of research on teacher education was the identification or the invention of transportable teacher-training procedures that produced the desired behaviors in prospective teachers. This effort in teacher education built on and paralleled the process-product research on teaching that was dominant during the time. With process-product research, the goal was to develop "the scientific basis of the art of teaching" (Gage, 1978) by identifying and specifying teacher behaviors that were correlated with pupil learning and applying them as treatments to classroom situations (Gage, 1963). The version of this that became prominent in research on teacher education was treating the independent variables of process-product research on teaching (i.e., observable teacher behaviors, such as question-asking strategies or clearly stated objectives, which were presumed correlated with student achievement) as the dependent variables in research on teacher preparation. Teacher-training procedures (e.g., microteaching, training prospective teachers to use interaction analysis or behavior modification, lecture, demonstration, and/or clusters of these procedures with and without different kinds of feedback) were the independent variables.

The training approach to teacher education was not without its critics. Some questioned the training approach at its very core by critiquing the effectiveness research on which it was based. They argued that the empirical research base for specific and generally applicable teaching behaviors was thin and that the competency-based, teacher-training programs that arose in the late 1960s and early 1970s did not have a greater amount of empirical support than other teacher education programs. Other critics argued that a more critical research stance was needed that made the existing social arrangements of schooling problematic and challenged taken-for-granted assumptions about definitions of professional competence. Still others raised methodological objections, pointing to obstacles to establishing causal relationships between particular aspects of teacher preparation and teacher performance given the many intervening variables and the months- or even years-long time lag. The most damaging critique, however, was that although the training research showed that prospective teachers could indeed be trained to do almost anything, the focus was on "empty techniques" (Lanier, 1982) rather than knowledge or decision making, and thus, the approach was atheoretical and even anti-intellectual.

TEACHER EDUCATION AS A LEARNING PROBLEM

During the period from roughly the early 1980s through the early 2000s, teacher education was defined primarily as a learning problem. This approach assumed that excellent teachers were professionals who were knowledgeable about subject matter and pedagogy and who made decisions, constructed responsive curriculum, and knew how to continue learning throughout the professional lifespan. The goal of teacher preparation programs was to design the social, organizational, and intellectual contexts wherein prospective teachers could develop the knowledge, skills, and dispositions needed to function as decision makers. Feiman-Nemser (1983) and others argued at the time that teacher education was not equivalent to formal teacher preparation programs. Rather, learning to teach also had to do with the beliefs, knowledge, and experiences prospective teachers brought with them into preparation programs; the ways their knowledge changed and was translated into classroom practice over time; the ways teachers interpreted their fieldwork and course experiences in light of their own school experiences; and how they developed professionally as teachers by observing and talking with others.

Based on the premise that teacher education was a learning problem, the point of research on teacher education was to build and explore the professional knowledge base, codifying not only how and what teachers should know about subject matter and pedagogy but also how they thought and how they learned in preservice programs and schools and the multiple conditions and contexts that shaped their learning. Not surprisingly, multiple research questions, methods, and approaches to interpretation and analysis developed during this time rather than adherence to a single, dominant paradigm. Although some studies continued to focus on teachers' behavior, many examined teachers' attitudes, beliefs, knowledge structures, predispositions, perceptions, and understandings as well as the contexts that supported and/or constrained these. In addition, teacher education research came to include more critical approaches, and a whole program of research emerged that explored how teachers learned to teach for diversity. During this time, there were also new investigators involved in teacher education research, including teacher educators who studied their own practices.

The learning approach to teacher education was extensively critiqued, especially in the years from the mid-1990s to the early 2000s. During this time, teacher preparation was often characterized by skeptics as substandard, attracting mediocre to poor prospective teachers who were out of touch with the public interest and too focused on progressive and constructivist perspectives. At the same time, reformers within the teacher education community called for higher standards as well as consistency across preparation, licensure, and accreditation and better recruitment and retention strategies. Characterized by some as nothing more than "touchy feely" self-awareness (Schrag, 1999), teacher education's emphasis on beliefs and attitudes was particularly hard hit by external critics, especially beliefs related to culture and diversity. Research on teacher education was also sharply criticized during this time from both within and outside the field for its weak methods and lack of generalizability.

No doubt, the most damning critique of teacher education as a learning problem was that it focused on teachers' knowledge, skills, and beliefs without adequate attention to pupils' learning. That is, when teacher education was defined as a learning problem, neither practitioners nor researchers concentrated on establishing the links between and among what teachers knew and believed, how they developed professional practice in the context of different schools and classrooms, and what their pupils learned that could be demonstrated on tests and other measures.

TEACHER EDUCATION AS A POLICY PROBLEM

In many of the major debates since the mid- to late 1990s, teacher education has been defined as a policy problem. Here, the goal is to identify which of the broad parameters of teacher education policy that can be controlled by institutional, state, or federal policymakers is most likely to have a positive effect. The point is to use empirical evidence to guide policymakers in their investment of finite human and fiscal resources in various aspects of the preparation and professional development of K-12 teachers.

Many policy-related studies of teacher preparation were conducted before the end of the 1990s. However, prior to that time, they were generally not part of the discourse of the professional community responsible for teacher education. In fact, as Kennedy (1996) has pointed out, in the past, policy research on teacher education was most familiar to skeptics and critics of teacher education, including economists and policy analysts, and least familiar to teacher educators themselves. This situation has changed considerably, and the most visible current debates about teacher education have concentrated to a great extent on policy.

Constructing teacher education as a policy problem means identifying both institution-level policies (such as entrance and course requirements or 4- and 5-year program structures) and state or larger scale policies and practices (such as state teacher tests, allowable entry routes, licensure regulations) that are presumably warranted by empirical evidence demonstrating positive effects on desired outcomes. At the local level, for example, practitioners are striving to develop evidence about the effect of teacher candidates' performance on pupils' learning. At state and larger levels, policymakers are seeking empirical studies, preferably experimental studies or correlational studies with sophisticated statistical analyses, that indicate which aspects of teacher preparation do and do not have a systematic and positive effect on pupils' learning, particularly scores on standardized tests.

The research designs that are considered by some to be best suited to studying teacher education as a policy problem are production function studies of educational resources and other multiple regression analyses that aim to establish correlations between resources and indicators of teacher effectiveness. On the other hand, some researchers take a broader approach to the study of teacher education as a policy problem, including a variety of accepted research methods and a range of indicators of effectiveness.

Although it now seems self-evident that certain policy decisions regarding teacher education ought to be informed by empirical evidence, the policy approach has also been sharply critiqued. Some have pointed out that in the absence of clear and consistent evidence, many policymakers either ignore research or focus on only the evidence that supports their a priori positions. Others argue that the aspects of teacher education studied from a policy perspective are "crude quantifiable indicators" (Kennedy, 1999, p. 89) that cannot make meaningful distinctions among the varied features of teacher preparation programs. Still others have noted that studies of teacher education as a policy problem generally do not account for the contexts and cultures of schools or for how these support or constrain teachers' abilities to use knowledge and resources. Finally, it is clear that when teacher education is constructed as a policy problem, pupil achievement scores are considered the most important educational outcome. A number of teacher education researchers and practitioners have argued that although test scores are one indicator of teachers' effectiveness, other outcomes, such as pupils' social and emotional growth, their preparedness to live in a democratic society, and teachers' retention in hard-to-staff schools, are also important.

THE PROBLEM OF TEACHER EDUCATION: A CONTEMPORARY PERSPECTIVE

In the first 4 years of the 21st century, we have seen the intensification of the policy focus. There is no question that the No Child Left Behind Act (2002) and its agenda to provide "highly qualified teachers" depend on a view of teacher education as a policy problem. Increasingly, it is assumed that the right policies can simultaneously solve the problems of teacher retention, teacher quality, and pupil achievement. The "right" policies are supposedly those based on empirical evidence about the value teacher preparation adds to pupils' scores on tests and on cost-benefit analyses of how to invest finite human and fiscal resources. Also underlying the policy focus is the assumption that the overarching goal of education—and teacher education—is to produce the nation's workforce and maintain its position in the global economy.

Folded into the current policy approach is also a return to the training view of teacher education. The argument is that subject matter, which can be assessed on a standardized teacher test, is what teachers need to know to teach well. Whatever else there is to know (e.g., techniques, classroom strategies, best practices) can be picked up on the job or in summer courses or school-based training sessions for teachers. Increasingly, then, the focus in discussions of teacher education is on training and testing to ensure that all teachers have basic subject matter knowledge and the technical skills to bring pupils' test scores to minimum thresholds.

There are many more concerns about the current policy approach to teacher education than can be included in a short editorial. I name just three. First, teacher education is a political problem, not just a policy problem. Policies regarding teacher preparation do not come about as the result of simple common sense or expediency alone, nor are they disconnected from values and ideology, from existing systems of power and privilege, or from assumptions about what is mainstream and what is marginal. Second, teaching has technical aspects to be sure, and teachers can be trained to perform these. But teaching is also and, more importantly, an intellectual, cultural, and contextual activity that requires skillful decisions about how to convey subject matter knowledge, apply pedagogical skills, develop human relationships, and both generate and utilize local knowledge. Finally, the purpose of education in a democratic society is not simply assimilating all schoolchildren into the mainstream or preparing the nation's workforce to preserve the place of the United States as the dominant power in a global society. Our democratic society depends on the preparation of a thoughtful citizenry (Gutman, 1999). How to prepare teachers to foster democratic values and skills must be acknowledged as a major part of the "problem of teacher education" if we are to maintain a healthy democracy.

NOTE

1. This editorial is based on a larger analysis of the history of teacher education research and reform (Cochran-Smith & Fries, 2005) that examines public documents, historical sources, and 30 syntheses of research on teacher education published between 1958 and 2003. The syntheses are treated as historical artifacts, assumed to reflect the ways of defining and studying teacher education that were prominent in particular time periods.

The larger analysis includes discussion of the historical, economic, and social contexts of each time period.

REFERENCES

Cochran-Smith, M., & Fries, M. (2005). The AERA panel on research and teacher education: Context and goals. In M. Cochran-Smith & K. Zeichner (Eds.), *Studying teacher education. The report of the AERA panel on research and teacher education*. Mahwah, NJ: Lawrance Erlbaum.

Feiman-Nemser, S. (1983). Learning to teach. In L. Shulman & G. Sykes (Eds.), *Handbook of teaching and policy* (pp. 150-170). New York: Longman.

Gage, N. (1963). Paradigms for research on teaching. In N. Gage (Ed.), *Handbook of research on teaching*. Chicago: Rand McNally.

Gage, N. (1978). *The scientific basis of the art of teaching*. New York: Teachers College Press.

Gutman, A. (1999). *Democratic education (with a new preface and epilogue)*. Princeton, NJ: Princeton University Press.

Kennedy, M. (1996). Research genres in teacher education. In F. Murray (Ed.), *The teacher educator's handbook: Building a knowledge base for the preparation of teachers* (pp. 120-154). San Francisco: Jossey-Bass.

Kennedy, M. (1999). The problem of evidence in teacher education. In R. Roth (Ed.), *The role of the university in the preparation of teachers* (pp. 87-107). Philadelphia: Falmer.

Lanier, J. (1982). Teacher education; Needed research and practice for the preparation of teacher professionals. In D. Corrigan (Ed.), *The future of teacher education: Needed research and practice* (pp. 13-36). College Station, TX: College of Education, Texas A&M University.

No Child Left Behind Act: Reauthorization of the Elementary and Secondary Act, Pub. L. No. 107-110, (2002). Retrieved June 2002 from http://www.ed.gov

Schrag, P. (1999, July). Who will teach the teachers. *University Business*, pp. 29-34.

Smith, B. (Ed.). (1971). *Research in teacher education: A symposium*. Englewood Cliffs, NJ: Prentice Hall.

23 Stayers, Leavers, Lovers, and Dreamers

Insights About Teacher Retention

Teacher shortages are not new. Periodically, throughout the past half century, there have been fewer teachers available than were needed, and policymakers at the state and federal levels have responded by stepping up recruitment efforts and issuing temporary teaching credentials to those without qualifications. Three things are new, however: the requirement that teachers in all schools be "highly qualified"; the realization that it is not so much teacher recruitment that is the problem in staffing the nation's K-12 schools but teacher retention; and growing evidence that, similar to every other problem that plagues the nation's schools, the problem of teacher retention is most severe in hard-to-staff schools.

In 1999, in an article in *Education Week*, John Merrow reported that recruitment was both the "wrong diagnosis" and a "phony cure" (p. 38) for the teacher shortage. By 2003, the National Commission on Teaching & America's Future (NCTAF) had announced that teacher retention was a "national crisis" (p. 21). Drawing heavily on Richard Ingersoll's (2001, 2002) analyses of retention and attrition patterns in K-12 schools and on other analyses of large-scale state and national data sets, the NCTAF (2003) report concluded that the teacher shortage was caused primarily by early attrition of those in the teaching pool rather than by insufficient numbers of people preparing to teach. The report also made it clear that the retention

SOURCE: *Journal of Teacher Education,* Vol. 55, No. 5, November/December 2004, pp. 387-392.

problem was most severe in urban and rural schools where there were large numbers of poor and minority students.

This editorial highlights five new analyses of teacher retention, which frame the problem in conceptually and methodologically different ways.[1] Due to space constraints, the editorial does not critique the five studies or offer extensive analysis that cuts across them, although this kind of analysis is needed. Rather, the purpose of the editorial is to highlight important insights about retention from each of the five pieces and invite readers to review each of them thoroughly.

IT'S RETENTION, NOT RECRUITMENT: THE NEED FOR "DEMAND-SIDE" ANALYSES AND SOLUTIONS

Throughout the past decade, Richard Ingersoll (2001, 2002, 2003, 2004) has conducted a series of studies about the teacher workforce from the perspective of the sociology of organizations, occupations, and work. In many of these studies, Ingersoll uses data from the Schools and Staffing Survey (SASS) and its Teacher Follow Up Survey (TFS) to look at patterns and trends in the supply and demand of teachers for the nation's K-12 schools. Ingersoll's analyses challenge the conventional wisdom that the teacher shortage in the United States is due to a simple imbalance between supply and demand caused by large numbers of teacher retirements, increased student enrollments, and an insufficient supply of new teachers. Instead, Ingersoll reveals that it is true that both student enrollments and teacher retirements have increased since the mid-1980s, that most schools now have job openings, and that a significant number of schools have been unable to find enough qualified teachers. However, it is not true that most teachers who leave teaching do so because of retirement, and it also is not true that an insufficient number of teachers is being produced. To the contrary, Ingersoll (2004) argues that although there are not necessarily enough teachers produced in every field, there are, overall, "more than enough prospective teachers produced each year in the U.S." (p. 8).

Ingersoll argues that the crux of the retention problem is the teacher turnover rate, that is, the number of teachers per year who move from one teaching job to another or leave teaching altogether. As Ingersoll (2004) points out, the sheer size of the teaching force coupled with its annual turnover rate (about 14%) means that almost one third of the teacher workforce (more than one million teachers) move into, out of, or between schools in any given year. Moreover, as is now widely known, teaching's "revolving door" (Ingersoll, 2003, p. 11) swings shut behind an unusually large number of those in the early years of teaching, with as many as 46% of new teachers leaving the profession by the end of 5 years (Ingersoll, 2002). According to Ingersoll (2003), retirement accounts for a relatively small portion of departures from teaching (about 1/8), whereas job dissatisfaction and the desire to pursue a better job inside or outside the education field account for a much bigger share (almost half of the leavers). Many leavers are dissatisfied with their jobs because of low salaries, student discipline problems, lack of support, and little opportunity to participate in decision making. Ingersoll argues that there is a high cost to teacher turnover in terms of time and other resources, school cohesion and community, teaching effectiveness, and students' achievement. Ingersoll argues that systemic and simultaneous changes in entry requirements, teacher preparation, teaching rewards, teacher autonomy, and teacher accountability are needed to change the "semi-professional" status of teaching as an occupation, bolster teacher retention, and ultimately provide a well-qualified teacher for every classroom.

LOVERS AND DREAMERS: WHY TEACHERS STAY

In contrast to Ingersoll's study of the macro-aspects of teacher retention, Sonia Nieto's (2003) recent book titled *What Keeps Teachers Going?* turns the retention question on its head by asking why some teachers "persevere, in spite of all the deprivations and challenges" (p. 7). To explore this question, Nieto formed an inquiry group of eight highly experienced educators "known as excellent teachers of students of racially, culturally and linguistically diverse backgrounds" (p. xi) in the Boston Public Schools. Based on the group's inquiry and on talk and writing with other urban teachers throughout a year, Nieto offers a "'counter narrative' to the prevailing wisdom" (p. 7) that the way to improve education is to "fix" teachers or "fill them up" (p. 8) with best practices. Instead, Nieto argues for an alternative viewpoint about what is worth preserving in public education by building on teachers' strengths.

Nieto's analysis suggests that good teachers stay in teaching—even in the most difficult of circumstances and with the most marginalized students—for reasons that have more to do with teaching's heart than with either its physical conditions or the availability of the latest techniques. Many of Nieto's chapter titles—"Teaching As Love," "Teaching As Hope and Possibility," "Teaching As Anger and Desperation," "Teaching As Democratic Practice"—are intended to reflect the emotional, relational, and personal aspects of teaching. Among the many noteworthy ideas in Nieto's book, a central theme is that part of why good urban teachers stay is that they love, believe in, and respect the students they work with and they can imagine possibilities for them other than the dire circumstances in which many of them live. Although the teachers in Nieto's group acknowledged the inequities of society, were frustrated by the urban educational bureaucracy, and were plagued by their own self-doubts, they believed that education and teachers could make a difference in students' lives. To persevere, they looked for options other than giving up on students and their dreams, such as participating in teacher communities and other opportunities to meet, talk, and work with others who saw teaching "as a way to live in the world" (p. 101).

This Is Not Your Mother's Teacher: The New Teaching Generation

Although Nieto is not explicit about the age of the teachers she worked with, their narratives reveal that many had been teaching for 20 and 30 years. In *Finders and Keepers: Helping New Teachers Survive and Thrive in Our Schools* (2004), Susan Moore Johnson and colleagues suggest that 1960s and 1970s teachers had quite different expectations and experiences from those of teachers currently entering the profession. Moore Johnson and colleagues' larger study of the new teaching generation used in-depth interviews and follow-ups throughout 4 years with 50 1st- and 2nd-year teachers who entered teaching from different pathways, including university-based teacher education programs and fast-track recruitment programs, and who worked in diverse Massachusetts public schools. The research team focused on 10 of those teachers, particularly on how they decided whether to stay, move to another school, or leave teaching in *Finders and Keepers*.

This book offers many important insights about teacher retention and the characteristics of schools that are organized to sustain teachers' work. Perhaps most important, Moore Johnson and colleagues argue that the previous generation of teachers made the decision to enter teaching in a different labor market from that of today: (a) there were fewer career opportunities for educated women and people of color; (b) although it was broadly assumed that people taught for altruistic reasons and thus the pay gap was acceptable, teaching was respected work; and (c) most teachers entered through the same route and expected to stay in the classroom. Moore Johnson and colleagues argue that the next generation of teachers is quite different,

> They expect to be paid well . . . for the important work that they do. They expect variety in what they do with differentiated roles and opportunities to advance in the profession. They want the chance to collaborate with colleagues and to work in organizations that support them. (p. xii)

Susan Moore Johnson and her colleagues argue that if we look closely at the experiences of new teachers who enter from different paths, stay in, move within, and leave the profession, we see that the current situation cannot be fully understood as a failure to retain teachers. Rather, we need to address the teacher supply problem from a generational perspective that requires a redefinition of career expectations, career paths, and school organizations.

TEACHING TO CHANGE THE WORLD: GETTING SOCIAL JUSTICE ON THE TABLE

Similar to the work of Johnson and colleagues, the Teacher Education Program Research Group (TEP) at Center X at the University of California, Los Angeles (UCLA), studies the career paths of teachers in public schools. Somewhat different, however, the work of the UCLA group is based on the assumption that teaching is a social justice project and teachers should be activists as well as educators. Elaborated in a set of recent articles,[2] the TEP is currently in the 5th of a 7-year longitudinal study of more than a thousand graduates from UCLA's urban teacher education program.

Just two of the many noteworthy insights in the TEP studies are mentioned here. The TEP group is finding that their teacher candidates, who are particularly at risk for early leaving because they are among the "best and the brightest," stay in urban teaching at higher rates than national averages (Quartz, Lyons, & Thomas, 2005; Quartz & TEP Research Group, 2003). Specialized recruitment and preparation for urban schools coupled with school- and community-based professional learning communities and other school conditions figure prominently in stayers' and switchers' decisions about remaining in high-poverty schools. Second, the TEP group is beginning to identify a social justice career pattern that differs from the now well-documented migration of teachers from less to more affluent schools: the switch from full-time classroom teaching in high- poverty schools to either the combination of part-time teaching with leadership roles or full-time leadership roles dedicated to social justice goals (e.g., literacy coach or supervisor in high poverty schools, teacher of university courses related to social justice, community activist; Olsen & Anderson, 2004; Quartz et al., 2004). The TEP group suggests that we may need an expanded notion of retention that recognizes the migration to leadership roles not as failure to retain but as an appropriate career path for some social justice educators. At the same time, however, they also argue for more dual roles so successful urban teachers can remain in classrooms while also having expanded career opportunities.

WHAT'S DIVERSIFICATION GOT TO DO WITH IT? KEEPING TEACHERS OF COLOR IN THE PIPELINE

Consistent with the work of the UCLA TEP group, recent analyses by Ana Maria Villegas and Tamara Lucas (2004) focus on equity and social justice aspects of the teacher workforce problem. Villegas and Lucas provide retrospective and prospective analyses of trends in the diversity of the nation's teacher workforce coupled with assessment of the empirical evidence for diversification. They conclude that the case for increasing the racial and ethnic diversity of the teacher workforce is compelling,

> If teachers of color are essential role models for all students, especially students of color, in a democratic society, and if the

life experiences of teachers of color infuse into the teacher workforce a critical source of cultural knowledge, then efforts to increase the diversity of the teacher workforce should be a key component in any system that aims to supply schools with well-prepared teachers for all students, particularly in light of the shifting demographics of the student population. (pp. 75-76)

Villegas and Lucas point out that during the 1980s, the shortage of minority teachers began to receive national attention, especially as the disparity between the growing minority student population and the diminishing minority teacher population steadily increased. The shortage of minority teachers was understood as a problem due to small numbers of minority students eligible for college, increased professional opportunities for minorities, teacher testing, and dissatisfaction with the teaching profession. Villegas and Lucas argue that since the 1990s, the shortage of minority teachers has been constructed as a supply problem, which has prompted many comprehensive policy initiatives by state and private agencies to increase minority recruitment. However, Villegas and Lucas argue that we must now move beyond recruitment if we are to have a diversified teacher workforce. They call for action in three critical areas: (a) Primarily White institutions and teacher preparation programs must improve the retention of minority prospective teachers by incorporating their perspectives into the curriculum and finding ways to decrease the alienation they often experience; (b) teacher education programs must regard the cultural, linguistic, and life experiences of minority prospective teachers as resources for meeting the needs of the diverse school population and build on these; and (c) the educational community in general needs to alter the conditions of urban and other schools so that minority and other teachers are more likely to remain in the profession.

CONCLUSION: UNDERSTANDING RETENTION

The teacher shortage problem in the nation's K-12 schools is not simply a supply problem that can be resolved by fast-track entry routes and other short-term recruitment schemes. As the five analyses mentioned here make clear, the teacher shortage is in large part a demand problem that can be solved only if we decrease demand by increasing retention. As the five studies also make clear, teacher retention is a multidimensional problem, requiring both macro- and micro-level analyses and policy initiatives. These will need to address teacher recruitment and entry requirements (especially in terms of diversification), teacher preparation and ongoing professional learning, the cultures and conditions of schools, the rewards and incentives of teaching, the definition of teaching career paths, and the balance between teacher autonomy and teacher accountability.

From my perspective as a teacher educator for more than 25 years, I believe that despite changing times, good teachers are still lovers and dreamers. Many enter teaching for idealistic reasons—they love children, they love learning, they imagine a world that is a better and more just place, and they want all children to have the chance to live and work productively in a democratic society. But these reasons are not enough to sustain teachers' work over the long haul in today's labor market and in the face of the extraordinarily complex and multiple demands today's teachers face. To stay in teaching, today's— and tomorrow's—teachers need school conditions where they are successful and supported, opportunities to work with other educators in professional learning communities rather than in isolation, differentiated leadership and advancement prospects during the course of the career, and good pay for what they do. But we also need to rethink what "staying" in teaching means as a goal for the educational community, especially whether it makes sense to argue that teaching is a profession at the same time that we claim that the ultimate goal is keeping teachers in the classroom and thus maintaining a flat career trajectory where entrants do essentially the same work as effective and experienced teachers. It is clear that staying needs to be redefined. On one hand, staying needs to include a variety of career trajectories with multiple avenues for leadership roles and advancement during the career span. On the other hand, it also needs to include majority institutions' efforts not only to get but to keep in the pipeline minority teachers and educators who "stay the course" of work for social justice across multiple roles and responsibilities. We face enormous challenges as we rethink teacher recruitment, preparation, and retention. There are many new role and partnership possibilities for the universities, professional organizations, school districts, and communities with the vision to imagine them and the will to implement them.

NOTES

1. The main ideas in this editorial were presented in "Stayers, Leavers, Lovers and Dreamers: Why People Teach," the Opening Convocation at Bank Street College of Education, September 2004.

2. Except where otherwise noted, this editorial treats as a set a group of recently published or in press articles and chapters from the UCLA Center X Teacher Education Program Research group (Lyons, 2004; Olsen & Anderson, 2004; Quartz et al., 2004; Quartz, Lyons, & Thomas, 2005; Quartz, Olsen, & Duncan Andrade, in press; Quartz & TEP Research Group, 2003). All of these articles are available at the UCLA Center X Web site: www.idea.gseis. ucla.edu/projects/utec/utecresearch/index.

REFERENCES

Ingersoll, R. (2001). Teacher turnover and teacher shortages: An organizational analysis. *American Educational Research Journal, 38*(3), 499-534.

Ingersoll, R. (2002). The teacher shortage: A case of wrong diagnosis and wrong prescription. *The NASSP Bulletin, 86*, 16-31.

Ingersoll, R. (2003). *Is there really a teacher shortage? A report co-sponsored by the Center for the Study of Teaching and Policy and the Center for Policy Research in Education.* Seattle: University of Washington, Center for the Study of Teaching and Policy.

Ingersoll, R. (2004). Four myths about America's teacher quality problem. In M. Smylie & D. Miretzky (Eds.), *Developing the teacher workforce: The 103rd yearbook of the National Society for the Study of Education* (pp. 1-33). Chicago: University of Chicago Press.

Lyons, K. B. (2004). *Specialized recruitment: An examination of the motivations and expectations of preservice urban educators.* Unpublished manuscript.

Merrow, J. (1999, October 6). The teacher shortage: Wrong diagnosis, phony cures. *Education Week*, pp. 38, 64

Moore Johnson, S., & The Project on the Next Generation of Teachers. (2004). *Finders and keepers: Helping teachers survive and thrive in our schools.* San Francisco: Jossey-Bass.

National Commission on Teaching & America's Future. (NCTAF). (2003). *No dream denied, a pledge to America's children.* Washington, DC: National Commission on Teaching and America's Future.

Nieto, S. (2003). *What keeps teachers going?* New York: Teachers College Press.

Olsen, B., & Anderson, L. (2004). *Courses of action: A qualitative investigation into urban teachers retention and career development.* Unpublished manuscript.

Quartz, K., Lyons, K. B., Masyn, K., Olsen, B., Anderson, L., Thomas, A., et al. (2004). *Retaining urban school professionals: Interim results from a longitudinal study of career development.* Unpublished manuscript.

Quartz, K., Lyons, K. B., & Thomas, A. (2005). Retaining teachers in high poverty schools: A policy framework. In N. Bascia, A. Cummins, A. Datnow, K. Leithwood, & D. Livingstone (Eds.), *International handbook of educational policy.* Dordrecht, the Netherlands: Kluwer.

Quartz, K. H., Olsen, B., & Duncan-Andrade, J. (in press). The fragility of urban teaching: A longitudinal study of career development and activism. In F. Peterman (Ed.), *Resiliency, resistance, and persistence in partnering to prepare urban teachers: A call to activism.* Los Angeles: University of California–Los Angeles Institute for Democracy, Education and Access (IDEA).

Quartz, K., & TEP Research Group. (2003). Too angry to leave: Supporting new teachers' commitment to transform urban schools. *Journal of Teacher Education, 54*(2), 99-111.

Villegas, A., & Lucas, T. (2004). Diversifying the teacher workforce: A retrospective and prospective analysis. In M. Smylie & D. Miretzky (Eds.), *Developing the teacher workforce: The 103rd yearbook of the National Society for the Study of Education* (pp. 70-104). Chicago: University of Chicago Press.

24 Taking Stock in 2005

Getting Beyond the Horse Race

D uring the summer of 2004, a new study of the impact of Teach for America (TFA) teachers on pupils' achievement was released by Mathematica Policy Research, Incorporated. Taking stock in 2005, this editorial uses the new TFA study to make several points about research on teacher preparation programs in general and about how this research is often used and misused in the discourse about teacher preparation reform. The editorial begins by reviewing two previous studies of TFA, noting that although they asked similar questions, they reached directly opposing conclusions and, not surprisingly, engendered directly opposing critique from those with differing political and professional agendas. Then the editorial briefly describes the Mathematica study, arguing that although it was not designed to compare the effectiveness of teachers prepared in university-based teacher education programs with that of teachers who entered teaching through alternate routes, it is nonetheless being constructed that way in the larger political discourse. The editorial makes the argument that the new study is one more indication that we need to get beyond the teacher education "horse race," which pits one route, program, or structural arrangement against another to declare the "winner" or the "one best" approach to teacher preparation. Instead, we need to focus directly on the essential ingredients in the preparation of all teachers and the ways these interact with what teacher candidates bring and with the contexts of programs and schools to produce desirable outcomes.

SOURCE: *Journal of Teacher Education,* Vol. 56, No. 1, January/February 2005, pp. 3-7.

Assessing the Impact of TFA Teachers: Previous Studies

In June 2004, a major national study (Decker, Mayer, & Glazerman, 2004) of the impact of TFA, an alternate teacher recruitment and training program, was released by Mathematica, an independent research firm that provides analyses of the socioeconomic issues that drive public policy. Not surprisingly, the Mathematica study generated immediate response. Since its inception in 1989, TFA has been a hot-button issue among teacher education researchers and practitioners and among educational policymakers. Indeed, in many of the most contentious debates, TFA has been constructed as both the poster child for alternate routes into teaching (even though it is technically not an alternate route but a teacher recruitment and initial training program) and a major battleground for larger discussions about who should teach, what they should know, how and where they should be prepared, and who should decide.

The Mathematica study is not the first analysis of the impact of TFA teachers on pupils' achievement as indicated by test scores. Raymond, Fletcher, and Luque (2001), for example, studied TFA teachers for the Center for Research on Education Outcomes (CREDO), a research group of the Hoover Institute. This study compared new TFA teachers hired in Houston with other new teachers hired there and concluded that TFA teachers were at least as good as others in terms of pupils' test scores and better than other new teachers in raising pupils' math test scores. The foreword to the study, written by Chester Finn and Marci Kanstoroom, concluded, "The TFA program, we learn from this study, proves that it's not necessary to spend an extended period in an ed school to be effective in a K-12 classroom" (p. ix). Spokespersons for major national organizations supporting professional teacher preparation were quick to critique the study, pointing out that because Houston has an unusually large number of uncertified teachers (including teachers without even a bachelor's degree), the study actually compared TFA teachers with teachers who were less well-qualified than they were. Critics concluded therefore that the study did not really "prove" anything about the effectiveness of teachers prepared in "ed school" programs in comparison with teachers entering through alternate routes. Critics also pointed out that the exceedingly high attrition rate of

TFA teachers in the Houston study (60% to 100% after 2 years) was a major concern.

A year later, Laczko-Kerr and Berliner (2002) published a study comparing the achievement test scores of pupils taught by recently hired, regularly certified teachers and by "under-qualified" teachers (i.e., emergency, temporary, and provisionally certified teachers, including a subset of TFA teachers) in five low-income school districts in Arizona. Based on an analysis of pairs of teachers matched for grade level and degree earned and within similar schools or districts, Laczko-Kerr and Berliner found both that the pupils of certified teachers scored substantially higher than those of under-certified teachers and that the pupils of TFA teachers performed no better than the pupils of other under-certified teachers. The authors concluded that educational policies that allow under-prepared teachers to teach, particularly in low-income schools with children who are most in need of good teachers, are harmful and will only exacerbate current achievement gaps. Critics of university-based teacher preparation were quick to respond, arguing that the Laczko-Kerr study failed to account adequately for both prior differences in students' achievement and biases in the assignment of students to teachers. Critics also argued that TFA teachers' credentials are not at all like those of "emergency" certified teachers, thus rendering comparisons completely inappropriate. According to the critics, the methodological flaws in the Laczko-Kerr study negated its potential to say anything useful about public policy decisions about teacher preparation and certification.

In addition to studies focusing on pupils' test scores, there have also been comparisons of TFA and other teachers' attitudes, sense of efficacy, and evaluations. The research on TFA has widely been used (and abused) to argue the case for and against alternate entry routes, alternate recruitment and training programs, traditional teacher preparation, and professional accreditation, certification, and licensure, depending on the larger purposes and political agendas of those involved.[1]

ASSESSING THE IMPACT OF TFA TEACHERS: THE MATHEMATICA STUDY

The new Mathematica study (Decker et al., 2004) compared the test score gains from fall to spring on the Iowa Test of Basic Skills of pupils randomly assigned to TFA teachers or "non-TFA" teachers, defined as all teachers who were never part of TFA, including traditionally certified, alternately certified, and uncertified teachers. The final sample included 2,000 students in 100 elementary classrooms (Grades 1 through 5) in 17 schools in Chicago, Los Angeles, Houston, New Orleans, and the Mississippi Delta, which accounts for 6 of the 15 regions where TFA teachers are placed. Two major analyses were conducted—one of the pupil test scores of TFA and non-TFA teachers and one of pupil scores of novice TFA teachers and novice control group teachers. The study found that in math, the gains of TFA pupils were significantly higher than those of non-TFA pupils, whereas in reading, the growth rates of pupils in both groups were equivalent. The impact of novice TFA in comparison with the impact of novice non-TFA teachers on pupil test scores was the same as or greater than the impact found in the overall comparison. Researchers concluded that TFA "supplies low-income schools with academically talented teachers who contribute to the academic achievement of their students. The success of TFA teachers is not dependent on their having extensive exposure to teacher practice or training" (Decker et al., 2004, p. xvi).

There is no question that the Decker et al. (2004) study represents a methodological breakthrough in the research on teacher preparation. It is one of the few studies in the broad field of teacher education that links teacher preparation with pupils' learning, and it is the first independent study of program structures and alternatives to use an experimental design and a large nationwide sample to assess the impact of TFA recruitment and training on pupils' test gains (Zeichner & Conklin, 2005).

The advantages of the study's unique experimental design have been noted—and lauded—by critics of all stripes. Nevertheless, although it was not the intention of the Decker et al. (2004) study to compare the effectiveness of university-based teacher preparation with that of alternate recruitment and entry programs—and the Decker study goes to some pains to point this out explicitly—such comparisons have been and will continue to be drawn. In fact, a number of dramatically different interpretations of the study's bottom-line implications for public policy followed quickly after release of the study. For example, the bulletin of the Southeast Center for Teaching Quality (SECTQ), an ardent advocate for professional teacher preparation, suggested that the study actually reveals more about the abysmal achievement of pupils in both the TFA and non-TFA teacher groups than it does about anything else (a point with which this editorial strongly agrees and to which it returns in a forthcoming edition). This point notwithstanding, the SECTQ critique also pointed out that when considering the implications of the study for teacher preparation policy, it is essential to note that the novice control group, which included emergency, temporary, and alternate route certification teachers, actually had less teacher preparation than the TFA novices. That is, during the year of the study, TFA novices had higher rates of certification, more master's degrees, and more student teaching experience than the control group of novices. Given these discrepancies, the SECTQ review argued that the Decker study actually tells us nothing about the merits of traditional or university-based preparation but does tell us a lot about the lack of preparation of novice teachers in high-poverty schools. On the other hand, in a short review of the Decker study in *The Education Gadfly*, Chester Finn's weekly newsletter for the Fordham Foundation and a strong opponent of certification and university-based teacher preparation, Porter-Magee (2004) concluded that the Decker study showed that bright teachers with little formal training could be at least as effective as "traditional teachers who are relegated to serve the hardest-to-teach students."

GETTING BEYOND THE HORSE RACE

Even assuming that the findings of the Decker et al. (2004) study hold up under rigorous methodological critique (and they seem to be doing so), it is extremely unlikely that this study will be the last word about either the impact of TFA in comparison with the impact of some other group of teachers or the value of university-based professional teacher preparation. Rather, it seems clear that although this study was not designed to compare traditional and alternate forms of teacher preparation, it is already and will continue to be used and misused as evidence in these very discussions, just as previous studies of TFA have been. I would argue that one of the lessons of the Mathematica study, is, as I have suggested elsewhere (Cochran-Smith & Fries, 2005), that we need to get beyond the "horse race"[2] mentality in discussions about how to recruit, prepare, and retain teachers for the nation's schools.

The horse race approach to teacher preparation makes three flawed assumptions: that teacher preparation is a matter of uniformly applied and received "treatments," that effectiveness can be defined in terms of test scores alone, and that empirical research is capable of proving which "treatment" produces better results and thus can definitively guide policy. It is not research that tries to determine "who wins" that is most important (nor is it conversations that use this research—either appropriately or inappropriately—to claim the winner). Rather, we need research and debate that identify and explain—with empirical evidence—what the active ingredients are in any programs, approaches, or routes where teachers have a positive impact as well as the conditions and contexts in which these ingredients are most likely to be present (Cochran-Smith & Zeichner, 2005).

Teacher preparation is conducted in local communities, institutions, and contexts where program components and structures interact with one another as well as with prospective teachers' different experiences and abilities. This point is explicit in Zeichner and Conklin's (2005) up-to-date analysis of the research on teacher education programs. In their critique of research on various teacher education programs and structural alternatives, including TFA, they suggest that in many areas of the country where TFA teachers are employed (such as Arizona, where the Laczko-Kerr study was done, and in some of the districts included in the Decker study), TFA teachers are now required to enroll in certification programs at universities. Likewise, in many of the places where TFA teachers are hired (such as Houston, where the Raymond study was done, as well as some other districts included in the Decker study), the other novice teachers to whom TFA teachers are compared are among the least prepared and least educated teachers in the nation, not only with no student teaching and no certification but also with no B.A. degrees. Unlike other critics, however, Zeichner and Conklin do not conclude that either TFA or university-based preparation is superior. Rather, they point out the many difficulties involved in any research (or research-based discussion) that attempts to compare approaches and draw conclusions at a very global level. Global comparisons tend to obscure the very real differences that do exist between and among recruitment and preparation programs (including the many different versions of TFA) and prevent us from developing important insights about specific programs we might want to emulate and others we might want to eliminate or drastically upgrade.

"Teacher preparation" and "teacher education" are neither monolithic nor unitary pursuits. To the contrary, even in the face of tightly specified policies, teacher education is enacted in ways that are highly local—embedded in the multiple and changing contexts of local institutions and regions and subject to the interpretations and social interactions of individuals and groups. Complexity and variation between and among teacher education structures, organizational arrangements, program types, institutional categories, and preparation paths or routes are the rule rather than the exception.

Given the variation of both TFA and other alternate and traditional recruitment and/or training programs, it is not likely that any study—no matter what its design—will produce findings that definitively tell policymakers whether to put their money into support for university-based teacher preparation programs or alternate route programs. It's time to get beyond the horse race.

NOTES

1. See Cochran-Smith (2005) for a discussion of research as a "weapon" in the battle for competing reform agendas in teacher education and Cochran-Smith and Fries (2002) for discussion of the notion of "forensic social science" as applied to research on teacher preparation policies.

2. David Imig initially used the "horse race" metaphor in his review of an early draft of Cochran-Smith and Fries (2005), which is the introductory chapter to *Studying Teacher Education: The Report of the AERA Panel on Teacher Education* (Cochran-Smith & Zeichner, 2005).

REFERENCES

Cochran-Smith, M. (Ed.). (2005). *Promises and politics: Images of research in the discourse of teacher education.* Washington, DC: National Reading Conference.

Cochran-Smith, M., & Fries, M. K. (2002). The discourse of reform in teacher education: Extending the dialogue. *Educational Researcher, 31*(6), 26-29.

Cochran-Smith, M., & Fries, K. (2005). The AERA Panel on Research and Teacher Education: Introduction. In M. Cochran-Smith & K. Zeichner (Eds.), *Studying teacher education: The report of the AERA Panel on Research and Teacher Education.* Mahwah, NJ: Lawrence Erlbaum.

Cochran-Smith, M., & Zeichner, K. (2005). *Studying teacher education: The report of the AERA panel on research and teacher education.* Mahwah, NJ: Lawrence Erlbaum.

Decker, P., Mayer, D., & Glazerman, S. (2004). *The effects of Teach For America on students: Findings from a national evaluation* (MPR Reference No: M-8792-750). Princeton, NJ: Mathematica Policy Research, Inc.

Laczko-Kerr, I., & Berliner, D. (2002). The effectiveness of "Teach for America" and other under-certified teachers on student academic achievement: A case of harmful public policy. *Education Policy Analysis Archives, 10*(37).

Porter-Magee, K. (2004, June 21). The effects of Teach for America on students: Findings from a national evaluation. *Education Gadfly.* Retrieved July 1, 2004, from http://www.edexcellence.net/foundation/gadfly

Raymond, M., Fletcher, S. H., & Luque, J. (2001). *Teach for America: An evaluation of teacher differences and student outcomes in Houston, Texas.* Washington, DC: Thomas B. Fordham Foundation.

Southeast Center for Teaching Quality. (2004). *Teach for America study reports some gains, but obscures failed teaching policies in urban schools.* Retrieved July 1, 2004, from http://www.teachingquality.org/resources/mathematicaresponse.htm

Zeichner, K., & Conklin, H. (2005). Teacher education programs. In M. Cochran-Smith & K. Zeichner (Eds.), *Studying teacher education: The report of the AERA Panel on Research and Teacher Education.* Mahwah, NJ: Lawrence Erlbaum.

25 *No Child Left Behind*

3 Years and Counting

Three years ago, President Bush signed the No Child Left Behind Act (NCLB) into law. Nearly everybody agreed with the bill's purpose—"to ensure that all children have a fair, equal, and significant opportunity to attain a high-quality education and reach, at a minimum, proficiency on challenging state academic achievement standards and state academic assessments" (U.S. Congress, 2001), which was to be accomplished by shifting funding formulas and sending more federal resources to high-poverty and struggling schools.

Despite its lofty goals, there was criticism of NCLB from the beginning, which was reflected in wordplays on its name, borrowed in the first place (some would say co-opted) from children's rights work. Robert Schaeffer of Fair Test, for example, suggested the "no child left untested act" (Toppo, 2002), and some academics quipped that the bill should be labeled "no psychometrician left unemployed." In other circles, where there was concern that the emphasis on testing would narrow the curriculum and deprofessionalize teachers' work, the bill was referred to as "no teacher left standing," and many social justice advocates feared the bottom line would be "same children left behind." Underneath the wit and cynicism of these wordplays were serious concerns about the enduring impact NCLB would have on schools, teachers, students, families, and, in a larger sense, the American system of public education.

This editorial focuses on how NCLB is being assessed 3 years later, contrasting the public conclusion that all is well with the

SOURCE: *Journal of Teacher Education*, Vol. 56, No. 2, March/April 2005, pp. 99-103.

conclusion of a number of other individuals and groups who, for very different reasons, assert that all is decidedly not well. The editorial suggests that three aspects of NCLB are particularly relevant to teacher education—stipulations regarding "highly qualified teachers" (HQT) and "adequate yearly progress" (AYP) and the bill's emerging consequences for minority students. Each of these has troubling— even dangerous—ramifications.

3 Years and Counting

At the time of this writing, NCLB was about to celebrate its third anniversary. It is an understatement to say that assessments of its legitimacy and success are conflicting. In testimony to the House Education and the Workforce Committee (*Hearings on NCLB*, 2004), for example, Republican Chairman John Boehner announced that as a result of NCLB, test scores all across the country are rising and the achievement gap is closing. The assessment of the most recent report from the Education Commission of the States (ECS; 2004) was somewhat more modest and mixed, although the report concluded that "the overall picture is encouraging" (p. vi). The ECS report found that although all 50 states are on track to meet at least half of NCLB's requirements, only five states are likely to meet all of them. Similarly, the commission found that although many states are improving student achievement, few will be able to meet requirements concerning highly qualified teachers.

Along similar lines, *Education Week*'s survey of state education departments (Olson, 2004b), titled "Taking Root," concluded that despite problems and complaints from various groups, NCLB has "become implanted in the culture" (p. S1) of the American public school system. The *Education Week* survey indicated that nearly half the states now have testing programs in place in reading and math for third through eighth graders and high schoolers, as required by NCLB, and all states are now using test results to determine AYP. On the other hand, the report also indicated that the number of schools identified as needing improvement has doubled since last year, and some states now have both AYP annual reports and, at the same time, yearly report cards based on statewide systems for assessing the performance of their schools. It is an understatement to say that these dual accountability systems, with different criteria and sometimes conflicting conclusions, are engendering confusion among education professionals, parents, and the broader public.

Meanwhile, many state and local leaders have objected that NCLB is one more unfunded educational mandate. More than 20 states and school districts across the country have officially protested NCLB regulations (Darling-Hammond, 2004), and several groups of federal legislators and education-related organizations have proposed changes in how the law is implemented (Olson, 2004a). Many of the proposed revisions have to do with how annual progress is defined and measured and whether annual goals are even remotely reachable. Perhaps in response to these and other concerns, some flexibility—particularly in how highly qualified teachers are defined in rural areas and how the test scores of disabled and other student subgroups are calculated in determinations of whether schools are meeting AYP requirements—has been introduced.

A number of groups and organizations have assessed particular aspects of NCLB in keeping with specific political and/or professional agendas. For example, a report from the libertarian-oriented CATO Institute (McCluskey, 2004) concludes both that the unprecedented authority NCLB gives the federal government over K-12 education is an unconstitutional intrusion into state matters that has not produced significant results. In contrast, researchers assessing the school choice provisions of NCLB (Hess & Finn, 2004) suggest that NCLB's choice option is serving too few students due in part to the bill's insufficient "muscle" (p. 295) to overcome administrators' resistance as well as practical implementation issues and schools' preferences for supplemental services rather than school choice. Along completely different lines, a status report from the Southeast Center for Teacher Quality (2004), a strong advocate of teacher professionalization, concludes that NCLB's narrow emphasis on content knowledge coupled with lack of funding have resulted in many states lowering rather than raising their standards for teachers. In a book sponsored by the Forum for Education and Democracy (Meier & Wood, 2004), a number of prominent progressive educators argue that NCLB is not simply failing to fulfill its promise of higher quality and more equitable and accountable schools for poor and minority students. Rather, the authors assert that under NCLB many poor and minority students actually have more limited learning opportunities than before, they are being pushed out of schools in order to raise test scores, and schools are becoming less rather than more accountable to the local communities they serve.

NCLB and Teacher Education

Just before this editorial went to press, George W. Bush was reelected president. It is impossible at this time to comment on the long-term ramifications of NCLB as sweeping educational policy or for teacher education in particular. It seems reasonable, however, to assume that the federal government—and thus the states—will continue to implement NCLB for at least the next 4 years with even greater intensity. Although many aspects of the law are important, as noted above, three are particularly relevant for the preparation of teachers and are of particular concern to the teacher education community.

Highly qualified teachers. NCLB requires that all students have teachers with at least a bachelor's degree, full state certification (including through alternate routes) or a passing score on a state teacher licensing exam, and demonstrated competence in the subjects they teach. Unfortunately, although NCLB's HQT regulations have the potential to drive improvement in teacher preparation, professional development, teacher recruitment and retention, and teacher professionalism, these promises are not being fulfilled (Southeast Center for Teaching Quality, 2004).

The HQT definition focuses almost exclusively on subject matter knowledge and ignores pedagogy and other professional knowledge and skills, a definition reinforced by the Secretary of Education's reports to Congress on teacher quality (U.S. Department of Education, 2002, 2003, 2004). These reports assert that in order to produce the teachers required by NCLB, states should get rid of teacher preparation requirements not based on scientific research, recruit candidates from other fields, and widely implement alternate route programs. Despite their lack of preparation as teachers, then, anyone enrolled in an alternative program is automatically deemed highly qualified. Furthermore, there is growing evidence that despite the fact that NCLB is designed to improve the achievement of disadvantaged students, these are the very students who are least likely to get well-qualified and experienced teachers (Education Commission of the States, 2004; Oakes, 2004), a situation exacerbated by the increased difficulty schools labeled "failing" have in attracting qualified teachers.

As noted above, recent assessments indicate that NCLB's requirements concerning HQT and high-quality professional development for experienced teachers are among those that states are finding most difficult to meet (Education Commission of the States, 2004). But the HQT requirements also have the most loopholes, and little attention from the Bush administration is being given to which schools and students do and do not have qualified teachers (Olson, 2004b). Rather, the HQT agenda obfuscates the acute and chronic problem of unequal distribution of resources to high-poverty schools. At worst, it defines the problem away, reducing the disparities in teacher qualifications between low- and high-poverty schools by simply changing the definition. The painful irony of NCLB is that its long-term legacy may be to decrease rather than increase the quality of the teaching force available to students in the neediest schools.

AYP. The centerpiece of NCLB is the AYP requirement, which is currently driving (and plaguing) efforts in many schools across the nation. AYP is the rate of improvement schools (and all subgroups within schools) must make each year on tests given by their states toward the goal of 100% competence by 2013. Schools that miss any of these multiple targets for 2 years are deemed "needs improvement" and must provide students the option to move to another school. Schools that miss targets for several years are eventually considered "failing" and are subject to progressive sanctions, including mandatory provision of vouchers for supplemental educational services, withdrawal of federal funds, reconstitution (replacing faculty), and restructuring (state takeover or imposed private management).

To a very great extent, NCLB equates teaching quality and students' learning with high-stakes test scores, which Elmore (2002) suggests is the worst aspect of the contemporary accountability movement. This equation precludes the use of multiple measures of progress toward goals and multiple assessments of learning (such as performance and other alternative assessments), which provide a more complex picture of both students' learning and effective teaching. In addition, AYP requirements are unrealistic, and given different tests and different standards, comparisons across states mean very little (e.g., Linn, 2004; Packer, 2004). Warning that almost all schools will fall short of AYP targets for the next few years, Linn (2004) has demonstrated statistically that students would have to improve at 10 to 15 times the current rate in order for schools and districts to meet AYP goals. The relatively small number of schools currently failing is a function of what Packer (2004) calls "the balloon payment" approach many states used to establish initial accountability targets—small goals at first with the promise of huge gains later. As the balloon payments become due, more and more schools will be deemed failing. Some researchers predict that in the next few years, most of the nation's public schools will be labeled "failing" according to AYP regulations, even if students' achievement scores are improving, with the likelihood of failing increasing in direct proportion to the diversity of the school population (Darling-Hammond, 2004). Some critics have even speculated that part of the point of the AYP accountability system may be to discredit public education and thus pave the way for increased school privatization through the voucher system (Meier & Wood, 2004).

NCLB defines teacher quality and student learning solely in terms of students' test scores as gauged by whether schools are or are not meeting AYP goals. It is only a small leap to defining the success of teacher preparation in terms of how the pupils of graduates score on tests, and indeed, teacher education programs across the nation are being urged not only to demonstrate their impact on pupils' learning but also to provide direct evidence of impact on test scores (The Teaching Commission, 2004). The slope here is exceedingly slippery, and the dangers involved in inventing a new kind of teacher education where pupils' test scores are not just the bottom line but the only line are enormous.

Consequences for minority students. NCLB's accountability goals must be met not only at the school level but also for all subgroups of students. There are separate AYP target goals for various subgroups of students (e.g., special education students, English language learners, African American students), each of which must have at least 95% of students take the test and each of which must make its yearly target goal toward 100% proficiency. On its face, the requirement that schools disaggregate and publicize achievement data for minority and other groups of students promises new attention to the inequities in quality of education provided for poor, immigrant, and minority students, and many civil rights group applaud this. In practice, however, what is developing is a "diversity penalty" for schools (Novak & Fuller, 2003), or the disproportionate labeling as needing improvement of those schools with the greatest diversity (and thus the largest number of AYP targets that must be met; Darling-Hammond, 2004).

A new study from the Harvard Civil Rights Project (Orfield, Losen, & Wald, 2004) adds another dimension to the consequences of NCLB for minority students. The report proclaims a "national crisis" in graduation rates of minority students, revealing that Black and Latino students are graduating from high school at rates far lower than Whites in even those states with the worst overall graduation rates. With reference to NCLB, the report suggests that even though there could be positive outcomes from a "sound system" of subgroup accountability for school achievement, case studies are exposing what appears to be a pattern: New regulations requiring that graduation rates be included in NCLB accountability provisions are not being enforced, whereas incentives for removing low-scoring students are rigidly followed. This means that there may now be "perverse incentives in many states to push low-performing students out the back door" (Orfield et al., 2004, p. 3) so districts can avoid test-driven sanctions.

WHAT'S BEHIND NCLB?

The stated goals of NCLB—to ensure that all children attain an equal and high-quality education and meet challenging academic standards—are unassailable. But the operating assumptions behind NCLB are not. As many critics have pointed out (e.g., Cuban, 2004; Darling-Hammond, 2004; Earley, 2004; Elmore, 2002), a fundamental flaw of NCLB is the set of assumptions behind it: A highly coercive accountability system, based on competitive pressure and including public shaming and punishments for failure, will improve schooling for disadvantaged students without the improvement of school capacity, increases in resources, and major investments in programs to improve the quality of professional teachers. As Cuban (2004) concludes quite succinctly,

The No Child Left Behind law has foundered on trying to improve the nation's worst schools with pennies and sledge-hammer tactics, as if dispirited schools could, alone, transform their students through a combination of sheer will and good intentions. They cannot.

They cannot. Neither schools nor teacher education programs alone can fix the nation's worst schools and improve the life chances of the most disadvantaged students without simultaneous investment in resources, capacity building, and enhancing teachers' professional growth. This is neither an excuse for schools and teacher preparation programs or a statement that should in any way be construed to mean that certain students are not capable of learning to high standards. Rather, it is a categorical acceptance of the goal of equal and high-quality education for all students and a flat-out rejection of NCLB's flawed assumptions about how to attain that goal.

REFERENCES

Cuban, L. (2004, March 17). The contentious "no child" law I: Who will fix it? And how? *Education Week*. Retreived November 20, 2004, from www.edwk.org/ew/articles/2004/03/17/27cuban.h23.html

Darling-Hammond, L. (2004). From "separate but equal" to "no child left behind": The collision of new standards and old inequalities. In D. Meier & G. Wood (Eds.), *Many children left behind: How the No Child Left Behind Act is damaging our children and our schools* (pp. 3-32). Boston: Beacon.

Earley, P. (2004). Searching for the common good in federal policy: The missing essence in NCLB and HEA: Title II. In N. Michelli & D. Keiser (Eds.), *Teacher education for diversity and social justice* (pp. 57-76). New York: Routledge/Taylor & Francis.

Education Commission of the States. (2004). *ECS report to the nation: State implementation of the No Child Left Behind Act, respecting diversity among states*. Denver, CO: Author.

Elmore, R. (2002). The testing trap. *Harvard Magazine, 105*(1), 35.

Hearings on No Child Left Behind. (2004). Washington, DC: U.S. House of Representatives.

Hess, F., & Finn, C. (Eds.). (2004). *Leaving no child behind? Options for kids in failing schools*. New York: Palgrave/Macmillan.

Linn, R. (2004, July). *Rethinking the no child left behind accountability system*. Paper presented at the Center on Education Policy forum on ideas to improve the accountability provisions under the No Child Left Behind Act, Washington, DC.

McCluskey, N. (2004). *A lesson in waste: Where does all the federal education money go?* Washington, DC: CATO Institute.

Meier, M., & Wood, G. (Eds.). (2004). *Many children left behind: How the No Child Left Behind Act is damaging our children and our schools.* Boston: Beacon.

Novak, J., & Fuller, B. (2003). *Penalizing diverse schools? Similar test scores but different students bring federal sanctions.* Berkeley, CA: Policy Analysis for California Education.

Oakes, J. (2004). Investigating the claims in *Williams v. State of California: An unconstitutional denial of education's basic tools? Teachers College Record, 106*(10), 1889-1906.

Olson, L. (2004a, August 11). Critics float 'no child' revisions. *Education Week,* pp. 1, 33.

Olson, L. (2004b, December 8). Taking root. *Education Week,* pp. S1, S3, S7. Retreived November 20, 2004, from www.edwk.org/ew/articles/2004/08/11/44alth23.htm

Orfield, G., Losen, D., & Wald, J. (2004). *Losing our future: How minority youth are being left behind by the graduation rate crisis.* Cambridge, MA: Harvard University, The Civil Rights Project; contributors: Advocates for Children of New York, The Civil Society Institute.

Packer, J. (2004, July). *No child left behind and adequate yearly progress fundamental flaws: A forecast for failure.* Paper presented at the Center on Education Policy forum on ideas to improve the accountability provisions under the No Child Left Behind Act, Washington, DC.

Southeast Center for Teaching Quality. (2004). *Unfulfilled promise: Ensuring high quality teachers for our nation's schools: No Child Left Behind: A status report from southeastern schools.* Chapel Hill, NC: Author.

The Teaching Commission. (2004). *Teaching at risk: A call to action.* New York: Author.

Toppo, G. (2002, January 7). Bush to sign education bill, but the debate over required testing goes on. *The Washington Post.* Available from www.washingtonpost.com

U.S. Congress. (2001). *No Child Left Behind Act of 2001: Conference report to accompany H.R. 1, report 107-334.* Washington, DC: Government Printing Office.

U.S. Department of Education. (2002). *Meeting the highly qualified teachers challenge: The secretary's annual report on teacher quality.* Washington, DC: Author.

U.S. Department of Education. (2003). *Meeting the highly qualified teachers challenge: The secretary's second annual report on teacher quality.* Washington, DC: U.S. Department of Education, Office of Postsecondary Education.

U.S. Department of Education. (2004). *The secretary's third annual report on teacher quality.* Washington, DC: Author.

26 The Politics of Teacher Education and the Curse of Complexity

S ome policy and political analysts assume that ambiguity, conflict, and competing goals are inherent in human societies. From this perspective, politics is a "creative and valued feature of social existence" (Stone, 1997, p. x) and the "process by which citizens with varied interests and opinions can negotiate differences and clarify places where values conflict" (Westheimer, 2004, p. 231). Following from this conception of politics, education (and with it, teaching and teacher education) are inherently and unavoidably political in that they involve the negotiation of conflicting values about curriculum, accountability, the role of schools in society, the children deemed eligible for particular services, and the persons and structures that govern and regulate all of these.

This view of the politics of education is quite different from the view that "being political" about education (or teacher education) is equated with being partisan about it and, thus, is a barrier to improving the processes of teacher preparation. Following from this latter conception of politics, it is assumed that it is possible—and desirable—to create a system of education that is politically neutral, value free, and above or outside of disagreements about educational means and ends (Westheimer & Kahne, 2004). From this perspective, public dissent and the acknowledgement of ideological

SOURCE: *Journal of Teacher Education,* Vol. 56, No. 3, May/June 2005, pp. 181-185.

differences are regarded as obstacles to policies leading to educational improvement, not to mention as threats to truth and patriotism (Ross, 2004).

This editorial is rooted in the premises of the first position elaborated above—that politics is an inevitable characteristic of human society and social institutions involving contested notions about public and, private interests and the role of education in society. The editorial focuses on two ideas that are useful in unpacking the issues involved in the contemporary politics of teacher education: the rhetoric of teacher education reform and the "curse" of complex understandings of teaching, learning, and schooling.

THE RHETORIC OF REFORM

During the past 10 years, reforming teacher education has become acutely politicized. Deborah Stone's *The Policy Paradox* (1997) is particularly helpful here. In her theory of public policy, Stone rejected both the market model of society and the production model of policy making, which, she suggested, are the cornerstones of much of contemporary public policy analysis. Stone argued instead for a model of society as a political community and a model of policy making as the struggle over ideas:

> Each idea is an argument, or more accurately, a collection of arguments in favor of different ways of seeing the world . . . there are multiple understandings of what appears to be a single concept, how these understandings are created, and how they are manipulated as part of political strategy. (p. 11)

Stone suggested that from a market model of policy making, the definition of policy problems is mistakenly regarded as a simple and straightforward matter of "observation and arithmetic" (p. 133)—the statement of a clear and fixed goal accompanied by an assessment of how far the status quo is from that goal. To the contrary, Stone posited that goals and positions are never fixed and problem definition is never a simple matter of arithmetic. Rather it is a matter of the strategic representation of situations wherein advocates "deliberately and consciously fashion their portrayals so as to promote their favored course of action" (Stone, 1997, p. 133).

One of the central ways groups, individuals, and government agencies promote their particular definitions of the problems of teacher education (and seek, ultimately, to control policy) is through the "rhetoric of reform," which includes how they use metaphor and analogy (Lakoff & Johnson, 1980), emblematic language and recurring arguments forwarding their own positions and discrediting the positions of others (Cochran-Smith & Fries, 2001), and symbols, stories, and literary devices (Stone, 1997). All of these can be understood as attempts by the proponents of particular positions to garner support—not simply for the solutions they favor but also for their ways of understanding particular problems in the first place—and, thus, for their worldviews (Stone, 1997).

This means that the rhetoric of reform is not a simple matter of semantics. It is a vital part of understanding the politics of teacher education. In debates about teacher education, for example, it matters whether market forces are described as "the cleansing waters of competition" (Hess, 2001a, p. 22), the "market bulldozer" of reform (Hess, 2001b, p. 4), the "discipline of the market" (Ballou & Podgursky, 1999, p. 67), or a system based on "competition, choice, winners and losers, and finding culprits" (Earley, 2000, p. 37). It matters whether access for all students to certified teachers is described as an "educational birthright" (National Commission on Teaching & America's Future, 1996, p. 21) or "regulatory overkill" (Abell Foundation, 2001, p. vi). And it matters whether the key to the improvement of the educational system is assumed to be the "development of a highly qualified teacher workforce imbued with the knowledge, skills, and dispositions to encourage exceptional learning in all the nation's students" (Sykes, 1999, p. xv) or the provision of "effective forms of professional development [that] reduce the differences [among teachers] to the point that every teacher should be good enough so that no child is left behind" (Whitehurst, 2002, p. 13). These strikingly different metaphors and assertions are based on different models of society and on different ideas about the role of education in a democratic society.

Debating teacher education reform by spinning out dramatic metaphors and powerful imagery is not a new phenomenon (although the extremely strategic uses of language that turn issues on their heads and make them hard to question does seem to be new) (Lakoff, 2002). Arthur Bestor (1953), a leader of 1950s efforts to bolster the academic curriculum of the schools, argued that "educationists" (i.e., those who studied education and prepared teachers in colleges and universities) were making the public schools into an "educational wasteland." Several decades later, John Goodlad (1990) concluded,

> The teacher education train is *not* on the tracks. Further, the engine is not coupled to the cars nor the cars to one another. The board of directors is not even sure where the train should go once it is on the tracks and coupled. (p. 270)

From a different perspective, the National Commission on Teaching & America's Future (1996) warned that unless they concentrated on teachers with know-how and schools with resources, the national, state, and district mandates governing the preparation of teachers—far from being the "magic wands" they seemed presumed to be—were "simply so much fairy dust" (p. 5). And finally, the U.S. Secretary of Education's report to Congress on supplying qualified teachers for the nation's schools charged that schools of education and formal teacher training programs constituted "a broken system" (U.S. Department of Education, 2002).

As these examples suggest, it is not an overstatement to say that in the discourse of teacher education reform, the metaphor is the message—that is, the powerful metaphors and images used to characterize teacher education convey equally powerful messages about the nature of society and the possibilities and limitations of particular directions for improving the quality of the nation's teachers. A wasteland, a decoupled train, and a broken system hold out very little hope for improvement through fortification or even restructuring. And a policy system based on fairy dust and magic has no corporeity, no connection with reality, and no chance. Instead, these metaphors are intended to conjure hopeless situations that can be remedied only by pursuing radically different directions, a conclusion that neatly paves the way for the policy recommendations of their architects. Understanding the rhetoric of reform, then, is central to deconstructing the politics of teacher education.

THE CURSE OF COMPLEXITY

The second aspect of the politics of teacher education, which I refer to as "the curse of complexity," is quite different from the first. Here I use not Stone's (1997) theory of political reasoning as I did above but instead, Gary Trudeau's (2003) well-known "Doonesbury" political comic strip. Regular readers of "Doonesbury" are familiar with the two radio journalists who are partners and often appear together in the comic strip—the mustached, flannel-shirted liberal and the clean-shaven, bow-tied conservative.

Like most of Trudeau's comics, the one I refer to here has virtually no action, just dialogue between the characters:

FRAME 1

[Coming from the TV]: Fox news! We report, YOU decide!

Liberal Radio Journalist [musing aloud]: That HAS to be the most cynical slogan in the history of journalism!

FRAME 2

Conservative Radio Journalist [to liberal's back]: Drives you crazy, doesn't it? You know why? Because you liberals are hung up on fairness! You actually TRY to respect all points of view!

FRAME 3

Conservative Radio Journalist [continuing]:   But conservatives feel no need whatsoever to consider other views. We know we're right, so why bother?

FRAME 4

Conservative Radio Journalist [continuing]:   Because we have no tradition of tolerance, we're unencumbered by doubt! So we roll you guys EVERY time!

FRAME 5

[The two journalists gaze directly at one another; the liberal looks thoughtful.]

FRAME 6

Liberal Radio Journalist: Actually, you make a good point . . .

Conservative Radio Journalist: SEE! Only a LOSER would admit that! (Trudeau, 2003, p. D11)

This cartoon gets at the crux of the curse of complexity—the tradition in teacher education (and in much of progressive educational scholarship) of trying to account for diverse viewpoints, subtle nuances, uncertainties, and the multiple facets involved in unraveling the relationships between and among teacher preparation and teaching, learning, schooling, and contexts. The curse is particularly vexing when many of the critics of university-based teacher education feel no such need to acknowledge uncertainty and complexity and, in fact, are quite ready to provide uncomplicated statements about how to solve simultaneously—through "rational" and "commonsense" approaches—the many problems related to teacher recruitment, preparation, and retention.

The concept of "teacher quality," a critical issue in debates about teacher education, works as a good illustration of the curse of complexity. Nationwide, there is an emerging consensus that teacher quality makes a significant difference in schoolchildren's learning and in overall school effectiveness. There is no such consensus, however, about how to define teacher quality and as the following two definitions suggest, multiple ways of thinking about this have been suggested.

Based on two decades of research on the impact of school inputs on students' achievement, economist Eric Hanushek (2002) defined teacher quality this way:

> This discussion begins with some evidence about the importance of teacher quality and moves to ideas about how the quality of teachers can be improved. Central to all of the discussion is the relationship between incentives and accountability. In simplest terms, if the objective is to improve student performance, student performance should be the focal point of policy. . . . I use a simple definition of teacher quality: *good teachers are ones who get large gains in student achievement for their classes; bad teachers are just the opposite* [italics added]. (pp. 2-3)

Hanushek defined and operationalized teacher quality in terms of pupil performance, period. From this perspective, the point is to identify major differences in student achievement gains that are linked to teachers and then suggest implications regarding incentives programs, school accountability systems, and policies regarding the placement of teachers and students. Throughout the chapter from which the above excerpt is drawn, titled only "Teacher Quality," Hanushek was crystal clear and consistent. Although he referred to complex econometric analyses, his point was straightforward and simple: teacher quality is test score gains; to improve gain scores, public policy and school incentives should be geared to test scores, not school inputs. The chapter concluded with a concise summary consisting of five declarative points.

In contrast, the definition of teacher quality posited by Gary Fenstermacher and Virginia Richardson (2005)—philosopher and teacher educator, respectively—is not at all straight forward. They began an article titled "On Making Determinations of Quality in Teaching" with these words: "What is quality teaching? Would we recognize it if we saw it? These modest questions hold a host of complexities" (p. 186). Five pages later (and only after first clarifying the prior notion of teaching itself), Fenstermacher and Richardson offered this definition of teacher quality:

> Quality teaching, we argue here, consists of both good and successful teaching. By *good* teaching, we mean that the content taught accords with disciplinary standards of adequacy and completeness, and that the methods employed are age appropriate, morally defensible, and undertaken with the intention of enhancing the learner's competence with respect to the content studied (a separate section on the notion of good teaching is just ahead.) By *successful* teaching we mean that the learner actually acquires, to some reasonable and acceptable level of proficiency, what the teacher is engaged in teaching. As we have just noted, however, learning is more likely to occur when good teaching is joined with the other three conditions (willingness and effort, social surround, and opportunity). Thus for the teacher to be successful—that is, to bring about learning—and do so in a manner that accords with standards for good teaching, the additional three conditions for learning should be in place. When they are, then all conditions for quality teaching have been met. (p. 191)

Fenstermacher and Richardson conceptualized teacher quality in ways that are complex, subtly nuanced, and qualified. Drawing on an array of conceptual and empirical work, they raised questions, pointed to differences in definitions of learning, and sorted out the psychological, logical, and moral aspects of teaching. No one would ever describe their definition of quality teaching as simple or straightforward.

Readers should note that from my own perspective as teacher education scholar and practitioner, I reject Hanushek's (2002) definition for many of the same reasons Fenstermacher and Richardson (2005) do, and I agree with a great deal of what they suggest about both conceptualizing teacher quality and considering its implications for policy. The point of this illustration, however, is not which of these two definitions of teacher quality is better or whether either one of them is right. The point is that the first is simple, linear, and causal, whereas the second is complex, nuanced, and contingent. Political debates about teacher education are to a great extent enacted in pithy face-to-face debates, sound bites, bold-printed newspaper headlines, and policy briefs with pie charts, bar graphs, and five or fewer bulleted points. In these arenas, to paraphrase the conservative radio journalist in Trudeau's (2003) comic strip, "simple, linear, and causal" rolls "complex, nuanced, and contingent" every time. In these arenas—where the politics of teacher education are played out—the necessity of acknowledging and capturing complexity may indeed be a curse with which the teacher education community will have to continue to struggle.

Quoting Plutarch, Stone (1997) pointed out that politics is an ever-changing and never-ending aspect of human societies:

> They are wrong who think that politics is like an ocean voyage or a military campaign, something to be done with some end in view, or something which levels off as soon as that end is reached. It is not a public chore, to be got over with; it is a way of life. (p. 34)

There is no question that politics has become a way of life in teacher education. The question is how we will live that political life. This includes whether we will be engaged in framing the questions that matter in the political arenas where they are debated and decided or whether we will allow others to frame the questions—and the answers—for us. This special issue of the journal takes on many of these important issues and suggests a number of ways that we need to be engaged in the politics of teacher education.

REFERENCES

Abell Foundation. (2001, November). *Teacher certification reconsidered: Stumbling for quality: A rejoinder*. Retrieved from http://www.abell.org

Ballou, D., & Podgursky, M. (1999). Teacher training and licensure: A layman's guide. In M. Kanstoroom & C. Finn (Eds.), *Better teachers, better schools* (pp. 31-82). Washington, DC: Thomas Fordham Foundation.

Bestor, A. (1953). *Educational wastelands: The retreat from learning in our public schools*. Urbana: University of Illinois Press.

Cochran-Smith, M., & Fries, K. (2001). Sticks, stones, and ideology: The discourse of teacher education. *Educational Researcher, 30*(8), 3-15.

Earley, P. (2000). Finding the culprit: Federal policy and teacher education. *Educational Policy, 14*(1), 25-39.

Fenstermacher, G., & Richardson, V. (2005). On making determinations of quality in teaching. *Teachers College Record, 107*(1), 186-213.

Goodlad, J. (1990). *Teachers for our nation's schools*. San Francisco: Jossey-Bass.

Hanushek, E. (2002). Teacher quality. In L. Izumi & W. Evers (Eds.), *Teacher quality* (pp. 1-12). Palo Alto, CA: Hoover Institution.

Hess, F. (2001a). *Tear down this wall: The case for a radical overhaul of teacher certification*. Washington, DC: Progressive Policy Institute.

Hess, F. (2001b). The work ahead. *Education Next*. Retrieved March 30, 2001, from http://www.educationnext.org/20014/7hess.html

Lakoff, G. (2002). *Moral politics: How liberals and conservatives think*. Chicago: University of Chicago Press.

Lakoff, G., & Johnson, M. (1980). *Metaphors we live by*. Chicago: University of Chicago Press.

National Commission on Teaching & America's Future. (1996). *What matters most: Teaching for America's future*. New York: Teachers College, Columbia University.

Ross, W. (2004). Negotiating the politics of citizenship education. *Political Science and Politics, XXXVII*(2), 249-251.

Stone, D. (1997). *The policy paradox: The art of political decision making*. New York: Norton.

Sykes, G. (1999). Teacher and student learning: Strengthening their connection. In L. Darling-Hammond & G. Sykes (Eds.), *Teaching as the learning profession: Handbook of policy and practice* (pp. 151-179). San Francisco: Jossey-Bass.

Trudeau, G. B. (2003, February 14). Doonesbury. *Boston Globe*, p. D11.

U.S. Department of Education. (2002). *Meeting the highly qualified teachers challenge: The secretary's annual report on teacher quality*. Washington, DC: Author.

Westheimer, J. (2004). The politics of civic education. *Political Science and Politics, XXXVII*(2), 231-234.

Westheimer, J., & Kahne, J. (2004). Educating the "good citizen": Political choices and pedagogical goals. *Political Science and Politics, XXXVII*(2), 241-247.

Whitehurst, G. (2002, March). *Scientifically based research on teacher quality: Research on teacher preparation and professional development*. Paper presented at the White House Conference on Preparing Tomorrow's Teachers, Washington, D.C.

27 *Studying Teacher Education*

What We Know and Need to Know

The most recent of the new teacher education reports is *Studying Teacher Education: The Report of the AERA Panel on Teacher Education* (Cochran-Smith & Zeichner, 2005), which reviews existing research and calls for a new research agenda. This editorial comments on the report from three perspectives: the emerging research in the field, the preparation of professionals in other professions, and the conclusions of other recent teacher education reports.[1]

STUDYING TEACHER EDUCATION[2]

The work of the American Educational Research Association (AERA) Panel on Research and Teacher Education began at a time when many conflicting claims were being made about what the research said about teacher education. The panel was charged with two tasks: (a) to present an even-handed, critical analysis of the weight of the empirical evidence about the impact of policy and practice in preservice teacher education in the United States and (b) to recommend a research agenda that acknowledged strengths and shortcomings of the extant research and that built on promising lines to move the field forward. Throughout its work, the panel took seriously its charge to produce a synthesis that was not beholden to any reform agenda and did not advocate for or against any particular political position.

SOURCE: *Journal of Teacher Education*, Vol. 56, No. 4, September/October 2005, pp. 301-306.

WORKING ASSUMPTIONS AND KEY QUESTIONS

The work of the panel is based on four assumptions. We assumed complexity and variation, rather than uniformity, across collegiate programs and alternate providers as well as in the language used to describe them. Thus, we focused primarily on components rather than on program types. Second, the panel assumed that many empirical approaches are needed in the study of teacher education, including experimental and correlational research but also including a variety of qualitative approaches. Thus, the panel worked from the assumption that pupils' learning, especially when defined solely by test scores, is a necessary but not sufficient way to conceptualize the outcomes of teacher preparation; we therefore considered a variety of outcomes. Finally, the panel assumed that there is a loose coupling among research, practice, and policy, which means that teacher preparation policies and practices can be profoundly influenced but never determined solely by empirical evidence.

Working from these assumptions, the panel developed three framing chapters and nine reviews of empirical research on (a) the demographic characteristics of the entering teaching force, (b) relationships between demographic characteristics and quality, (c) the outcomes of coursework in the arts and sciences and foundations of education, (d) the outcomes of methods courses and fieldwork, (e) the outcomes of various teacher education pedagogies, (f) the outcomes of preparing teachers to work with diverse populations, (g) the outcomes of preparing teachers to work with students with special needs, (h) the outcomes of accountability processes, and (i) the outcomes of teacher preparation program types. For each area, the panel analyzed the findings, strengths, and weaknesses of the research and also identified needed research topics and methods.

FINDINGS AND RECOMMENDED RESEARCH AGENDA

Just a few highlights of the panel's findings and recommendations are noted here. The panel found that despite growth in alternate routes, most teachers are still prepared in undergraduate programs in public colleges and universities with more majoring in arts and sciences subjects than ever before. College graduates in secondary teacher education have SAT or ACT scores comparable to those of other college graduates, although elementary teachers have slightly lower scores. The research comparing the impact of different types of teacher education programs and pathways (4-year to 5-year programs, traditional-alternate routes) does not point to the superiority of any one path. However, across the research, there is evidence that certain program components and characteristics are related to teacher quality and pupils' achievement, such as consistent vision, strong collaborations between universities and schools, certain course work and school/community fieldwork, and effective use of certain teacher education strategies. There is more research about teacher preparation in mathematics than in other areas, with the evidence favoring certification and candidates' study of mathematics. There is little research on the impact of preparing teachers for diverse populations or on teacher education's major accountability processes—teacher testing, accreditation, and certification.

The panel recommends an extensive new research agenda that expands the concept of student achievement beyond test scores and that examines how teacher quality and demographic variables interact to influence student learning. In particular, we need more and better research on the outcomes of teacher education, including research that uncouples the impact of preparation from that of teachers' entering characteristics. We need research that explores the interrelationships of teacher education strategies and arrangements, what teacher candidates actually learn, how they use what they learn in schools and classrooms, and what and how much their students learn. We need to know how these relationships vary within differing school and accountability contexts and conditions. In addition, we need research on the outcomes of preparing teachers in subject areas and grade levels besides secondary mathematics as well as research on preparing teachers for diverse populations, English-language learners, and students with special needs. We need research on the effectiveness of the teacher education accountability mechanisms that are in place in nearly every state. We also need research on the impact on students' achievement of teacher retention and distribution patterns, low numbers of minority teachers, and differing pathways into teaching.

To accomplish this ambitious agenda, the panel calls for investments in long-term and sustained research on teacher preparation, quality, and career effects. This requires better data collection and analysis tools for studying outcomes and consistent use of these tools across individual studies. This, in turn, requires consistent definitions of terms, common outcomes measures, common research instruments for measuring learning and performance, and development of reliable data sets and resources, including better coordination of the data that already exist as a result of institutional, state, and national reviews of individual programs. Especially important is the development of major programs of research in teacher education, which are driven by theory and where researchers can build on prior studies and accumulated knowledge in particular areas over time. Finally, the panel recommends more cross-disciplinary and multiple methods research as well as cross-institutional and longitudinal studies.

SO WHAT? NOW WHAT? COMPARED TO WHAT?

As this editorial went to press, the AERA panel report was receiving a fair amount of attention in the education media and the profession. Below, I suggest three ways to consider the report within a larger context.

Researching Outcomes in Teacher Education

The report of the AERA panel is not the first review of the literature to call for more research on teacher education, especially on its outcomes, and to argue that we need the tools and the infrastructure to do so. Fifteen years ago, Grant and Secada (1990) argued that the major need in teacher education research was "more information about the scope of effective educational practice and the combinations of practice that result in optimal outcomes" (p. 413). Along the same lines, all of the recent syntheses of teacher education research have called for more and better research, and the federal government has explicitly recommended causal research in this area.

So why do we not already have this research? One reason is certainly the historical marginalization and underfunding of research related to teacher education in general. Another is the heavy research emphasis from the mid-1980s to the early 2000s on teachers' knowledge and beliefs, thinking, and learning in communities (Cochran-Smith & Fries, 2005), which tended to overshadow other questions. But a third reason is that rigorous outcomes research in teacher education (and in many other complex enterprises) is difficult and expensive to do. To get from teacher education to impact on pupils' learning requires a chain of evidence with several critical links: empirical evidence demonstrating the link between teacher preparation programs and teacher candidates' learning, empirical evidence demonstrating the link between teacher candidates' learning and their practices in actual classrooms, and empirical evidence demonstrating the link between graduates' practices and what and how much their pupils learn. Individually, each of these links is complex and challenging to estimate. When they are combined, the challenges are multiplied: There are often substantial time lags between the teacher preparation period and the eventual measures of pupils' achievement or other outcomes; there are many confounding and intervening variables (which themselves are difficult to measure) that influence what teachers are able to do and what their pupils learn; and the sites where candidates complete fieldwork and eventually teach are quite different from one another in context, school culture, resources, students, and communities.

Outcomes research is not impossible, but it requires resources and the research capacity to pose and untangle very complex issues. Researchers from different fields have begun to work together on these. For example, as part of the Teacher Quality Project in Ohio, researchers from measurement, psychology, literacy, and teacher education are using both value-added assessment and qualitative studies to try to sort out the relationships of variations in teacher preparation, classroom discourse and instructional practices, and pupils' learning. Labor market economists, teacher educators, and policy analysts have teamed up to work on the New York City Pathways project, which is examining teachers' entry paths, knowledge and skill, and outcomes. Louisiana's Teacher Quality Initiative is measuring pupils' growth in achievement and linking that to information about where and how candidates were prepared. In addition, in a number of the universities that are part of the Carnegie Corporation's Teachers for a New Era project, researchers from many education, social and natural sciences, and humanities fields are working together on new ways to assess the impact of teacher education and to use that information for program improvement.

These projects have begun to demonstrate that the field has the conceptual and methodological capacity to pose complex questions and to carry out cross-disciplinary research that relies on sophisticated research designs and analyses to get at impact. Despite these and other examples of research in progress, however, the issue of whether adequate resources will be available to sustain the development of rich programs of research on teacher preparation and quality is entirely open to question.

Comparing Teacher Education to Preparation in Other Professions

The panel's report makes it clear that we do not have empirical evidence demonstrating the positive impact of many of the policies that currently govern teacher education (e.g., teacher testing and accreditation) or of the curricular and instructional practices that are common in teacher education programs across institutions (e.g., requiring courses in education foundations or using journaling as a way for teacher candidates to track and reflect on their developing practices). Likewise, the report reveals that there is not a clear empirical mandate for many of the reforms that are being advocated and/or implemented in state and national initiatives (e.g., moving teacher preparation outside of colleges and universities through the development of alternate routes and pathways into teaching or, along entirely different lines, improving collegiate teacher preparation through closer collaboration between education and arts and sciences faculty). Although there are extensive and, in some cases, persuasive rationales for these practices and reform policies, which are based on politics, on "common sense," or on professional consensus, they are not supported by empirical evidence about their efficacy.

At first glance, this seems to suggest that as a profession, teacher education is in sorry shape, operating from tradition and from normative positions rather than from solid research. But closer analysis reveals that compared with the preparation of professionals in other fields, teacher preparation may actually be at the forefront. A new report from the Finance Project, *Preparing and Training Professionals: Comparing Education to Six Other Fields* (Neville, Sherman, & Cohen, 2005), compares the preparation of professionals in education with that of professionals in law, accounting, architecture, nursing, firefighting, and law enforcement. The report is worth a thorough read because it points out many differences and some similarities between teacher education and the preparation of professionals in other fields. But the final point in its executive summary is most relevant here:

Faced with great pressure to improve student achievement, districts and policymakers demand evidence that investments in professional development will pay off in better teachers and student performance. No field in this study systematically assesses the effect of its training programs on professional performance. (p. 5)

This last sentence is worth repeating: "No field in this study systematically assesses the effect of its training programs on professional performance." Because critics so often compare teacher education to other professions—and find it wanting—it is imperative to note that other professions do *not* operate according to standards and policies that have been verified by systematic evidence of their impact on professional performance.

Another of the major conclusions of the Finance Project is that in comparison with other professions, teacher education lacks consistent national standards for program accreditation and approval, entry examinations, in-service training, and induction programs. The report suggests that education's continued "grappl[ing] with a lack of consensus" (p. 3) about effective teaching and preparation makes it difficult to ensure that all teachers meet particular levels of competency (a position, by the way, that advocates of the professionalization agenda for teacher education have long endorsed). But there is a rock-and-a-hard-place situation here for teacher education. On one hand, teacher education is exhorted to be more like other "grown-up" professions by relying on consistent standards for the preparation of new professionals that reflect consensus in the field. This is the rock. At the same time, however—and this is the hard place—as the Finance Project report makes clear, the policies and practices of other professions are not based on evidence of their effectiveness for professional performance. Thus, teacher education is caught—and squeezed—between two demands that are, at least right now, mutually exclusive.

Reading the AERA Report in Light of Media Response and Other Reports

Since its release at a press conference at the National Press Club in mid-June of 2005, there have been articles about the AERA panel report in most of the major education news outlets and on the Web sites or updates of teacher education–related organizations, such as the National Commission on Teaching and America's Future and the National Council for Accreditation of Teacher Education. Not surprisingly, the news media—at least in their headlines—have tended to focus on the lack of definitive research in teacher education. For example, *Inside Higher Education*'s (Jaschik, 2005) headline was "What They Don't Know," which although ambiguous about who actually does not know something (teacher educators? policymakers? reformers?), critics of teacher education may use headlines like these (and the report itself) to undermine the profession. A different spin on this, however, would be to note, as I have above, that teacher education is ahead of other professions in taking a hard look at the research in its own field and beginning to develop the data collection and analysis tools to track the effectiveness of its preparation programs on the performance of professionals and their clients.

The *Education Week* story (Viadero, 2005) located the panel's report in the context of the recent spate of reports about teacher education and raised some interesting questions about how the panel's conclusions relate to others. Here, I consider two recent reports, each of which has been discussed in previous *JTE* editorials: *Preparing Teachers for a Changing World* (Darling-Hammond & Bransford, 2005), the report of the Committee on Teacher Education of the National Academy of Education (NAE), and *Teaching at Risk* (Teaching Commission, 2004), the report of the Teaching Commission, chaired by former IBM CEO Louis Gerstner.

The NAE report focuses on the knowledge bases for teaching and is intended to make research-grounded recommendations about what core knowledge for beginning teachers should be included in teacher education curricula. The NAE report draws on research, to be sure, but it asks questions that are quite different from those asked by the AERA panel.

The key questions of the NAE committee are in part normative— What are the domains in which all teachers should have knowledge?— and in part research based—What do we know about these domains? The report uses four kinds of research evidence as the grounding for its curricular recommendations: research on how people learn and develop; research on how specific teaching practices influence pupils' learning; research on the relationships among preparation, practices, and pupils' learning; and research on what and how prospective teachers learn in particular contexts. The NAE report does not claim that there is definitive research evidence about the impact of including the topics they recommend for the teacher education curriculum on desired outcomes. Rather, their recommendations are informed by basic teaching and learning research, by research about teachers' professional development, and by professional consensus about what knowledge for teaching is of most worth. As the Finance Project's report so clearly indicates, this is entirely consistent with the way the professional curriculum is established in other professions. The AERA panel report, on the other hand, is specifically intended to assess the weight of the evidence about the impact of teacher education policies and practices on professional performance, pupils' learning, and other important school outcomes.

The report of the Teaching Commission, which is a call for action to improve the quality of teaching in the United States, is quite different from either the NAE or the AERA reports. The Teaching Commission report is a political document intended to create a sense of national urgency about the need to improve teaching. The Teaching Commission pushes four major reforms, the second and third of which are directly related to teacher preparation: (a) up teachers' salaries with bonuses for teachers who increase pupils' test scores or work in shortage areas, (b) hold college and universities accountable for improving teacher preparation through tougher admissions and ensuring that teachers who deliver have knowledge of scientifically based practices, (c) revamp licensure and certification with more tests and alternate routes, and (d) increase autonomy for school principals to hire teachers who deliver and fire teachers who fail to deliver by raising pupils' test scores. The Teaching Commission draws on research in only the loosest way, which is selective and political. It uses sidebar references to selected studies and initiatives that support the policy positions taken in the report. Of course, this is entirely different from the task of the AERA panel, which was to examine the full range of evidence about the impact of teacher education policies and practices and to draw conclusions about the weight of the evidence, not governed by an a priori professional position or in support of, or opposition to, an existing policy position.

During the past 10 years, there have been scores of new reports, surveys, research syntheses, policy reviews, and empirical studies about teacher preparation. Blue-ribbon panels have weighed in about the future of teacher preparation, and foundations and professional groups have launched new initiatives. Notwithstanding considerable debate about the meanings of teacher quality and highly qualified teachers, it is no exaggeration to say that the national focus on these issues rivals that of any previous period. During the past 10 years, there have also been many competing claims about the relationships that do and do not exist among teacher qualifications; about the policies and practices governing teacher preparation, teaching performance, and educational outcomes; and about the research or evidentiary bases for these claims. Although it will clearly not be the last of the teacher education reports, the contribution of the AERA panel is its attempt to speak to some of the important issues in the field by carefully weighing the empirical evidence and by crafting a new research agenda to generate the information we need.

NOTES

1. Clearly, this editorial reflects a biased perspective on the work of the American Educational Research Association (AERA) panel, which I cochaired with Ken Zeichner and whose report I coedited. However, the book is highly appropriate for the *JTE* audience and is consistent with many previous editorials about new reports and initiatives.

2. This description of the AERA project draws directly on the report's executive summary, its three framing chapters, and its press-kit materials prepared when the book was released. In addition to its cochairs, panel members include Renee Clift, Mary Dilworth, Dan Fallon, Bob Floden, Susan Fuhrman, Drew Gitomer, Pam Grossman, Etta Hollins, Jackie Jordan Irvine, Ann Lieberman, Marleen Pugach, Ana Maria Villegas, Suzanne Wilson, and Karen Zumwalt. Kim Fries served as project manager.

REFERENCES

Cochran-Smith, M., & Fries, K. (2005). Paradigms and politics: Researching teacher education in changing times. In M. Cochran-Smith & K. Zeichner (Eds.), *Studying teacher education: The report of the AERA panel on research and teacher education*. Mahwah, NJ: Lawrence Erlbaum.

Cochran-Smith, M., & Zeichner, K. (2005). *Studying teacher education: The report of the AERA panel on research and teacher education*. Mahwah, NJ: Lawrence Erlbaum.

Darling-Hammond, L., & Bransford, J. (Eds.). (2005). *Preparing teachers for a changing world: Report of the Committee on Teacher Education of the National Academy of Education*. San Francisco: Jossey-Bass.

Grant, C., & Secada, W. (1990). Preparing teachers for diversity. In W. R. Houston, M. Haberman, & J. Sikula (Eds.), Handbook of research on teacher education (pp. 403-422). New York: Macmillan.

Jaschik, S. (2005). What they don't know. *Inside Higher Education*, June 21.

Neville, K. S., Sherman, R. H., & Cohen, C. E. (2005). *Preparing and training professionals: Comparing education to six other fields.* New York: Finance Project.

Teaching Commission. (2004). *Teaching at risk: A call to action.* New York: Author.

Viadero, D. (2005). Review panel turns up little evidence to back teacher ed. practices. *Education Week,* June 22.

28 *Teacher Education and the Outcomes Trap*

S ome time ago in this journal and elsewhere (Cochran-Smith, 2000, 2001), I began to write about what I called "the outcomes question in teacher education," by which I meant the ways that the effects, results, consequences, and impacts of teacher education were conceptualized and operationalized as well as how, by whom, and for what purposes these were measured and disseminated. My argument then was that how we as a professional community constructed and answered the outcomes question (or how it got constructed for us) would define the field of teacher education over the next several decades, shaping the experiences of a generation of teachers and thus influencing the learning opportunities and life chances of thousands of American schoolchildren.

Perhaps more obvious than prescient, this prediction appears to have been correct. Teacher education in the 2000s is frontally about outcomes, and the language of "results," "consequences," "effectiveness," "impact," "bottom lines," and "evidence" has been stitched into the logic of teacher education so seamlessly that it is now nearly imperceptible. It is now widely assumed that teacher preparation programs and pathways can and ought to be evaluated for programmatic, institutional, accreditation, or regulatory purposes in terms of their outcomes. This editorial makes two points. First, I suggest that the current outcomes focus in teacher education is not an isolated or inexplicable phenomenon but is instead deeply rooted in the history of teacher education and is also part of a larger shift in how we

SOURCE: *Journal of Teacher Education,* Vol. 56, No. 5, November/December 2005, pp. 411-417.

define educational accountability. Second, the editorial agues that the new focus on outcomes—if narrowly defined only or even predominantly in terms of test scores—is a trap for teacher education that ignores the broader purposes of education in a democratic society and inappropriately places the onus for improving schools and schooling on teachers and teacher educators alone.[1]

WHERE DID THE OUTCOMES FOCUS COME FROM?

Prior to the mid-1990s, the emphasis in teacher education was not on outcomes. It was primarily on process—how prospective teachers learned to teach, how their beliefs and attitudes changed over time, what contexts supported their learning, and what kinds of content, pedagogical, and other knowledge they needed. Teacher education assessment focused on what is now retrospectively referred to as "inputs" rather than outcomes—institutional commitment, qualifications of faculty, content and structure of courses and fieldwork experiences, and the alignment of all of these with professional knowledge and standards.

The shift in teacher education from inputs to outcomes was part of a larger sea of change in how we think about educational accountability. Along these lines, Cuban (2004) points out that, contrary to the popular belief that accountability is a relatively new development in education, public schools have, in actuality, never been "*un*accountable." Rather, Cuban argues, definitions of accountability and quality schooling have changed. Prior to and immediately following World War II, what was most important to school boards, administrators, and the public was the efficient use of resources to accommodate all of those going to school. School leaders were accountable for providing equipment, supplies, and facilities. Schools that did so were considered good schools. After the war, however, social, economic, and political changes produced what Cuban calls a "more dramatic" notion of accountability that hinged on results.

The turning point was the passage of the Elementary and Secondary Act (ESEA) of 1965 and the many events, acts, and court cases leading up to or concurrent with it, including *Brown v. Board of Education*, the launching of *Sputnik*, and the Coleman Report (Cuban, 2004). The idea with ESEA was not only to provide funds for improving education but also to attach those funds to new accountability requirements. The reform reports of the 1980s that linked mediocre pupil performance on national and international tests to mediocre economic performance globally spurred new standards and accountability measures in nearly every state, including revised curricula, increased graduation requirements, and new performance standards (Fuhrman, 2001). There were somewhat parallel developments in higher education, which Graham, Lyman, and Trow (1995) refer to as the "increasing clamor to apply quantitative measures of academic outcomes to guarantee educational quality for consumers" (p. 7).

The history of the standards and accountability movement helps to make the point that the shift from inputs to outcomes in teacher education was part of a sea of change in educational accountability writ large rather than an isolated occurrence in one area. With this said, however, it is also important to note that teacher education is currently the only area of professional education (Neville, Sherman, & Cohen, 2005) that is expected to justify its existence by demonstrating direct impact on professional performance and client outcomes.[2]

Undoubtedly, part of the reason teacher education has been singled out in this way is the fact that teaching is a public profession that serves the entire nation, employs a larger number of workers than any other professional field, and involves huge public investment of funds (Ingersoll, 2004). Another reason, however, is its historically low status in the world of professional work and as a field of study within the institutional hierarchy of the university. The fact that teaching has long been "women's work" as well as an initial route into the middle class for members of the working class and for minorities has contributed to its low status (Labaree, 2004; Lagemann, 2000). In addition, as Labaree (2004) points out in his insightful history of education schools, during the early and mid-20th century, normal schools evolved from teacher training institutions into general purpose universities. This boosted their institutional status dramatically while at the same time dramatically decreased the status of teacher education within them. Labaree concludes that, in part, because of teacher education's overall low status, it has historically been an easy target for critics who are unconcerned about what those inside the profession think and thus feel at liberty to make demands and issue critiques that they may not make of higher status professions.

The New Outcomes Focus of Teacher Education

An early indication of the emerging outcomes focus in teacher education was the highly contentious debate of the mid-to-late 1990s and early 2000s about whether collegiate teacher education and state-regulated certification were warranted as broad educational policies. Played out in the pages of academic journals, face-to-face debates, and reports/counterreports from foundations and professional organizations, these debates zeroed in on the impact of teacher education, primarily on pupils' achievement. A well-known example that reflects the emerging outcomes focus was the Abell Foundation's (2001a) report, which challenged teacher certification as educational policy primarily with the claim that there was no solid research demonstrating a positive correlation between teacher preparation/certification and pupil achievement. This conclusion was soundly rejected in a critique by Linda Darling-Hammond (2001) on behalf of the National Commission on Teaching and America's Future, which was followed by multiple rejoinders from the Abell Foundation (2001b). Other well-publicized examples of teacher education's focus on outcomes are the many recent studies comparing the test scores of pupils whose teachers entered teaching through alternate and more traditional routes (e.g., Darling-Hammond, 2001; Decker, Mayer, & Glazerman, 2004; Laczko-Kerr & Berliner, 2002; Raymond, Fletcher, & Luque, 2001), the results of which are mixed and contentious.

In addition to outcomes studies of teacher education as broad educational policy, there are also now a number of state and regional initiatives, such as those in Ohio, New York City, and California, involving the collective efforts of teacher educators and researchers in economics, educational measurement, and other areas to trace the impact of variations in teacher preparation on educational outcomes.[3] In addition, under larger umbrellas such as the National Council for the Accreditation of Teacher Education, the Teacher Education Accreditation Council, and Teachers for a New Era teacher education reform project sponsored by the Carnegie Corporation and other funders, many individual institutions are studying the outcomes of their teacher preparation programs in terms of teacher candidates' knowledge growth, pupils' learning, and teacher retention. Finally, there are state-level projects underway, such as Louisiana's (Noell, 2004) teacher quality initiative, whose fourth stage is designed to evaluate teacher education programs in the state on the basis of the achievement gains of the pupils of teachers who were prepared at different teacher education institutions and with different amounts of experience.

Clearly, there are important philosophical and methodological variations within teacher education's new focus on outcomes, including especially whether test scores are the only outcomes examined or whether other outcomes—such as teacher candidates' knowledge growth or their classroom practices—count as well. There are also differences in what are suggested as the logical or possible implications of focusing on outcomes. These differences notwithstanding, however, the central tenet of the new outcomes approach to teacher education is that the effectiveness of teacher preparation policies, programs, and pathways can and ought to be assessed in terms of outcomes—especially pupils' achievement gains—and that the results of these assessments should be publicly disseminated.

THE OUTCOMES TRAP

There is much about teacher education's new focus on outcomes that is positive and commendable. For example, it is a decidedly positive development that schools of education—and some alternate providers of teacher preparation—are thinking hard about the goals of their programs and inventing new ways to trace the impact all the way to the ultimate destination—the nation's schoolchildren. As noted above, this is virtually unheard of in professional education. Although providers of medical and legal education keep track of their graduates' scores on board certification and bar exams, for example, they generally do not follow their graduates into hospitals and courtrooms, trying to work backward from the number of lives saved to conclusions about particular medical schools or backward from the court cases lost and won to conclusions about particular law schools. In this sense, the work in teacher education on outcomes is groundbreaking in professional education and it may establish what has heretofore been a missing program of research, that is, research that connects what happens in professional preparation to its consequences in classrooms and in the world.

It is also a very positive development that many interdisciplinary groups of researchers are working together on the outcomes question in teacher education. Their projects are inventing new ways to think about outcomes and systematically examining the complex links among variations in teacher preparation programs and pathways, teacher candidates' learning, varying accountability contexts, and pupils' learning. Most of these interdisciplinary efforts involve mixed-method or multiple-method research designs. They work from the idea that pupils' test scores on state assessments are a necessary part of evaluating the outcomes of teacher preparation, but they also make clear that test scores alone are an insufficient way to do so. In addition, at some teacher education institutions, particularly those that prepare teachers for urban schools (e.g., University of California–Los Angeles; Montclair State University; University of Illinois–Chicago; and Boston College), educators are working to conceptualize and measure teaching for equity and social justice as an outcome of teacher preparation in and of itself.

Despite these positive developments, however, the more narrow and reductionist version of the new focus on outcomes—evaluating teacher preparation predominantly on the basis of test scores—may well prevail. And in fact, several of the proposed bills to the reauthorization of the Higher Education Act, which is currently being considered by Congress, called for federal-level evaluation of teacher preparation programs based on the contribution of their graduates to annual increases in pupil achievement.

In an article titled "The Testing Trap," Richard Elmore (2002) argued that No Child Left Behind and its supporting bills and policies were accelerating the accountability movement's focus on test scores only as measures of teachers' and students' performance. Elmore argued that this test-based accountability system had a narrow rather than an expansive view of performance and was utterly uninformed about the relationships and realities of local and state educational capacity, on one hand, and accountability, on the other. He argued that this system was unlikely to increase test scores in low-performing schools and was in fact likely to increase rather than close the gap between high- and low-performing schools and districts.

In teacher education, we are now in danger of being ensnared by "the outcomes trap," which in a nutshell is the working theory that evaluating policies and programs related to teacher education on the basis of test scores will bring about major teacher education reform and ultimately solve the teacher-quality problem. A series of problematic assumptions underlies this theory, which are the springs in the trap: the equating of teacher quality and pupils' learning with test scores, the belief that teachers alone can save the schools, the assumption that the goal of urban teacher preparation is to do no harm, and the belief that providing the nation's workforce is the primary purpose of public education. What makes this a trap is that accepting the premise that teacher education programs and policies ought to be evaluated according to their impact on test scores means implicitly accepting and even bolstering these problematic assumptions, each of which is described below.

The first part of the outcomes trap is equating both pupils' learning and teacher quality with test scores. Increasingly, under the current educational regime, this is the case. This equation is far too simplistic a way to conceptualize the complexities of teaching and learning. Teaching does not simply involve transmitting bits of information that can be tested, and learning is not just receiving information about subject matter. Both are far more complex. In addition, schools and teacher education programs have purposes in addition to pupils' academic learning, including their social and emotional development and their ability to participate in a democratic society. To represent all of the complex aspects involved in teacher quality and pupils' learning in one number derived from increases in achievement test scores is a trap—it reflects impoverished notions of teaching and learning not at all in keeping with research or experience in these areas and ignores broader commitments.

The second part of the outcomes trap is the premise that teachers are *the* critical components in boosting pupils' achievement. Many critics before me (Cohen, 1995; Fullan, 1993) have noted the paradox here—the assumption that teachers are both the most intractable problem educational policymakers must solve (because, it is alleged, it is teachers' meager knowledge and skills that are the cause of the failure of the schools in the first place) and, at the same time, that teachers are the best solution to that problem (because, it is assumed, improved teacher quality is the cure for all that ails the schools). The 2004 report of the Teaching Commission chaired by the former chief executive officer of IBM is particularly straightforward on this point:

Bolstering teacher quality is, of course, not the only challenge we face as we seek to strengthen public education. There are social problems, financial obstacles, and facilities issues, among other concerns. But The Teaching Commission believes that quality teachers are the critical factor in helping young people overcome the damaging effects of poverty, lack of parental guidance, and other challenges. . . . In other words, the effectiveness of any broader education reform . . . is ultimately dependent on the quality of teachers in classrooms. (pp. 14–5)

Teachers (and teacher education programs) alone cannot fix the nation's worst schools and improve the life chances of the most disadvantaged students without simultaneous investments in resources, capacity building, and enhancing teachers' professional growth, not to mention changes in access to housing, health, and jobs. The trap here is that making a statement such as the one I just made gets construed by some critics of teacher education (e.g., Haycock, 2005) as an "excuse" or "apology" for teacher education or as evidence of its low expectations for its own teachers. This construal is completely wrongheaded. Acknowledging that the problems of the nation's schools include, but go far beyond, teachers and that the problems of the nation include, but go far beyond, the schools is not an excuse. It reflects a categorical acceptance of the goal of equal and high-quality education for all students and a flat-out rejection of the outcomes trap—that holding teachers and teacher preparation accountable for everything will fix everything without attention to much larger problems.

The third piece of the outcomes trap relates in particular to efforts to determine which teacher preparation approaches are effective for urban areas. A recent study by Decker et al. (2004), which compared the effect on pupils of Teach for America (TFA) and non-TFA teachers, has been heralded as a methodological breakthrough because it used a randomized field trial and thus met the "gold standard" of today. My critique here is not of the TFA program itself or of the science used to study it but of the question with which it began: "Do TFA teachers improve (or at least not harm) student outcomes relative to what would have happened in their absence?" (Decker et al., 2004, p. xi). As one critique pointed out shortly after the TFA study was released (Southeast Center for Teaching Quality, 2004), it did not ask whether TFA or the control teachers in the regions studied were effective for the students they taught: "If they had, the answer would be, 'no.' Students of both TFA and control group teachers scored very poorly." Rather, the study asked whether having teachers who were not fully prepared and certified did any harm to pupils by making their achievement scores any worse than they would have been anyway, given the reality that high-poverty schools often have to hire poorly educated, uncertified, and unqualified teachers. Decker et al. (2004) were explicit on this point:

> The consistent patterns of positive or zero impacts on test scores across grades, regions, and student subgroups suggests that there is little risk that hiring TFA teachers will reduce achievement, either for the average student or for most subgroups of students. (p. xvi)

The trap here is the premise of costs-benefit studies such as this one. They assume that the goal of policies for high-poverty, hard-to-staff, and minority schools is providing teachers who will do no harm because they cost no more and are "good enough" to maintain or slightly increase existing very low levels of achievement rather than investing in approaches that interrupt the cycle of inadequate resources, low expectations, and poor achievement.

The last piece of the outcomes trap is that it assumes that the primary purpose of public education (and thus teacher education) in our society is to produce the nation's workforce in keeping with the changing demands of a competitive and increasingly global and knowledge-based society. Grubb and Lazerson (2004) refer to education systems "whose purposes are dominated by preparation for economic roles" as "vocationalist" (p. 2), a trend that first emerged at the turn of the 20th century and is now paramount in the 21st century. Although vocationalism has always had both individual goals (e.g., social mobility and/or individual economic advantage) and public goals (e.g., providing an educated workforce and/or meeting the needs of employers), its narrow focus on producing the nation's workforce coupled with excessive attention to the tests used to compare it to other countries has pushed out other traditional goals and purposes of schooling and of teacher education (Cuban, 2004; Michelli & Keiser, 2004). Chief among these is the goal of preparing teachers who know how to prepare future citizens to participate in a democratic society. Amy Gutman (1999) argues that the key to what she calls "deliberative democracy" is democratic education: "Deliberative democracy underscores the importance of publicly supported education that develops the capacity to deliberate among all children as future free and equal citizens" (p. xii). If all free and equal citizens of a society are to have the benefit of a democratic education, all teachers will need to have the knowledge, skills, and dispositions to teach toward the democratic ideal and all teacher preparation programs ought to be measured—at least in part—by their success at producing teachers who teach for democracy. When pupils' test scores and teachers' scores on tests of content knowledge only are the outcomes most heavily emphasized in teacher education, attention to preparing teachers to teach for democratic goals is squeezed out.

CONCLUSION: AVOIDING THE TRAP

As I have noted, there is much about the new outcomes focus of teacher education that is positive and encouraging, but there is also the very real danger that we will evaluate and reform teacher education primarily according to pupil gains on achievement tests, thus implicitly accepting that the goal of teacher preparation (and of the policies governing teacher preparation) is to raise test scores. This is the essence of the outcomes trap. In conclusion, I urge that we rethink outcomes, making the bottom line of teaching and teacher education learning, not outcomes narrowly defined as tests. When teacher education is learning driven, there is a focus on ensuring that all schoolchildren—including those in poor schools—have rich opportunities to learn, not just opportunities to be held accountable to the same high stakes.

As a teacher education community, we need to help change the terms of the debate about the purpose of schooling (and teacher education) in society. Surely, the major purpose is not to produce pupils who can pass tests. As a community, we need to take the lead in challenging the whole doctrine of school outcomes as test scores, which is linked to the idea of producing workers to maintain the dominant place of the United States in the global economy. We certainly want to ensure that schoolchildren develop basic skills as well as depth of knowledge. We certainly want high school graduates to be well-prepared for college and/or meaningful work. But we also need to make civic education a priority goal and social justice an outcome of teacher preparation. From a social justice perspective, the purpose of education needs to be understood not simply as constructing a system where pupils' test scores and wise monetary investments are the bottom lines. Rather, the purpose of education also must be understood as preparing students to engage in satisfying work, function as lifelong learners who can cope with the challenges of a rapidly changing global society, recognize inequities in their everyday contexts, and join with others to challenge them.

My conclusions here should not be construed as a call for restoration of some previous form of teacher education from the "good ole days" or as a call for preservation of the status quo. There is much that needs to be improved about teacher education, there are many existing programs and entry routes that are not sufficient to provide the teachers we need, and there are many new research possibilities on the horizon. Neither restoration nor preservation is the answer. But the teacher education community must work against the emerging reductionist view of teacher education outcomes as test scores and help to change the terms of the debate. This will not be easy but our democracy depends on it.

NOTES

1. Discussion of "the outcomes trap" in teacher education is based on a point made in the American Educational Research Association (AERA) 2005 Presidential Address, "The New Teacher Education: For Better or For Worse?" (Cochran-Smith, 2005a).

2. See the *Journal of Teacher Education* (*JTE*) editorial "Studying Teacher Education," (Cochran-Smith, 2005b), which describes the Neville, Sherman, and Cohen (2005) study of six areas of professional education, pointing out similarities and differences among the fields.

3. A number of these projects will be described in the special double issue of *JTE* on "Evidence, Efficacy, and Effectiveness in Teacher Education" (January/February and March/April 2006). See especially articles by Lasley, Siedentop, and Yinger; Noell and Burns; Pecheone and Chung; Darling-Hammond; Boyd, Grossman, Lankford, Loeb, Michelli, and Wyckoff; and Schalock, Schalock, and Ayres.

REFERENCES

Abell Foundation. (2001a, October). *Teacher certification reconsidered: Stumbling for quality*. Retrieved from http:// www.abell.org.

Abell Foundation. (2001b, November). *Teacher certification reconsidered: Stumbling for quality. A rejoinder*. Retrieved from http://www.abell.org.

Cochran-Smith, M. (2000). The questions that drive reform. *Journal of Teacher Education, 51*(5), 331-333.

Cochran-Smith, M. (2001). Constructing outcomes in teacher education: Policy, practice and pitfalls. *Educational Policy Analysis Archives, 9*(11). Retrieved from http://epaa.asu.edu/epaa/vol9.html/.

Cochran-Smith, M. (2005a). The new teacher education: For better or for worse? *Educational Researcher, 34*(6), 3-17.

Cochran-Smith, M. (2005b). Studying teacher education: What we know and need to know. *Journal of Teacher Education, 56,* 301-306.

Cohen, D. (1995). What is the system in systemic reform? *Educational Researcher, 24*(9), 11-17, 31.

Cuban, L. (2004). Looking through the rearview mirror at school accountability. In K. Sirotnik (Ed.), *Holding accountability accountable* (pp. 18-34). New York: Teachers College Press.

Darling-Hammond, L. (2001). The research and rhetoric on teacher certification: A response to "teacher certification reconsidered." Retrieved October 2001 from http://www.nctaf.org.

Decker, P., Mayer, D., & Glazerman, S. (2004). *The effects of Teach for America on students: Findings from a national evaluation* (MPR Reference No. 8792-750). Princeton, NJ: Mathematica Policy Research, Inc.

Elmore, R. (2002). The testing trap. *Harvard Magazine, 105*(1), 35.

Fuhrman, S. (Ed.). (2001). *From the capitol to the classroom: Standards-based reform in the states, 100th yearbook of the national society for the scientific study of education.* Chicago: University of Chicago Press.

Fullan, M. (1993). *Change forces: Probing the depths of educational reform.* London: Falmer.

Graham, P., Lyman, R., & Trow, M. (1995). *Accountability of colleges and universities: An essay.* New York: Columbia University.

Grubb, W. N., & Lazerson, M. (2004). *The education gospel: The economic power of schooling.* Cambridge, MA: Harvard University Press.

Gutman, A. (1999). *Democratic education (with a new preface and epilogue).* Princeton, NJ: Princeton University Press.

Haycock, K. (2005). Choosing to matter more. *Journal of Teacher Education, 56*(2), pp. 256-265.

Ingersoll, R. (2004). Four myths about America's teacher quality problem. In M. Smylie & D. Miretzky (Eds.), *Developing the teacher workforce: The 103rd yearbook of the national society for the study of education* (pp. 1-33). Chicago: University of Chicago Press.

Labaree, D. (2004). *The trouble with ed schools.* New Haven, CT: Yale University Press.

Laczko-Kerr, I., & Berliner, D. C. (2002). The effectiveness of "Teach for America" and other under-certified teachers on student academic achievement: A case of harmful public policy. *Education Policy Analysis*

Archives, 8. Retrieved September 23, 2002, from http://epaa.asu.edu/epasa/v10n37/.

Lagemann, E. (2000). *An elusive science: The troubling history of education research*. Chicago: University of Chicago Press.

Michelli, N., & Keiser, D. (Eds.). (2004). *Teacher education for diversity and social justice*. New York: Routledge/Taylor & Francis.

Neville, K. S., Sherman, R. H., & Cohen, C. E. (2005). *Preparing and training professionals: Comparing education to six other fields*. New York: The Finance Project.

Noell, G. (2004, August 24). *Assessing teacher preparation program effectiveness: A pilot examination of value added approaches*. Baton Rouge: Center for Innovative Teaching and Learning, Louisiana State University.

Raymond, M., Fletcher, S. H., & Luque, J. (2001). *Teach for America: An evaluation of teacher differences and student outcomes in Houston, Texas*. Washington, DC: Thomas B. Fordham Foundation.

Southeast Center for Teaching Quality. (2004). *Teach for America study reports some gains but obscures failed teaching policies in urban schools*. Retrieved June 11, 2004, from http://www.teachingquality.org/resources/html/TFA_Report.htm.

The Teaching Commission. (2004). *Teaching at risk: A call to action*. New York: Author.

29 Taking Stock in 2006: Evidence, Evidence Everywhere

In her history of education research, Ellen Lagemann (2000) suggested that during the 20th century, education had a "romance with quantification" (p. ix), which was reflected in its penchant for counting, measuring, and calculating and in order to resemble the hard sciences as closely as possible. In this editorial, I argue that while education has in no way broken off its love affair with quantification, its current paramour is evidence, and the affair is hot and heavy in teacher education. In fact, it is not an exaggeration to say that evidence—or at least talk about evidence—is now everywhere in teacher education research, policy, and practice. This editorial describes and critiques the current focus on evidence, making the argument that while it has great potential to improve teacher education, it also has troubling aspects that need to be acknowledged and debated.[1]

EVIDENCE EVERYWHERE

Teacher education's current preoccupation with evidence is consistent with the way the standards movement has evolved and with the trend toward evidence-based practice in education writ large. It is important to note, however, that although there have long been several lines of research related to the effects of teacher education

SOURCE: *Journal of Teacher Education,* Vol. 57, No. 1, January/February 2006, pp. 6-12.

(Cochran-Smith & Fries, 2005: Kennedy, 1999), the current intense focus on evidence in teacher education practice and policy is a significant departure from far and recent past. The major reforms of the 1980s and early 1990s, for example, demanded that teacher education be more coherent and intellectually rigorous (e.g., Carnegie Forum on Education and the Economy, 1986; Holmes Group, 1986), while reformers like John Goodlad (1990) argued that school renewal and teacher education reform should proceed simultaneously based on moral purposes. During this same time period, revised National Council for the Accreditation of Teacher Education (NCATE) accreditation standards pushed teacher education to concentrate on the professional knowledge base and be explicit about the conceptual frameworks that guided programs (Christensen, 1996). None of these reforms had much to do with evidence.

Currently, however, in debates about large-scale teacher education policies and in the federal and state regulations related to individual teacher preparation programs and pathways, evidence is front and center. For example, advocates of differing teacher education pathways often support their positions by citing empirical evidence that they claim demonstrates a positive relationship between particular pathways and school outcomes and, conversely, reject the positions of their opponents on the grounds that the opponent's evidence is flimsy or faulty (e.g., Ballou & Podgursky, 2000; Darling-Hammond, 2000). Along similar lines, critics of collegiate teacher education and state certification often make their arguments on the basis of the claim that there is an absence of evidence about their efficacy (e.g., Abell Foundation, 2001; Hess, 2001), and thus conclude that new approaches are needed.

The Title II teacher quality reporting requirements that went into effect in 1998 following the reauthorization of the Higher Education Act are perhaps the most striking example of the current emphasis on evidence in teacher education. Title II requires that all states provide annual evidence to the federal government about the quality of teacher preparation, which in turn depends on institutions providing annual evidence to the state about the qualifications (especially scores on state teacher tests) of every candidate recommended for certification. The fourth annual report to Congress on teacher quality (2005)—the first issued by Secretary of Education Margaret Spellings—states that the collection of "objective data" from every state regarding teacher preparation and certification has made possible the "first national systematic and comprehensive data resource about teacher preparation" (p. 2), which is intended to ensure "world class" (p. 1) teachers who can keep the nation "competitive" (p. xii).

The report concludes that the overall picture of teacher preparation in the nation shows "mixed results" (p. xi) with some, but not enough, improvement. The report lauds, for example, the fact that all but one state now have quality standards regulating all teaching fields and grade levels and 85% of states now have alternate pathways into teaching. In addition, the report notes that 39 states and outlying areas now require a content-specific bachelor's degree for teacher certification, although, on the other hand, 15 still have no content-specific bachelor's requirement. The report criticizes the fact that although much attention has been given to the typical 95% pass rate on state teacher tests, states have still not raised the minimum passing score. The secretary's report makes it clear that all teachers must know how to use multiple kinds of data and evidence in order to make instructional decisions in their classrooms, must know how to teach diverse learners, and must be knowledgeable about and able to use research-based techniques in the classroom. The report is crystal clear about the role of teacher education: "Teacher preparation programs have a responsibility to ensure their students are skilled in applying the latest proven techniques for instruction in their subject matter area" (p. 11).

In addition to the focus on research, evidence, and data-driven practice that is clear in governmental regulations regarding teacher preparation, there is also a strong emphasis in the profession on gathering local empirical evidence about what and how much prospective teachers learn in their course and fieldwork experiences, where and how long they teach, and what and how much their pupils learn. NCATE's accreditation process, for example, now requires institutions to provide "compelling evidence" (Williams et al., 2003, p. xiii) of teacher candidates' content knowledge and performance and to have in place data-driven assessment systems. The Teacher Education Accreditation Council (TEAC) requires "valid and reliable evidence" that would be credible to "disinterested experts" in support of the professional claims a faculty wishes to make about its teacher graduates (Murray, 2005). Teachers for a New Era, a major teacher education initiative funded primarily by the Carnegie Corporation, has three design principles, the first of which is "respect for evidence" (cf. Fallon, 2006). This means building into the teacher education program a process wherein research guides curriculum and arrangements, evidence is continuously fed back into decisions, and effectiveness is measured in large part by evidence of students' learning. Also at the national level is the new initiative of the American Association of State Colleges and Universities (the former normal schools) titled "Credible and Persuasive Evidence," which features a national survey of how colleges and universities are assembling evidence as well as discussions with policymakers and others about what forms of evidence actually are convincing (cf. Wineburg, 2006).

As these and other examples demonstrate, at many colleges and universities across the country related to teacher preparation, more and more of the people engaged in teacher preparation are also engaged in assembling evidence about their practices and their graduates. This is partly to satisfy their evaluators, but it is also to see whether programs are measuring up to their own standards for excellent teaching. Examples include Montclair State University's data base system tracking the progress of every teacher candidate toward meeting every NCATE standard and Michigan State University's systematic documentation of growth in teacher candidates' pedagogical and content knowledge as a result of coursework. Similarly, faculty at many TEAC schools run multiple forms of statistical analyses comparing teacher candidates and other college students, such as comparing the grades of education and arts and science majors in the same subject-matter courses in order to assess content knowledge.

Along related but somewhat different lines, many teacher educators in institutions around the country—and internationally—are engaged in practitioner inquiry and self-study. The focus of this work is often on what teacher candidates learn from courses and program experiences, how their knowledge, attitudes, and beliefs change over time, how particular pedagogies provide different kinds of learning opportunities, and how candidates understand and interpret their experiences in programs. AERA's special interest group, the Self-Study of Teacher Education Practices (S-STEP), has attracted a large number of members over the past decade based on the idea that teacher educators ought to be engaged in research and self-critical reflection about their own biographies and assumptions and about the impact of the work they do with prospective teachers.

It is clear that there are significant variations in breadth, method, and even fundamental assumptions among the examples I have just mentioned. Some focus explicitly on evidence of impact, while others interrogate process and interpretations. These differences notwithstanding, however, what all of these have in common is that they are intentional and systematic efforts to unlock the "black box" of teacher education, turn the lights on inside it, and shine a spotlight—or any number of differently directed flashlights—into its corners, rafters, and floorboards. If the "black box" metaphor works at all to describe teacher education—and in many respects it does not—it helps to reveal the central tenet of the current evidence focus of "the new teacher education"(Cochran-Smith, 2005): with clear goals, more evidence, and more light, practitioners and policymakers at all levels will make better decisions, and teacher preparation will improve.

EVIDENCE-BASED PRACTICE

For years a refrain of the critics has been that teacher education is idiosyncratic and insulated, guided more by tradition, fashion, or ideology than by cutting-edge research and solid evidence. The numerous initiatives now underway to study the meaning and impact of teacher preparation variations using new approaches and mixed-method research designs are likely to shine new light on some of the old problems of teacher education, particularly in cases where the new evidence produced is counter-intuitive. On a more local level, many teacher education programs now know more than they ever did about whether and where their candidates teach, how long they stay, and how well prepared they are for the challenges of beginning teaching. It is also clear that many teacher educators are engaged in self-study and practitioner inquiry projects wherein they treat their own and others' work as sites for systematic and intentional inquiry. These related but differing activities are very promising. They have the potential to make teacher education more evidence based and to transform its culture by shifting the focus of accountability from external policy only to external policy plus local internal practice.

There are also aspects of the evidence focus, however, that are troubling. These derive from the narrow version of evidence-based practice and policy that is part of the current education agenda, whose theory is explicit in the recommendations to the Department of Education by the Coalition for Evidence-Based Policy (2002):

Education is a field in which a vast number of interventions . . . have gone in or out of fashion over time with little regard to rigorous evidence. As a result, over the past 30 years the United States has made almost no progress in raising the achievement of elementary and secondary school students . . . despite a 90 percent increase in real public spending per pupil. . . . The Department should undertake a focused and sustained effort to . . . (i) Build the knowledge base of educational interventions that have been proven effective through randomized controlled trials . . . (ii) Provide strong incentives for the widespread use of such proven, replicable interventions by recipients of federal education funds. In this strategy, we believe, lies the key to reversing decades of stagnation in American elementary and secondary education, and bringing cumulative, evidence-driven progress—for the first time—to the U.S. educational enterprise. (pp. 1–2)

Although this strategy is crafted primarily for K–12 education, its hand reaches far into teacher education, as a report for the White House Conference on Preparing Tomorrow's Teachers made clear: "Unfortunately experimental methods have not yet found their way to research on teacher training" (Whitehurst, 2002, p. 10).

The source of the evidence-based education movement in the U.S. is evidence-based medicine in the U.K., which focuses on randomized clinical trials. In a critical appraisal of evidence-based practice in the U.K based on case studies in a number of fields, Liz Trinder (2000) concludes that in the disciplines most similar to hospital medicine, the development of evidence-based practice has progressed the furthest and retained the greatest fealty to the original formulation. In areas not close to hospital medicine, and here she specifically names education, social work, and resource management, there have been greater divergence from the original model and much less consensus about the value of evidence-based practice. As Trinder points out, hospital medicine deals with single individuals, and the point is usually to get rid of something (pain, disease, broken bones)—a fairly clear goal. Teacher education, in contrast, deals with groups, and the idea is to instill or provide something (knowledge, strategies, problem-solving skill), which are not as clear goals, so that the members of that group (teacher candidates) can in turn instill or provide something (again, knowledge, information, problem-solving skill) to yet another group (K–12 schoolchildren). This does not mean that randomized trials are any more difficult in teacher education than in social work, juvenile justice, and other "sprawling enterprises"(Weiss, 2001). But it may suggest that as the practice in question is further away from what economist Richard Nelson (2003) describes as the kind of "technical know how" involved in surgical practice and closer to the social and often tacit knowledge involved in education and economics, the more difficult it is for large-scale statistical studies to illuminate the most important problems.

Trinder (2000) suggests that in the early 1990s, evidence-based medicine was heralded as "profound enough" to be referred to as a paradigm shift (p. 212). However, over time and across many fields, "a number of cracks are beginning to show and its claim to be a new paradigm appears to be premature or over-inflated" (p. 236). When applied to teacher education, the narrow version of evidence-based practice does not offer a new paradigm either. In fact, many of the underlying assumptions are quite similar to those of the training model of teacher education and the process-product research on teaching that were predominant in the 1960s and 1970s (Cochran-Smith & Fries, 2005). Then teaching was regarded as a technical transmission activity, and teaching and learning were assumed to be related in a more or less linear way with teaching behaviors the beginning point and pupil learning, primarily reflected in test scores, the endpoint. Using a variety of experimental and correlational research designs, the point at the time was to develop a body of rigorous empirical research about how to produce effective behaviors in prospective teachers so that program and policy decisions could be empirically rather than normatively based.

The research from this period revealed that prospective teachers could indeed be trained to exhibit almost any targeted teaching behavior and that some techniques were more effective than others in producing those behaviors (Lanier & Little, 1986). Although research on the effects of teaching did not disappear, the training model ebbed in teacher education (as did the process-product research on teaching) at least in part because it did not account for how teachers' knowledge and beliefs mediated their behavior in classrooms (Shulman, 1986), nor did it account for the fact that teaching and learning are cultural practices embedded in the uncertain and dynamic contexts of classrooms, schools, and communities (Erickson, 1986). Although the new notion of evidence-based teacher education is not exactly the same as the training model, its underlying assumptions about the nature of teaching, the purposes of teacher preparation, and the power of science are very similar. The problem with the old paradigm, to use

Patti Lather's (2004) words, is that evidence-based practice "rein-scrib[es] the idealized natural science model ... [and] disavows decades of critique" (p. 27). At the end of the day, then, with the very narrow version of evidence-based education, the new paradigm is really the old paradigm, or as Lather concludes a bit more bluntly, "This IS your father's paradigm" (p. 15).

THE POLITICS OF EVIDENCE

In responding to the report of the National Research Council (2001) on scientific research in education, which provides examples of educational questions that warrant research, Fred Erickson (2005) also critiqued the narrow view of scientific research currently being forwarded. Erickson suggested that questions of prediction, explanation, and verification are inappropriately overriding questions of description, interpretation, and discovery. He argued that many of the most fruitful questions in education cannot be answered by causal research designs and offered a list of other possible questions in education worth pursuing. His list included: "What is it like to be a child in the bottom reading group in a particular first grade class? What happened as the math department at Washington High School seriously tried to shift their teaching away from math as algorithms to math as reasoning? How do children who come to school speaking Spanish use their mother tongue in learning to speak and read English?"(p. 9).

Inspired by Erickson's list, I would suggest that there are many fruitful questions about teacher education that deserve exploration. Some of these can be answered by the evidence produced in causal and correlational studies, while others cannot. All, I think, are worth asking: Are there any variations in teacher preparation associated with teachers' retention in hard-to-staff and other schools? What experiences do teacher candidates of color have in mostly white teacher education programs and institutions? Is this important? Are there differences in the ways college graduates with and without teacher preparation construct lessons, interact with pupils, and interpret what they see in classrooms? Are these differences related to pupils' learning? Is caring a quality that can be taught in a teacher preparation program or learned on the job, or is it something people simply have or don't have? Does this matter in teaching? How do we know? How do teacher candidates make sense of the roles parents do and do not play in their children's school lives—what do they make of the "no shows" at back to school night and parent conferences? Does this make a difference in how teachers act in the classroom? Why do new teachers migrate from urban to suburban schools, even if they were prepared specifically for urban classrooms? Is it fair that suburban school districts have a wide range of choices about which teachers to hire and urban and rural schools do not? How do we make a judgment about fairness in this case? What are the school conditions that make it possible for new teachers to take advantage of the resources available to them? How do teacher candidates know if their pupils are learning? What do they count as evidence of learning and how do they use that evidence to alter curriculum and instruction?

As my list of questions (and Erickson's) suggest, there are many important issues related to the preparation of teachers, some of which may be answered by randomized clinical trials, but many others— just as important—require empirical evidence that describes, interprets, and discovers. There are also many questions on my list and elsewhere that cannot be answered by empirical evidence at all. In *Policy Paradox,* Deborah Stone (1997) suggests that much of public policy analysis is part of "the rationality project," or the attempt to remove public policy from the "irrationalities and indignities" of politics, with the intention, instead, of building policy using "rational, scientific, and analytic" methods (p. 6). Stone asserts that policy can never be removed from politics. Diane Massell (2001) makes a similar point, questioning the assumption that data and evidence can inject a kind of "super rationality" into local decision making and pointing out that evidence of or about a problem does not necessarily tell us what we should do about it.

These cautions do not mean that we should not gather good evidence. Evidence can have a tremendous impact on the shape of teacher education for the 21st century, but it cannot tell us what to do. Even on that grand day when all the evidence is in, we will still need to make decisions based in part on values, moral principles, priorities, available resources, trade-offs, ethics, and commitments. Along the way, as we gather more and more evidence in teacher education (and in education more broadly), we must not forget to ask— Evidence of what? For what purpose? Collected by whom and under what circumstances? In order to serve whose interest and (perhaps) ignoring or disadvantaging whom? Do different things count as evidence in different contexts? What should count? Who decides?

There are many positive aspects to the emerging evidence focus of teacher education. As noted, this has the potential to transform the culture of teacher education. But the danger is a too narrow version of evidence grounded in "scientific research" as causal studies only. The teacher education community, and all of those who care about the preparation of teachers and public education, need to develop a perspective on evidence that includes but is not limited to clinical trials and a broad and inclusive view of science that includes but is not limited to the investigation of causal questions. Teacher education needs to be informed by empirical research of many kinds. To move forward, teacher education also needs to be informed by inquiry and scholarship that are not empirical. Perhaps this could be along the lines of what Margaret Eisenhart (2005) recently referred to as a "postpositivist" perspective on science that incorporates experimental research as well as qualitative research, with the latter accepted on its own terms rather than forced into an overarching framework governed by the assumptions of the former. Eisenhart called for educational practice and policy that were informed by "science plus," or the historical, theoretical, critical, and ethical scholarship that many members of the education research community would not call "science" but would deem essential to making good decisions about teaching and teacher education.

Following Eisenhart, I use the term "evidence plus" to make the point that teacher education should be informed by a wealth of critical and theoretical inquiry. In particular, it should be informed by the large bodies of work that now exist about teacher learning in communities and about the preparation of teachers for a diverse society, which come from critical and multicultural perspectives intended to interrupt the norms of conventional teacher education. A more inclusive view of research and evidence would also account for the local knowledge generated by teacher educators examining their own programs and policies and help to conceptualize inquiry and making decisions based on evidence as a stance rather than the beginning point in a causal chain.

NOTE

1. This discussion of the possibilities and the pitfalls of the evidence focus of teacher education is based on my analysis of three key features of "the new teacher education," presented for the 2005 AERA Presidential Address (Cochran-Smith, 2005).

References

Abell Foundation. (2001, October). Teacher certification reconsidered: Stumbling for quality. 2001, from http://www.abell.org

Ballou, D., & Podgursky, M. (2000). Reforming teacher preparation and licensing: What is the evidence? *Teachers College Record, 102*(1), 5-27.

Carnegie Forum on Education and the Economy. (1986). *A nation prepared: Teachers for the 21st century.* New York, NY: Carnegie Corporation.

Christensen, D. (1996). The professional knowledge-research base for teacher education. In J. Sikula, T. Buttery, & E. Guyton (Eds.), *Handbook of research on teacher education* (2nd ed., pp. 38-52). New York, NY: Macmillan.

Coalition for Evidence-Based Policy. (2002). *Bringing evidence-driven progress to education: A recommended strategy for the U.S. Department of Education.* Washington, DC: Council for Excellence in Government.

Cochran-Smith, M. (2005). The new teacher education: For better or for worse? *Educational Researcher, 34*(6), 3-17.

Cochran-Smith, M., & Fries, K. (2005). Researching teacher education in changing times: Paradigms and politics. In M. Cochran-Smith & K. Zeichner (Eds.), *Studying teacher education: The report of the AERA panel on research and teacher education.* Mahwah, NJ: Lawrence Erlbaum Associates.

Darling-Hammond, L. (2000). Reforming teacher preparation and licensing: Debating the evidence. *Teachers College Record, 102*(1), 28-56.

Eisenhart, M. (2005). Science plus: A response to the responses to scientific research in education. *Teachers College Record, 107*(1), 52-58.

Erickson, F. (1986). Qualitative methods on research on teaching. In M. Wittrock (Ed.), *Handbook of research on teaching* (3rd ed., pp. 119–161). New York, NY: Macmillan.

Erickson, F. (2005). Arts, humanities and sciences in educational research and social engineering in federal education policy. *Teachers College Record, 107*(1), 4-9.

Fallon, D. (2006). The buffalo upon the chimneypiece: The value of evidence. *Journal of Teacher Education, 57*(2).

Goodlad, J. (1990). *Teachers for our nation's schools.* San Francisco, CA: Jossey-Bass.

Hess, F. (2001). *Tear down this wall: The case for a radical overhaul of teacher certification.* Washington, DC: Progressive Policy Institute.

Holmes Group. (1986). *Tomorrow's teachers.* East Lansing, MI: Author.

Kennedy, M. (1999). The problem of evidence in teacher education. In R. Roth (Ed.), *The role of the university in the preparation of teachers* (pp. 87-107). Philadelphia, PA: Falmer Press.

Lagemann, E. (2000). *An elusive science: The troubling history of education research.* Chicago, IL: University of Chicago Press.

Lanier, J., & Little, J. (1986). Research on teacher education. In M. Wittrock (Ed.), *Handbook of research on teaching* (3rd ed., pp. 527-569). New York: Macmillan.

Lather, P. (2004). This is your father's paradigm: Government intrusion and the case of qualitative research in education. *Qualitative Inquiry, 10*(1), 15-34.

Massell, D. (2001). Theory and practice of using data to build capacity: State and local strategies and their effects. In S. Fuhrman (Ed.), *100th yearbook of the National Society for the Scientific Study of Education, from the capitol to the classroom: Standards-based reform in the states* (pp. 148-169). Chicago: University of Chicago Press.

Murray, F. (2005). On building a unified system of accreditation in teacher education. *Journal of Teacher Education, 56*(4), 307-317.

National Research Council. (2001). *Scientific research in education.* Washington, DC: National Academy Press.

Nelson, R. (2003). On the uneven evolution of human know-how. *Research Policy, 32,* 909-922.

Shulman, L. S. (1986). Paradigms and research programs in the study of teaching: A contemporary perspective. In M. C. Wittrock (Ed.), *Handbook of research on teaching* (pp. 3-36). New York: Macmillan.

Stone, D. (1997). *The policy paradox: The art of political decision making.* New York: W.W. Norton and Company.

Trinder, L. (2000). A critical appraisal of evidence-based practice. In L. Trinder & S. Reynolds (Eds.), *Evidence-based practice, a critical appraisal* (pp. 212-241). London, UK: Blackwell Science.

U.S. Department of Education. (2005). *The secretary's fourth annual report on teacher quality: A highly qualified teacher in every classroom.* Washington, DC: U.S. Department of Education, Office of Postsecondary Education.

Weiss, C. (2001). What to do until the random assigner comes. In F. Mosteller & R. Boruch (Eds.), *Evidence matters, randomized trials in education research* (pp. 198-224). Washington, DC: Brookings Institution.

Whitehurst, G. (2002). *Scientifically based research on teacher quality: Research on teacher preparation and professional development.* Paper presented at the White House Conference on Preparing Tomorrow's Teachers, Washington, D.C.

Williams, B., Mitchell, A., & Leibbrand, J. (2003). *Navigating change: Preparing for a performance-based accreditation review.* Washington, DC: National Council for the Accreditation of Teacher Education.

Wineburg, M. (2006). Evidence in teacher preparation: Establishing a framework for accountability. *Journal of Teacher Education.* 57(1), 51-64.

Epilogue

The Future of Teacher Education: Promises and Pitfalls

The very first editorial I wrote for the *Journal of Teacher Education* was titled, "Teacher Education at the Turn of the Century" (Cochran-Smith, 2000). This editorial introduced a special issue of the journal on the topic of teacher education's future with the sentence, "Teacher education is under attack" (p. 163). These words were followed in later paragraphs with, "The future of teacher education is at best uncertain," and, "The teacher education profession finds itself responding to the charges against it as well as the complex demands placed upon it" (p. 163). These dire words were appropriate at the time with new teacher tests (and some pretty stunning failures broadly publicized) just implemented in many states, new Title II reporting regulations looming ahead, and some teacher education programs (and schools of education) across the nation threatened with closure. Six years later, it is not an exaggeration to say that the future of teacher education, at least teacher education as it has been organized and located for many years, is still uncertain and that it continues to respond to the many demands placed upon it by the public and policymakers as well as by its external evaluators, its sponsors, its clients, and its own practitioners and researchers. It seems only fitting to return to the topic of teacher education's future in this Epilogue that bookends the editorials collected in this volume.

This Epilogue has a single purpose—to comment on the future of teacher education in terms of both promises and pitfalls, or in other words, in terms of both promising practices and developments that are, in my view, strengthening teacher education as well as trends and circumstances that threaten the profession and its capacity to prepare the teachers the nation needs. The good news is that there are indeed a number of very promising practices and trends in teacher education. These have the power to reinvent the profession by diversifying its forms, expanding its scope, and strengthening its research and professional bases. On the other hand—and this is of course the bad news—these very same trends also have the potential to impair teacher education by expanding routes and pathways that do not adequately prepare teachers, limiting the goals and purposes of teacher education, and narrowing its epistemological and professional grounding.

The Epilogue examines four aspects of teacher education that may be thought of as both promising trends and potential pitfalls. These include: (1) continuing heightened public *and* institutional attention to a whole array of issues regarding teacher quality and teacher preparation; (2) increasing use of sophisticated new research designs and instruments to study the complexity of teacher preparation and the components necessary in the preparation all teachers; (3) growing emphasis on research and empirical evidence as the basis for decision making about curriculum, policy, and practice in teacher education; and, (4) working simultaneously within and against the teacher education system in keeping with the critique of prevailing views about teacher education policies and practices and as part of larger social movements to expand the ways we think about teacher education's role in society and its broader goals and purposes.

ATTENTION TO TEACHER QUALITY AND TEACHER PREPARATION

For some time now, there has been an enormous amount of public and institutional attention to matters related to teacher quality and preparation. Although education is a perennial concern of the public as indicated by public opinion polls (Hart & Teeter, 2002; Mosle, 1996; Rose & Gallup, 2003), it has not always been the case that there was so much interest in teachers, teaching, and teacher preparation (as opposed to, say, school resources and facilities, school funding formulae, or the required content of the curriculum). Likewise although there have been debates about the liberal and technical aspects of teacher preparation (Borrowman, 1956) among university scholars and critics for more than a hundred years, it has not always been the case that university administrators at the highest levels have taken an active role in decisions related to the education of teachers.

Today there is widespread and nearly universal agreement that teachers are engaged in vitally important work and that they determine to a great extent the success or failure of their students. Three examples of current initiatives make the point that current public interest in teaching and teacher education is at an all-time high. As this book went to press, it was formally announced that under the auspices of the National Academies of Science, Congress had charged the National Research Council to "conduct a study that synthesizes data and research on teacher preparation programs in the United States" (NRC Current Projects, 2005). Congress mandated that the study pay particular attention to: the characteristics of teacher candidates in various programs and pathways, the specific coursework and experiences provided to teacher candidates in various programs and pathways, and the consistency of required course and field experiences in reading and mathematics across programs and with scientific evidence. The committee will be co-chaired by Ellen Condliffe Lagemann, former dean of the Harvard Graduate School of Education, as well as former president of the Spencer Foundation and the National Academy of Education, and Kenneth Shine, former president of the Institute of Medicine and professor of medicine emeritus at the University of California, Los Angeles. The NRC study has been referred to informally as a "Flexner-like" report by many insiders, linking it to the famous 1920s study that transformed the face of medical education in this country. A mandate from Congress for a study of teacher education programs signifies the current importance attached to teacher preparation as well as the perceived need to analyze, assess, and—perhaps—alter it.

A second example of the very high current level of attention to teacher quality and teacher preparation, mentioned in several editorials, is the Teachers for a New Era initiative to improve teacher preparation, sponsored by the Carnegie Corporation of New York with additional support from the Ford and Annenberg Foundations. Funded at a level exceeding $125 million (including the matching funds that each of 11 selected institutions must provide), the project is intended to transform how institutions of higher education allocate resources, organize academically across education and arts and sciences, evaluate faculty efforts, relate to public schools, and utilize internal accountability measures to improve the preparation of teachers (Carnegie Corporation of New York, 2005). The third example of heightened public and institutional interest in teacher education is the collection of recent resolutions regarding teacher preparation that conceptualize teacher preparation as an all-university activity: the American Council on Education's "To Touch the Future: Transforming the Way Teachers Are Taught—An Action Agenda for College and University Presidents," the American Association of Universities' "Resolution on Teacher Education," and the American Association of State Colleges and Universities "Call for Teacher Education Reform: A Report of the AASCU Task Force on Teacher Education." The important thing here is that these resolutions were not issued by organizations like AACTE, which is explicitly concerned with teacher preparation. Rather, they represent the collective viewpoints of organizations for college and university presidents and thus signal interest in the preparation of teachers at the highest levels of leadership in the academy. Each of the resolutions calls upon university presidents to provide leadership concerning teacher preparation and to consider this work as an all-university responsibility rather than one that resides only in schools, colleges, and departments of education.

These three examples, and many others that are described in the editorials throughout this book, attest to the strong national interest in teaching and teacher preparation on the part of the public, policymakers, major foundations whose scope of interests include education, and institutions of higher education. One interpretation of this mounting interest is that, as a nation, we have finally and rightfully acknowledged the importance of teachers and the incredible impact their work can have on the achievement and life chances of the students they teach. Parents and those who work as and with teachers have long known how important teaching is and have periodically protested that this was not adequately recognized by policymakers and politicians. It is extremely promising for the future of teacher education that the nation's leaders now seem to acknowledge that teaching and teacher preparation are important.

Another interpretation, however, and a theme of the editorials in this book, is that the current emphasis on teachers as *the* determining factor in students' success ignores other complex and confounding variables, such as school resources, leadership, and investments in teachers' capacity building and professional development, as well as family structure, poverty, housing, health, and employment. The future of American teacher education depends to a great extent on how this all-time-high level of interest in teaching quality and preparation plays out over time. Of particular importance is whether it is acknowledged that the problems of the nation's schools include but are much bigger than teachers and that the problems of the nation include but are much bigger than the schools. As I have argued repeatedly, teachers teaching better—either alone or collectively— cannot fix everything, even if they are held accountable for everything. If we approach teacher quality and preparation as one part of much larger educational and societal problems that must be attacked in a variety of ways and on a variety of fronts, the future of teacher education looks bright. There is a very real danger, however, that we will use teachers and teacher educators as scapegoats for the other parties who are also responsible for the current state of public education—the policymakers who make monetary, trade, and industrial policies that influence economic competitiveness; the leaders of business and industry who lobby for and benefit from those policies; the testing and textbook industries that profit from the nation's current obsession with testing and accountability regimes; and the various layers of school bureaucracy caught up in the red tape of schooling and far removed from the daily work of classrooms. If we hold teachers and teacher educators accountable for everything without acknowledgement of the other major actors in the educational scene and without attention to the complex problems involved, then the future of teacher education is not so bright.

Focus on the Complexity and Components of Teacher Preparation

For nearly 40 years there has been debate about teacher education program types and organizational structures. To make their points, debaters often refer to research studies intended to identify which programs (e.g., four or five year, undergraduate or master's level) are "best," or most effective in terms of teacher retention, principals' evaluations, or students' achievement (Zeichner & Conklin, 2005). However, these studies have not provided convincing evidence of the superiority of one program type or another, and their research methods (and results) have almost always been disputed. Many of the recent studies along these lines compare "alternative" and "traditional" routes. As has been pointed out repeatedly (Wilson, Floden, & Ferrini-Mundy, 2001; Zeichner & Conklin, 2005), however, there is no consistency in definitions of "alternative" and "traditional" pathways, and not surprisingly, there has also been no consistency in the results of the comparison studies. Rather, each new major study seems to contradict its predecessor by reaching the opposite conclusion.

By now it has become clear that there will likely never be definitive research showing the one best way to prepare teachers. This is the case because "the horse race approach" (Cochran-Smith, 2005; Cochran-Smith & Fries, 2005), which pits one program type or pathway against another, is hopelessly flawed by its faulty assumptions about the uniformity rather than the variability of teacher education programs of the same "type," the linear rather than interactive and confounding relationships among the variables that influence outcomes, and the simplicity rather than the complexity involved in preparing teachers and assessing their preparation. One current development in the field that shows promise for the future of teacher education is growing acknowledgement of the complexity of the entire teacher education enterprise and growing recognition that studying that complexity, including concentrating on components rather than program or pathway types, is more likely to yield fruitful results.

Today's richer data sources, more powerful analytical techniques, and increasingly sophisticated researchers are making it possible for the field to develop more complex understandings of teacher preparation programs and pathways. Three examples make this point. Ohio's Teacher Quality Project, formerly the Ohio Partnership for Accountability (2002), which is mentioned in several of the editorials in this book, is directed by Robert Yinger at the University of Cincinnati in cooperation with researchers from Ohio State University and the University of Dayton. The Ohio project is a collaboration among all 50 of Ohio's teacher certification institutions, the state department of education, and the state board of regents as well as representatives from the teachers' union, the business community, and other relevant stakeholders. The project takes a mixed-methods approach, combining three different studies—value-added assessment of teachers' impact on achievement, qualitative studies of classroom interactions, and surveys of teacher candidates and graduates—to try to sort out the relationships of teacher preparation, classroom discourse and instructional practices, and pupils' learning. What makes this project exemplary is not simply its mixed-methods approach or its multidisciplinary, cross-institutional research team (although these are important, to be sure), but also its attempt—by design—to understand the interrelationships of the features of teacher preparation, school students' learning as indicated on tests as well as in classroom performance, and multiple systems of accountability.

A second example is the New York City Pathways Project, a collaboration among labor market economists, teacher education researchers, and the City University of New York, under the leadership of Donald Boyd, Pamela Grossman, Hamilton Lankford, Susanna Loeb, Nick Michelli, and James Wyckoff. Like the Ohio project, the New York City Pathways project is "complex by design" (Boyd, Grossman, Lankford, Loeb, Michelli, & Wyckoff, in press) in that it attempts to sort out the multiple pathways into teaching that are currently possible in New York City and study their impact on the composition of the teacher workforce and on students' achievement. The study is using New York City and state teacher data bases to analyze outcomes by pathways, including traditional and a variety of alternate route programs. Three aspects of the New York study reflect the emergence of increasingly sophisticated and complex research designs and tools in teacher education. First, the study explicitly eschews the notion of uniform and monolithic program types by carefully delineating the characteristics and features of the various alternate pathways existing in New York City rather than lumping them into one category. Second, the researchers conceptualize impact as an intricate combination of recruitment effects, features of preparation, and retention/attrition outcomes rather than simply test score gains. Third, the study combines multiple research methods and designs to analyze impact by pathway (not by individual as is the case in accountability systems based on value-added assessment)—impact on test scores, on teachers' perceptions of their preparation, and on retention and attrition. Like the Ohio project, the New York project is exemplary in combining econometric analyses with analyses based on interviews, surveys, and document collection that get at the variations in pathways that influence candidates' opportunities to learn.

A third example is a recent study of Teach for America and other teachers (Decker, Mayer, & Glazerman, 2004). In appraising this study in a *JTE* editorial, I was critical of the question with which the study began—whether TFA teachers did any harm to students' achievement in comparison to the effect of the teachers these students otherwise would have had given the reality that the urban and poor areas served by TFA are often forced to hire unqualified and poorly prepared teachers. I stand by this criticism. But my point here is a different one, and I include the study by Decker and colleagues as part of the emerging and promising practice in teacher education of using more complex and sophisticated research designs to study teacher education. The Decker, Mayer, and Glazerman study used a national sample and randomized assignment of pupils to TFA or non-TFA teachers, a rarity in teacher education research. They also included detailed information about the components and features of the teacher preparation program under study rather than simply identifying it by type or category. In fact, as Zeichner and Conklin (2005) point out, the Decker, Mayer, and Glazerman study goes to some pains to avoid assuming that all alternate routes—or even all TFA sites—are the same. Instead, they describe the context and content of the actual TFA program the subjects of their study experienced. This suggests that variations in context and content matter and that, even in the case of a national model like TFA, it is a particular combination of selection, preparation, and placement features that have an impact rather than the model itself.

These examples and others suggest that a current trend in teacher education is the development of multiple-methods research studies that conjoin the efforts of scholars from different fields. The positive interpretation of this trend is not only that the field has the capacity to do the kind of sophisticated research that is required in teacher education, but also that those engaged in that research are beginning to acknowledge the complexity of teacher education as something that must be accounted for and thus get beyond the horse race approach.

The pitfall in this emerging approach is its potentially too heavy buy-in to defining teacher education as a policy problem (Cochran-Smith, 2005b) and to assessing the effectiveness of pathways and programs using cost-benefit and other econometric analyses with test scores as the primary outcome. The future of teacher education depends in part on whether accounting for teacher education's complexity, which has the potential to be a very positive step, plays out, on the one hand, as the development of more and more sophisticated econometric models that are still basically linear with students' test scores the end point, or, on the other hand, plays out as the development of multifaceted studies that pose a range of questions, include multiple research paradigms on their own terms, and construct pupil learning outcomes in ways broader and richer than tests scores.

USING RESEARCH AND EVIDENCE TO MAKE POLICY AND PRACTICE DECISIONS

For almost as long as it has existed, teacher education has been critiqued and exhorted to reform and improve. Today there is widespread emphasis on using research and evidence to make decisions, a trend that is somewhat different from previous foci on content and foundations. This relatively new development in teacher education is part of larger national efforts in education and in health, social work, and law enforcement. Several examples make the case that teacher education has turned toward research and evidence.

In 2005, two landmark books were published that focus on the research base of teacher education—*Preparing Teachers for a Changing World: The Report of the Committee on Teacher Education of the National Academy of Education,* edited by Linda Darling-Hammond and John Bransford (2005), and *Studying Teacher Education: The Report of the AERA Panel on Teacher Education,* edited by myself and Ken Zeichner (Cochran-Smith & Zeichner, 2005). These books are similar in that each represents the collective efforts of a larger group—a 28-member Committee on Teacher Education in the case of the Darling-Hammond/Bransford book, and a 17-member AERA Panel on Research and Teacher Education in the case of the Cochran-Smith/Zeichner book—and each is sponsored by a major national organization whose mission is the development and dissemination of research to improve education. The books are also different, however, in that each asks a different question about the strength and role of research in teacher education policy and practice and each reaches different conclusions.

As discussed in several of the editorials in this book, the purpose of the National Academy Committee on Teacher Education (CTE) and the Darling-Hammond and Bransford book was to articulate the knowledge bases for teaching and to make research-grounded recommendations about how core knowledge for beginning teachers could be included in teacher education curricula and pedagogies. Based on careful analysis of this research in several of the key domains related to teaching, learning, and schooling, the CTE report concluded that there was indeed a body of well-defined and significant research that ought to inform the preparation of every new teacher. Also mentioned in several editorials, the purpose of the AERA Panel on Research and Teacher Education and the Cochran-Smith and Zeichner book was quite different from that of the CTE. The AERA Panel set out to assess the weight of the empirical evidence on the impact of teacher education about several key areas and to recommend a research agenda for the future. Based on critical analysis of the empirical research that met its criteria for rigor and relevance, the AERA Panel concluded that research about the impact of teacher preparation practices and policies is generally weak and inconclusive. The panel called for an extensive new research agenda, better research designs and instruments, and programs of research that cohere theoretically and methodologically. (My editorials comment in some detail on the different questions these projects posed and the different answers they found.)

A second example of the current focus on research and evidence is somewhat different from the two projects noted above. There are many institutional and regional initiatives to foster local research about what and how much prospective teachers learn in their course and fieldwork experiences, where and how long they teach, and what and how much their pupils learn. And in fact, more and more teacher educators all over the country are currently engaged in gathering evidence about the knowledge, skills, experiences, perceptions, beliefs, and performances of their teacher candidates and the pupils of those teachers. As several editorials note, this turn toward evidence is partly because teacher educators are trying to hold themselves accountable to their own commitments and goals. But the empirical turn in teacher education is to a great extent a response to new accreditation standards at the national level and new program approval requirements at the state level, all of which are influenced by the larger national trend toward evidence-based education. For example, National Council for Accreditation of Teacher Education current standards require institutions to show evidence of teacher candidates' subject matter knowledge and classroom performance and to have data-driven assessment systems built into their programs that allow them to track candidates' progress over time. Teacher Education Accreditation Council requires valid and reliable evidence about candidate performance and knowledge, and the Teachers for a New Era reform project has as its first design principle, "respect for evidence" (Carnegie Corporation of New York, 2005). What these have in common is the idea of building into teacher education a process wherein research guides curriculum and arrangements, evidence is continuously fed back into decisions, and effectiveness is measured in large part by evidence of pupils' learning.

These examples, and many others that are described in the editorials in this book, suggest that teacher education has made an empirical turn—at least on the surface—and is currently striving to use research and evidence to improve practice. One interpretation of this trend is that it shows great promise for the profession. It reflects efforts to build the capacity within teacher education programs themselves to assess progress and effectiveness, to shift accountability from external policy to internal practice, and to generate knowledge that can be used in both local programs and more broadly. Transforming teacher education into an enterprise that is grounded in research, revolves around continuous assessment of learning, and makes decisions driven by evidence is very promising and would be nothing short of a culture shift in our field. Another positive read on this current trend is that it puts teacher education at the forefront of other professions in that it has taken a hard look at itself by assessing the research bases for its actions and has concluded that much more rigorous and systematic research is needed. As noted in an editorial, no other profession currently evaluates its success by assessing the impact and performance of its graduates once they are in the profession.

Another interpretation, however, is that the current emphasis on research and evidence has the potential to narrow the kinds of questions that are asked in teacher education and to exacerbate the current dangerous trend to define accountability solely in terms of pupils' test scores. As I have argued many times, teaching and learning are much more complex than raising test scores and there are many important questions in teacher education that cannot be answered solely on the basis of assembled evidence. Even in the face of more and more evidence, teacher educators and others will still have to make decisions based on values, moral purposes, and priorities, and there will still be many critically important questions that are not of the "what works?" variety.

There is also a very real danger that the current preoccupation with evidence is simply the latest development in teacher education's long history of being reactive rather than proactive—continuously buffeted about by pressure from outside evaluators, creditors, and critics. Wineburg's (2006) recent national survey of institutional members of the American Association of State Colleges and Universities is titled "Credible and Persuasive Evidence." Preliminary analysis reveals that although nearly all teacher education institutions reported that they were involved in time-consuming and labor-intensive efforts to gather evidence about teacher education, they were much less certain about what the purposes and possible uses of this evidence might be, not to mention uncertain about whether the evidence gathered was valid and reliable. Teacher education will not get better just because more people gather evidence, and decisions based on evidence are not necessarily better than decisions based on moral purposes or decisions based on experience over time. In the rush to be "empirical" and "evidence-based," teacher education will have to work hard to avoid the pitfall of empiricism, which eschews theory in favor of observation and experiment, on the one hand, and the pitfall of scientism, which assumes that science alone can explain phenomena. Ultimately the point is not simply to focus on evidence but also to ask—evidence of what? for what purposes? under whose direction? and to serve whose larger ends (while perhaps doing a disservice to others)? What all this means is that although the current trend of focusing on research and evidence has the potential to help transform the culture of teacher education in very positive ways, its promise will only be realized if evidence is considered in light of larger agendas, commitments, and values.

WORKING WITHIN AND AGAINST THE SYSTEM

Finally, a small but promising trend in teacher education is the effort by some teacher educators to work simultaneously within and against the larger educational system by critiquing prevailing views about teacher education policies and practices and expanding the ways we think about teacher education's role in society and its broader goals and purposes. I use just one example here to make this point, and in doing so I return to the work of Larry Cuban (1992), whom I mentioned in the Prologue. Following Cuban and others, I suggested in the Prologue that as teacher educators, we must also be public intellectuals, using our expertise, our evidence, and our freedom to challenge policies and practices that do not serve the interests of school students and to try to lead the way in other directions that are more productive and more democratic. I suggested that in order to do so, teacher education scholars and practitioners would have to work simultaneously against and within the system. This means offering critique in whatever public realms one has influence and access at the same time that one continues to do the work of teacher education within the boundaries of current policy and practice.

For example, a number of teacher educators have pointed out problems with equating accountability with testing. While there is general consensus among teacher educators regarding the importance of accountability, serious questions have been raised about how best to assess the impact of teacher education and what should count as measures of its success. In particular, critics of the recent accountability movement have questioned narrow definitions of success that focus exclusively on how the students of teacher education program graduates perform on standardized tests. They have also criticized the lack of attention to other outcomes such as preparing teachers for diverse populations, ensuring equitable learning opportunities for all pupils, and working to make schools more caring and just (Oakes, 2004). Along these lines, at some institutions—particularly those that prepare teachers for urban schools—educators are working within the system by focusing on outcomes, but also working against the system by conceptualizing equity, social justice, and preparation for participation in a democratic society as legitimate and justifiable outcomes of teacher preparation in and of themselves with an array of "just measures" for assessing results.

For example, at UCLA, the teacher education group has worked for the last 7 years to track the placement and retention patterns of their graduates who work in Los Angeles' most difficult schools, counting as an outcome of their program their graduates' commitment to and retention in careers as social justice educators (Quartz & Teacher Education Program Research Group, 2003). At Boston College, researchers and practitioners from teacher education, educational measurement, and psychology are working together to develop a multimethods instrument for assessing how teacher candidates "learn to teach for social justice," by combining surveys with vignette analysis, interviews, and school observations of teachers and pupils. At the University of Illinois-Chicago, educators are linking their program completer information to the Illinois Teacher Data

Warehouse, which tracks all Illinois public school teachers, to see whether they meet their own program goal of serving children who live in extraordinary poverty. And at Montclair State University, educators have developed a data base system tracking the progress of every teacher candidate toward meeting every NCATE standard, including in particular learning to teach for diverse populations. What this small group of examples has in common is the assumption that one essential outcome of teacher education is preparing teachers who effectively teach all students (including those who attend the poorest and most neglected schools) *and* at the same time work to make their schools and communities more caring and more just places.

One interpretation of these efforts—and this is the promising aspect—is that teacher educators and their colleagues are not simply trying to prove their points using the same kinds of evidence and reasoning that already dominate debates about teaching, learning, and schooling. Rather, they are working to change the terms of the debate in the first place. In other words, instead of simply trying to find new ways to gather evidence showing that teacher candidates and teachers who create caring and just classrooms have an impact on pupils' test scores, some educators are arguing for different outcomes in the first place and developing ways to assess and measure those outcomes. The downside here—and this is the pitfall, of course—is that although efforts like these are tolerated—and even applauded at times—they are generally regarded as so supplementary and peripheral to the "real" outcomes of schooling that they are largely ignored.

CONCLUSION: THE FUTURE

As noted in the discussions above, for many years teacher education has been pushed to change and pressed to improve by policymakers, the public, critics within and outside the university, and those with a variety of political agendas. That teaching is a highly visible, very large, and very public profession is surely part of the explanation for all this criticism, which has not been the case for most other professions. But, as one of the editorials in this book notes, another part of the explanation is teacher education's historically low status in the world of professional work and as a field of study within the institutional hierarchy of the university (Lagemann, 2000). As historian David Labaree (2004) concludes, in part because of teacher education's overall low status, it has historically been an easy target for critics who are unconcerned about what those inside the profession think and thus feel at liberty to make demands and issue critiques that they may not make of higher-status professions.

In the face of a long history of criticism and in light of its low status, teacher education's response to calls for change has been primarily reactive rather than proactive, a response often interpreted by others as defensive—a circling of the wagons intended to conserve current practice and maintain the status quo rather than make fundamental change. In a certain sense, this charge is simply not true (Imig & Switzer, 1996). There have always been local pockets of dramatic change and innovation in teacher education. But teacher education writ large has also made many changes over the years—changes such as new organizational arrangements (e.g., five-year, fifth-year, and master's-level initial teacher preparation programs), new structures and contexts for teacher preparation (e.g., professional development schools, teacher learning communities), and new curricular emphases (e.g., coursework in multicultural education, fieldwork experiences in schools and communities that begin at the earliest points of teacher education programs rather than coming simply at the end of the formal preparation period). In other ways, however, it is also true that in the main, teacher education has retained the same basic structure for more than 50 years—courses in subject matter and in general education, courses in educational foundations and pedagogy, and graduated fieldwork experiences. Even in areas such as multicultural education, which has been emphasized for the last 20 years, a number of policy and program analyses have concluded that most change has been on the surface and at the margins rather than at the core of teacher education, and many of what appear to be new approaches are more rhetorical than real (Gollnick, 2001; Ladson-Billings, 1999).

As the preceding sections have suggested, there are a number of current developments in teacher education that are very promising—recognition of the importance of teaching and teachers' work as part of a complex constellation of factors regarding school, community, health, employment, and economic conditions; new research that focuses on teacher education's complexity; the emergence of a culture of evidence wherein decisions are informed by both empirical data and ethical commitments; and the emergence of a cadre of educators working both within and against the educational system.

These have the potential to bring about real, not just rhetorical, change in teacher education. But in order for that to happen, we will have to avoid the very deep pitfalls I have noted above. Pitfalls are often unanticipated and disguised in some way—camouflaged with tree branches and built with sides so steep that, once the fall occurs, escape is impossible. We are *not* at a point in teacher education where it is impossible to avoid the pitfalls. Their sides are indeed steep and treacherous, but they are not so difficult to anticipate and they are avoidable. To do so and to make real change, it will take concerted efforts, clear-eyed analyses, and public critique of emerging and prevailing views. As importantly, it will take great care not to be co-opted by those with larger political and professional agendas that run counter to the greater purposes of teacher education in a democratic society.

REFERENCES

Borrowman, M. (1956). *The liberal and technical in teacher education: An historical survey of American thought.* New York, NY: Teachers College Press.

Boyd, D., Grossman, P., Lankford, H., Loeb, S., Michelli, N., & Wyckoff, L. (in press). Complex by design: Investigating pathways into teaching in New York City Schools. *Journal of Teacher Education, 57*(2).

Carnegie Corporation of New York. (2005). *Teachers for a new era.* September 1, 2005, from http://www.carnegie.org/sub/program/teachers_execsum.html

Cochran-Smith, M. (2000). Teacher education at the turn of the century. *Journal of Teacher Education, 51*(3), 163-165.

Cochran-Smith, M. (2005a). Taking stock in 2005: Getting beyond the horse race. *Journal of Teacher Education, 56*(1), 2-7.

Cochran-Smith, M. (2005b). The new teacher education: For better or for worse? *Educational Researcher, 34*(7), 3-17.

Cochran-Smith, M., & Fries, K. (2005). Paradigms and politics: Researching teacher education in changing times. In M. Cochran-Smith & K. Zeichner (Eds.), *Studying teacher education: The report of the AERA panel on research and teacher education.* Mahwah, NJ: Lawrence Erlbaum.

Cochran-Smith, M., & Zeichner, K. (2005). *Studying teacher education: The report of the AERA panel on research and teacher education.* Mahwah, NJ: Lawrence Erlbaum Associates.

Cuban, L. (1992). Managing dilemmas while building professional communities. *Educational Researcher, 21*(1), 4-12.

Darling-Hammond, L., & Bransford, J. (Eds.). (2005). *Preparing teachers for a changing world. Report of the Committee on Teacher Education of the National Academy of Education.* San Francisco: Jossey Bass.

Decker, P., Mayer, D., & Glazerman, S. (2004). *The effects of Teach for America on students: Findings from a national evaluation.* Princeton, NJ: Mathematica Policy Research, Inc.

Gollnick, D. (2001). National and state initiatives for multicultural education. In J. Banks & C. Banks (Eds.), *Handbook of research on multicultural education* (pp. 44-64). San Francisco, CA: Jossey-Bass.

Hart, P., & Teeter, R. (2002). *A national priority: Americans speak on teacher quality* (Public Opinion Research). Princeton, NJ: Educational Testing Service.

Imig, D., & Switzer, T. (1996). Changing teacher education programs: Restructuring collegiate-based teacher education. In J. Sikula, T. Buttery & E. Guyton (Eds.), *Handbook of research on teacher education* (2nd ed., pp. 213-226). New York, NY: Macmillan.

Labaree, D. (2004). *The trouble with ed schools.* New Haven, CT: Yale University Press.

Ladson-Billings, G. (1999). Preparing teachers for diverse student populations: A critical race theory perspective. In A. Iran-Nejad & D. Pearson (Eds.), *Review of research in education* (Vol. 24, pp. 211-248). Washington, DC: American Educational Research Association.

Lagemann, E. (2000). *An elusive science: The troubling history of education research.* Chicago, IL: University of Chicago Press.

Mosle, S. (1996, October 27). The answer is national standards. *New York Times.*

National Research Council Current Projects. (2005). Teacher preparation programs in the United States. Retrieved October 14, 2005, from www4 .nas.edu/webcr.nsf/5c50571a75df494485256a95007a091e/49ecf39f5d 0deaba85257098004884c6?OpenDocument

Oakes, J. (2004). Investigating the claims in *Williams v. State of California:* An unconstitutional denial of education's basic tools? *Teachers College Record, 106*(10), 1889-1906.

Ohio Partnership for Accountability. (2002). *Teacher education and student achievement in complex contexts of accountability.* Dayton, OH: Author.

Rose, L., & Gallup, A. (2003). The 35th annual Phi Delta Kappa/Gallup poll of the public's attitudes toward the public schools. *Phi Delta Kappan,* 41-56.

Weiss, C. (2001). What to do until the random assigner comes. In F. Mosteller & R. Boruch (Eds.), *Evidence matters, randomized trials in education research* (pp. 198-224). Washington DC: Brookings Institution.

Wilson, S., Floden, R., & Ferrini-Mundy, J. (2001). *Teacher preparation research: Current knowledge, gaps, and recommendations.* Washington, DC: Center for the Study of Teaching and Policy.

Wineburg, M. (2006). Evidence in teacher preparation: Establishing a framework for accountability. *Journal of Teacher Education, 57*(1), 51-64.

Zeichner, K., & Conklin, H. (2005). Research on teacher education programs. In M. Cochran-Smith & K. Zeichner (Eds.), *Studying teacher education: The report of the AERA panel on research and teacher education* (pp. 645-736). Mahwah, NJ: Lawrence Erlbaum Associates.

Index

About the Author

 **Marilyn Cochran-Smith** holds the John E. Cawthorne Millenium Chair in Teacher Education for Urban Schools at Boston College's Lynch School of Education where she directs the doctoral program in curriculum and instruction. Dr. Cochran-Smith earned her PhD in language and education from the University of Pennsylvania in 1982 where she was a tenured faculty member at the Graduate School of Education until going to Boston College in 1996.

An active participant in the national and international teacher education communities, Dr. Cochran-Smith has long been a member of AACTE committees and groups. From 2000 to 2006, she was the editor of AACTE's journal, *The Journal of Teacher Education,* along with a team of nine Lynch School of Education associate editors. The journal, which is published five times a year, addresses issues of research, practice, and policy in teacher education. From 1998 to 2006, Dr. Cochran-Smith was also a member of AACTE's Committee on Publications and the JTE. In 2004, Dr. Cochran-Smith won AACTE's highest honor, the "Pomeroy Award for Outstanding Contributions to the Field of Teacher Education." In 1999, she was awarded AACTE's "Margaret Lindsay Award for Distinguished Research in Teaching and Teacher Education," and in 1995 her book, *Inside/Outside: Teacher Research and Knowledge* (co-authored with Susan Lytle), won AACTE's "Annual Award for Excellence in Professional Writing in Teaching and Teacher Education." Most recently, *Studying Teacher Education: The Report of the AERA Panel on Research and Teacher Education*, co-edited with Kenneth M. Zeichner, won the 2006 AACTE "Outstanding Publication Award-Book."

Dr. Cochran-Smith was president of the American Educational Research Association for 2004–2005, serving on the Executive

Board and Council in 1998–2000 and again in 2003–2006. She is the co-chair of AERA's National Panel on Research and Teacher Education and co-editor (with Ken Zeichner) of *Studying Teacher Education: The Report of the AERA Panel on Research and Teacher Education* (Erlbaum, 2005). Dr. Cochran-Smith was also a member of the National Academy of Education's Committee on Teacher Education. She is co-editor of the Teachers College Press series on Practitioner Inquiry as well as co-editor of the *Third Handbook of Research on Teacher Education,* which is currently in preparation. In addition Dr. Cochran-Smith is on the advisory board for many national projects and committees, including the New York City Pathways Project, the Ohio Teacher Quality Project, and the UCLA/Center X Urban Teacher Educators Network.

Dr. Cochran-Smith is a member of the Executive Committee and the Leadership Team for Boston College's Teachers for a New Era (TNE) project, funded primarily by the Carnegie Corporation of New York, and chair of the Evidence Team for this project. She is also a member of the Research Coordinating Council for the TNE national cross-site group.

Dr. Cochran-Smith has written many award-winning articles and books on diversity in teaching and teacher education and on teacher education policy and practice, teacher research, teacher learning, and the growth and development of knowledge for teaching. *Walking the Road: Race, Diversity and Social Justice in Teacher Education* was published by Teachers College Press (2004). Many of her recent articles, book chapters, and books focus on teacher preparation research and policy, teaching quality, and competing agendas for education reform. Dr. Cochran-Smith's AERA Presidential Address, "The New Teacher Education: For Better or For Worse?" appeared in the October 2005 issue of *Educational Researcher.*

Dr. Cochran-Smith is a frequent keynote speaker nationally and internationally—most recently at the U.S. Office of Special Education Programs Project Director's Conference (Washington), the OISE/UT Conference on Teacher Education for the Schools We Need (Toronto), the North-South Conference on Teacher Education (Dublin), and the International Conference on the Education of Teachers (Hong Kong). In 2004, Dr. Cochran-Smith won the "Carl Grant Research Award for Outstanding Research on Multicultural Education," and in 2005, she was the recipient of the first National Impact Award from the New York State Association of Teacher Educators and the New York Association of Colleges for Teacher Education.